The Routledge Handbo Attachment: Implicatic Interventions

The Routledge Handbook of Attachment: Implications and Interventions offers an introduction to therapies produced as a result of the popularity of attachment studies. These therapies can be divided into two categories: those that are 'attachment-based', in that they use evidence-based attachment assessments in their development, or 'attachment-informed', in that the theories of attachment have been integrated into the practice of existing schools of therapy.

The book reviews the field and provides a range of interventions for children, adults and parents, beginning with a detailed review of both evidence-based and evidence-informed interventions including individual psychotherapy, family therapy and parenting. The remaining chapters provide accounts, from the practitioner's perspective, of interventions that address issues of attachment from the level of one-to-one therapy, family and social work to social interventions involving courts and care proceedings, illustrated with examples from day-to-day practice.

Discussing how an understanding of formal assessments of attachment can be used to inform therapeutic, social and legal interventions to assist and protect children, *The Routledge Handbook of Attachment: Implications and Interventions* is an indispensable guide for clinical psychologists, psychiatrists and social workers working with children and families, clinicians in training and students.

Paul Holmes is a child and adolescent psychiatrist who also trained as an adult psychotherapist. He worked in community child and adolescent mental health teams for many years, and with specialist services for fostered and adopted children. He has increasingly applied his long-standing interest in attachment theory to his work in providing expert psychiatric opinions to the British courts in child care proceedings.

Steve Farnfield is a Senior Lecturer and established the MSc in Attachment Studies at the University of Roehampton, UK. He is a social worker and play therapist with many years' experience and a licensed trainer for the Dynamic-Maturational Model of Attachment Infant CARE-Index, Preschool Assessment of Attachment and Adult Attachment Interview developed by Patricia Crittenden.

The Routledge Handbook of Attachment: Implications and Interventions

Edited by
Paul Holmes and Steve Farnfield

Routledge
Taylor & Francis Group

LONDON AND NEW YORK

First published 2014
by Routledge
27 Church Road, Hove, East Sussex, BN3 2FA

and by Routledge
711 Third Avenue, New York, NY 10017

Routledge is an imprint of the Taylor & Francis Group, an informa business

© 2014 Paul Holmes and Steve Farnfield

British Library Cataloguing in Publication Data
A catalogue record for this book is available from the British Library

Library of Congress Cataloging in Publication Data
  The Routledge handbook of attachment :
  implications and interventions /
  edited by Paul Holmes and Steve Farnfield.—First Edition.
  pages cm
  1. Attachment behavior. 2. Child psychotherapy.
  3. Dependency (Psychology) I. Holmes, Paul, editor of compilation.
  II. Farnfield, Steve, editor of compilation.
  BF575.A86R684 2014
  155.9'2—dc23
  2014003036

ISBN: 978-1-138-01672-9 (pbk set)
ISBN: 978-1-315-76509-9 (ebk set)
ISBN: 978-0-415-70611-7 (hbk)
ISBN: 978-0-415-70612-4 (pbk)
ISBN: 978-1-315-76428-3 (ebk)

Typeset in Times New Roman
by Swales & Willis Ltd, Exeter, Devon

This book is dedicated to those professionals who are the essential players in improving child welfare and protection, and to our partners who have supported us and nurtured us during the long gestation of this book.

Contents

Contributors

Elaine Arnold taught social work students (MSW courses) at Goldsmiths College and Sussex University, UK. She was Director of Training at Nafsiyat Intercultural Therapy Centre, UK. She researched the adverse effects of separation and loss and sometimes traumatic reunions among some families of African Caribbean origin, due to immigration from the West Indies to Britain. She is Director of the Separation Reunion Forum, the aim of which is to raise awareness of the importance of secure early attachment in the life of the individual; the phenomenon of broken attachments and traumatic reunions is also applicable to children separated through various circumstances and to other groups in society. Elaine currently lectures at various colleges and voluntary groups on the Theory of Attachment, Separation and Loss and its applicability to practice in the caring professions.

Marian J. Bakermans-Kranenburg is Professor at the Centre for Child and Family Studies, Leiden University, the Netherlands. She is interested in parenting and parent–child relationships, with a special focus on neurobiological processes and the interplay between genetic and environmental factors. Intervention studies and adoption studies as (quasi-) experimental manipulations of the environment have their natural place in this line of research. She was awarded the Bowlby-Ainsworth award of the New York Attachment Consortium (2005) and was VIDI (2004) and VICI (2009/2010) laureate of the Netherlands Organization for Scientific Research. She is a Fellow of The Royal Netherlands Academy of Arts and Sciences and a Fellow of the Association for Psychological Science, both since 2012.

Chip Chimera is a systemic family psychotherapist and a psychodrama psychotherapist. She is the director of the intermediate level of systemic training at the Institute of Family Therapy. She is also a founder member of the London Psychodrama Network. For many years Chip has been interested in the integration of attachment theory into clinical practice and into systemic training. As course director of Child Focused Practice at IFT she teaches attachment across the life cycle as an integral part of the training.

In clinical practice Chip has worked as an expert witness in private law high-conflict divorce cases and public law care proceedings, using an attachment-based approach to family assessment and treatment in complex situations. Chip has a thriving independent practice with individuals, families, couples and groups. She also offers consultation and training to professionals. She is based in London and Surrey and can be contacted at chipchimera@btinternet.com.

Steve Farnfield is a Senior Lecturer in Attachment Studies and convenor of the MSc in Attachment Studies at the University of Roehampton, UK. He is a social worker and play therapist with over 40 years' experience in the field of child and family welfare, and formerly taught on the Social Work and Post Qualifying Child Care Programmes at the University of Reading, UK. Steve is a licensed trainer for the Dynamic-Maturational Model of Attachment Infant CARE-Index, Preschool Assessment of Attachment and Adult Attachment Interview developed by Dr Patricia Crittenden. He has also developed a system for analysing attachment and mentalising using narrative story stems with pre-school and school-aged children.

Mary Ann Harris has been a member of the Law Society Children Panel for many years. She came to Britain from the United States in 1969 and initially worked as a paralegal and then graduated in Law in 1981. She obtained an LL.M (Cantab) in Public and International Law from Cambridge University, UK. She then lectured in the Law Department at Trent Polytechnic, UK, before qualifying as a solicitor. Since then she has practised in many small and medium sized law firms in Lincolnshire, a City Council and latterly for a firm in London specializing in family and children's law where she became a partner and joint head of the Family Department.

Her work ranged from probate work, advising on ecclesiastical law, civil litigation, divorces, and in the last 20 years specialising in the law relating to children, including adoption law, domestic violence and forced marriages.

She is now retired and lives on a livestock farm in Lincolnshire where she and her husband breed British Shorthorn cattle.

Jeremy Holmes is a psychiatrist and psychoanalytic psychotherapist. For 35 years he worked as Consultant Psychiatrist and Psychotherapist in the NHS, providing a district psychotherapy service in North Devon, focusing especially on people with Borderline Personality Disorder. He was Chair of the Psycho-therapy Faculty of the Royal College of Psychiatrists 1998–2002. Now partially retired, he has a small private practice; set up and co-runs a Masters and now Doctoral psychoanalytic psychotherapy training programme at Exeter University, UK, where he is visiting Professor; and lectures nationally and internationally. He has written more than 120 papers and book chapters in the field of Attachment Theory and Psychoanalysis, and 15 books including *John Bowlby and Attachment Theory* (Routledge, 1992), and *Oxford Textbook of Psychotherapy* (2005, co-edited with Glen Gabbard and Judy Beck). His latest is *Exploring in Security: Towards an Attachment-informed Psychoanalytic*

Psychotherapy (Routledge, 2010). He was recipient of the 2009 New York Attachment Consortium Bowlby-Ainsworth Founders Award.

Paul Holmes is a Consultant Child and Adolescent Psychiatrist with extensive clinical experience in community child mental health teams and in specialist services working with looked-after and adopted children, their families and their carers. In his private practice he undertook over 500 child psychiatry assessments for the courts in children's proceedings where he has used his expertise in attachment theory to inform his work. He has trained both as a psychoanalytic and psychodrama psychotherapist and is the author of the *Inner World Outside: Object Relations Theory and Psychodrama* and the editor of three other books on psychodrama.

David Howe is Emeritus Professor in the School of Social Work at the University of East Anglia, Norwich, UK. He has research and writing interests in emotional development, empathy, developmental attachment theory, and child abuse and neglect. His most recent books include *Child Abuse and Neglect: Attachment, development and intervention* (Palgrave Macmillan, 2005), *The Emotionally Intelligent Social Worker* (Palgrave Macmillan, 2008), *A Brief Introduction to Social Work Theory* (Palgrave Macmillan, 2009), *Attachment Across the Lifecourse: A brief introduction* (Palgrave Macmillan, 2011) and *Empathy: What it is and why it matters* (Palgrave Macmillan, 2012).

Daniel Hughes, PhD, is a clinical psychologist with a limited practice near Philadelphia, PA. He has specialised in the treatment of children who have experienced abuse and neglect and demonstrate ongoing problems related to attachment and trauma. This treatment occurs in a family setting and the treatment model has expanded to become a general model of family treatment. He is engaged throughout the US, Canada, Europe and Australia in conducting seminars and providing extensive training toward certification of therapists in his treatment model, as well as providing ongoing consultation to various agencies and professionals. Daniel is the author of many books and articles. These include *Building the Bonds of Attachment* (2nd ed.) (Jason Aronson, 2006), *Attachment-Focused Parenting* (W.W. Norton & Co., 2009), *Attachment-Focused Family Therapy Workbook* (W.W. Norton & Co., 2011) and *Brain-Based Parenting* (W.W. Norton & Co., 2012).

Marinus H. van IJzendoorn is a Professor of Child and Family studies at Leiden University and a Research Professor of Human Development at Erasmus University Rotterdam in the Netherlands. His major research interests include attachment across the life-span and in various contexts; gene-by-parenting interventions and differential susceptibility; neural and hormonal concomitants of parenting and emotional development. He was awarded the Aristotle Prize of the European Federation of Psychologists Associations (2011), the Bowlby-Ainsworth Founder Award of the New York Attachment Consortium (2011), an Honorary Doctorate of the University of Haifa, Israel (2008), the Distinguished

International Contributions to Child Development award of the Society for Research in Child Development (2007), and the Spinoza Prize awarded by the Netherlands Organization for Scientific Research (2004). He is a Fellow of the Royal Netherlands Academy of Arts and Sciences (elected in 1998).

Femmie Juffer is Professor of Adoption Studies at the Centre for Child and Family Centre, Leiden University, the Netherlands. She is interested in the life-long consequences of adoption and foster care, children's resilience and recovery from adversity, sensitive parenting, and effects of attachment-based early childhood interventions for families. Together with colleagues she is involved in several longitudinal and meta-analytic studies of adopted children and in studies testing the effectiveness of the attachment-based intervention developed at Leiden University: the Video-feedback Intervention to promote Positive Parenting (VIPP). For her efforts to translate science into practice she was awarded the Piet Vroon Prize in 2004 and a royal decoration of Officer in the Order of Orange-Nassau in 2010.

Jeanne Kaniuk is Managing Director of Coram's Adoption Services, based in London, UK, which has developed since her appointment as Head of Service in 1980. She has a long-standing interest in the needs of children who cannot remain in their birth families, and was involved in the longitudinal adoption attachment research study undertaken by Great Ormond Street Hospital, the Anna Freud Centre and Coram (Kaniuk *et al.* in *Adoption and Fostering*, 2004, 28.2, pp. 61–67). She was also instrumental in developing Coram's concurrent planning project, which is now in its 15th year. In 2006 Jeanne set up Coram's adoption partnership with LB Harrow, the first such partnership between a local authority and a voluntary adoption agency in the UK, aimed at ensuring improved adoption outcomes for Harrow's children. This partnership has now been replicated in other local authorities including Cambridgeshire, Kent and LB Redbridge.

Graham Music is Consultant Child and Adolescent Psychotherapist at the Tavistock and Portman Clinics and an adult psychotherapist in private practice. His publications include *Nurturing Natures, Attachment and Children's Emotional, Sociocultural and Brain Development* (Psychology Press, 2011) and *Affect and Emotion* (Icon Books, 2001). He has a particular interest in exploring the interface between developmental findings and clinical work. Formerly Associate Clinical Director in the Tavistock Child and Family Department, he has worked therapeutically with maltreated children for over two decades, has managed a range of services concerned with the aftermath of child maltreatment and neglect and organised community-based therapy services, particularly in schools and in GP practices alongside health visitors. He has recently been working at the Portman clinic with forensic cases. He organises training for therapists in the Child and Adolescent Mental Health Services (CAMHS), leads on teaching on attachment, the brain and child development, and teaches and supervises on the Tavistock Child Psychotherapy Training and other psychotherapy training programmes in Britain and abroad.

Preface

This volume is a companion to *The Routledge Handbook of Attachment: Theory* (Holmes & Farnfield 2014) and *The Routledge Handbook of Attachment: Assessment* (Farnfield & Holmes 2014).

We have both had a long-standing professional interest in child welfare, child protection and therapeutic services: Paul Holmes as a child psychiatrist and adult psychotherapist, Steve Farnfield as a social worker, play therapist and university lecturer. Like many professionals involved in these fields, in recent years we have become increasingly interested in using attachment theory and the associated evidence-based assessments, presented in these books, to underpin our work as therapists, supervisors and (for Paul Holmes) as an expert witness in children's legal proceedings. These three books were designed to cover the areas of expertise we draw on in this work.

Attachment theory and assessments can be used to assist in making decisions about the possible therapeutic and social interventions that might assist families and children. These may be either based on attachment theory and assessments (i.e. they are logical, evidence-based, developments arising from theory) or attachment-informed, in which existing therapeutic modalities or social interventions incorporate concepts and knowledge from attachment theory and research.

Attachment strategies, first developed in infancy to assist in gaining protection from danger, may later in life no longer assist the individual in the way they once did. Indeed, they can subsequently be counterproductive to the formation of close, trusting and secure relationships. Change can occur, through therapy or through other life experiences, but this is a complex process which can take time.

The authors in this book consider therapeutic, social and legal steps that can assist in this journey, from individual psychotherapy to, for a child, a change of carer through fostering or adoption. However, the reorganisation of strategies towards security or balance can be actually hard, particularly when a child or adult has been traumatised by abuse or loss. In such cases professionals have to decide if the problems are better worked through or worked around (Moran *et al.* 2008).

That said, all the chapters in this book consider interventions that offer the possibility of growth and change.

References

Farnfield, S. & Holmes, P. (eds) (2014) *The Routledge Handbook of Attachment: Assessment*, London and New York: Routledge.

Holmes, P. & Farnfield, S. (eds) (2014) *The Routledge Handbook of Attachment: Theory*, London and New York: Routledge.

Moran, G., Bailey, H. N., Gleason, K., DeOliveira, C. A. & Pederson, D. R. (2008) 'Exploring the mind behind unresolved attachment: Lessons from and of attachment-based interventions with infants and their traumatized mothers', in H. Steele & M. Steele (eds), *Clinical Applications of the Adult Attachment Interview* (pp. 371–398), New York: The Guilford Press.

Chapter 1

Introduction

Steve Farnfield and Paul Holmes

> A great deal of work needs doing before we can be confident which disorders of attachment and care-giving behaviour are treatable by psychotherapy and which not and, if treatable, which of various methods is to be preferred.
>
> (Bowlby 1979/2005: 171)

John Bowlby, the founding father of attachment theory and research, trained both as a psychiatrist and as a psychoanalyst. His early seminal book *Child Care and the Growth of Love* (1953) grew out of a report he wrote for the World Health Organization commissioned to study the needs of 'children who are orphaned or separated from their families for other reasons and need care in foster homes, institutions or other types of group care' (Bowlby 1953: 7).

Bowlby's interest in developing a research-based understanding of the consequences of childhood trauma, loss and separation was always linked to consideration of effective and logical therapeutic interventions. He struggled with his own personal psychoanalytic heritage and always intended his contribution as 'an up-to-date version of psychoanalytic object relations theory, compatible with contemporary ethology and evolution theory, supported by research, and helpful to clinicians in understanding and treating child and adult patients' (Ainsworth & Bowlby 1991: 9).

Clinical applications of his theory were slow to materialise and more has been achieved since his death, at the age of 83 in 1990, than during his lifetime. It is impossible to provide a comprehensive over view in a book of this length on all the implications and treatments associated with issues of attachment. However, the authors contributing to this volume open windows onto the wide range of therapies and interventions which use attachment theory and/or research to inform their practice.

Attachment theory

This book does not aim to provide a detailed account of attachment theory but a brief summary may be useful.

Attachment is first and foremost a relational theory. It has given us a way of describing what we do when we are anxious and how we use past experience to make predictions about what is most likely to keep us safe in the future. Bowlby described this information as being stored as Internal Working Models (Bowlby 1973/1985; Bretherton 2005) whereas Crittenden uses the term Dispositional Representations (Crittenden & Landini 2011). These memories of attachment-based experiences are not *things* we have in our heads so much as the sum of expectations of future situations, especially those involving danger, developed in interaction with attachment figures in the past.

The consequences of this process for an individual infant were neatly captured by Mary Ainsworth and her work on the Strange Situation procedure (SSP) (Ainsworth *et al.* 1978) which explored an infant's responses to a brief separation from their mother. Ainsworth's analysis of these observations provided the ABC notation on which much of the subsequent empirical work has been based.

- *Type A*   Carers of infants in Type A are predictably rejecting of 'unnecessary' signals of attachment from their child and tend to be protective but not comforting. Consequently the infant inhibits the display of anxiety; tries to fit in with the expectations of the outside world; takes responsibility for what happens; and finds intimacy in close relationships makes her defensive. Type A uses cognition as a source of information, i.e. there is a reliance on cause and effect at the expense of arousing feelings such as anger or desire for a cuddle.
- *Type B*   Carers of infants in Type B are predictably protective and comforting and attuned to their child's needs. The infant comes to learn that the expression of arousing negative feelings can lead to resolution of problems after which attachment-seeking behaviour can be terminated and he can go back to exploration. Children and adults in Type B develop a high level of emotional literacy.
- *Type C*   Carers of infants in Type C are inconsistently available to meet their infant's needs and may reinforce behaviour in the infant that they say they do not want, for example smiling approvingly when telling the child off for doing something 'wrong'. Life in Type C is never clear: the child's feelings and own perspective are a better guide to how he should proceed than the perspective of other people. He uses affective logic to solve relationship problems and force others to feel what he feels; finding the right distance in close relationships is a problem.

One starting point – two theories of attachment

Not all infants and children assessed in the early SSP samples fitted into one of these three types. Scrutiny of anomalous examples led to a divergence of theory by two of Ainsworth's students, Mary Main and Patricia Crittenden. Main and her colleagues developed a fourth category, disorganised-disorientated (Main & Solomon 1986), setting in motion the development of the ABC + D model of attachment. Crittenden interpreted the same data in a different way: as alternating A and C strategies and then early signs of more complex A and C strategies which she was later to describe in the Dynamic-Maturational Model (DMM) of attachment (Crittenden 1985, 1995), which integrates all types of strategic attachment behaviour under the three broad headings of A, B or C.

Other related theories

Neither the ABC + D or DMM model offers a phenomenology of attachment. Yet it is the feeling of being insecurely attached, and how this affects other people, which may bring people to therapy and interest professionals when trying to understand individuals or families.

Object Relations Theory (ORT) provides one way of trying to give subjective meaning to the internal processes that underpin Bowlby's 'inner working model' of the world or, to use different language, Crittenden's 'dispositional representations'. Concepts such as splitting or projective identification are useful in explaining not just the internal defences employed in the Type A and C strategies but also their effect on other people. ORT can flesh out the meaning attachment strategies have for specific individuals and the impact on their relationships. It is thus of considerable clinical use in attachment-informed treatments with both adults and children (Holmes 1992; Steele & Steele 2008a; Steele *et al.* 2007; Fonagy 2001).

The work of Peter Fonagy and colleagues has added the theory of mentalisation to the classical theories of psychoanalysis and has shifted attention from the classification of strategies to how people process information. Mentalising refers to the peculiar human ability to take an intentional stance with regard to our own and others' behaviour; our ability to read the minds of other people and think about our own thought processes. This can happen at a conscious or non-conscious level and high-level mentalising is associated with secure attachment; the parent–child relationship is a meeting of minds in which mentalising/secure attachment in the parent is transmitted to the child (Fonagy *et al.* 2004; Allen *et al.* 2008).

What are 'attachment-based' interventions?

Writing on clinical work with adults, Obegi and Berant (2009) make the useful distinction between attachment-informed and attachment-based psychotherapy. The former refers to the use of attachment theory and research to aid with assessment, formulation and aspects of treatment but with a reliance on established therapeutic modalities in terms of approach and technique. The latter attachment-based therapies make explicit use of attachment theory as a conceptual and operational framework for intervention and use validated assessment procedures to establish whether changes in attachment behaviour or representations of behaviour have occurred following a particular treatment. At a minimum this requires pre/post research designs and at best randomised controlled clinical trials.

The first reaction to reading the above might be that we should be striving for attachment-based interventions that meet the demand for evidenced-based practice. Certainly if increasing attachment security in our clients is the primary aim of our treatment then we should be able to give an account of our success. However, the progress in establishing formally attachment-based interventions is patchy at best. This is partly due to both the difficulty and the cost of mounting studies of effectiveness. But, a more central reason is that, as Music observes in Chapter 2, attachment theory and research cannot provide a whole theory about therapeutic work.

Do we need specific attachment-based treatments?

The chapters in this book are a testament to the likely balance between attachment-informed and attachment-based interventions in present clinical practice. In our opinion only one chapter (Juffer and colleagues in Chapter 5) describes a formal attachment-based intervention, while all the others are attachment-informed. In the other chapters the authors have used their training as therapists and their professional experiences to integrate the concepts of attachment into their work using their clinical judgement and creativity rather than following 'evidence-based' procedures. However, we would hope that therapeutic interventions that are 'felt to work' will result in the establishment of proper evidence-based outcome studies.

A prominent view, and one that we share, has been that attachment theory should be used to inform the use of existing interventions rather than create new ones (see Slade 1999: 577). The authors in this book discuss a number of therapeutic and social interventions informed by attachment studies in this way.

'Holding therapy'

Even a cursory search of the internet reveals all manner of 'attachment therapies' and cures for 'attachment disorders' together with other sites devoted to people complaining that they have suffered at the hands of intrusive and abusive therapists. These sites are reminders of an issue that came to a head in professional circles around 2005 regarding 'therapy' which included enforced holding and eye contact to reconfigure the social brain of traumatised children. This produced an outcry in professional circles (e.g. BAAF 2006; Chaffin et al. 2006; Prior & Glaser 2006). Our impression is that in this country the use of overt holding and other forms of enforced 'therapy' has now abated or indeed ceased.

'Holding' was certainly the antithesis of a 'secure base' and it also reminds us that psycho-social therapies are not neutral; if they can benefit people then they can also do damage. Doctors and therapists can do harm (Fonagy & Bateman 2006: 1 2).

Wheels within wheels: systems within systems

This book considers interventions from a wide perspective, moving from one-to-one individual psychotherapy through family therapy and parent training to the input of social workers and the interventions of society through legal activity.

Attachment can be conceptualised as an intra-personal, inter-personal and a social psychological theory which considers different spheres of existence or systems that all have an interlinked and hierarchical relationship to each other.

System

Genetic	That which is inherited but which is open to change after birth through the epigenetic process.
Biological	The nervous, neurobiological, system which grows and adapts over time from infancy consequent upon life experiences.
Intra-personal	The individual's psychology.
Inter-personal	The dynamics of families and close relationships with other people.
Cultural	The dynamics between people in the local community and national and international relationships.

(adapted from Holmes 1989: 244 and Holmes 1992: 20)

To take a very brief, simple, example:

Inter-personal system	The difficulties caused by a distressed and angry acting-out teenager will impact on those closest to him in a way that might be assisted by family therapy.
Intra-personal system	But the stresses in the home might make both the boy and his mother depressed and have an impact on the family. Individual psychotherapy or even antidepressant medication might help.
Social system	Likewise a change in any one system (say the family) may impact on the boy's peers and teachers at school. Should this lad's behaviour cross certain social and cultural boundaries he may become involved with social services and even the police and the criminal justice system.

Family systems theory describes how a change in any person in the family will impact on all the constituent parts of that system (Marvin 2003). This process will also result in changes in the other systems in the hierarchy. If the family therapy is successful the boy's mother might become less depressed (which some would see as a change in her nervous/biological system). Further pressure could be taken off the school and social services systems and, indeed, the police.

It must be stressed, however, that there are always reciprocal interactions between these systems. It is not a case of just blaming this boy or indeed anyone else. He might be reacting to a depressed mother, marital discord, or dysfunction in the classroom consequent upon the skills of teachers who are incompetent or who are overly stressed by changes in the government's education policy.

Further, our teenager may deploy an insecure (Type C) attachment strategy developed in infancy, with a tendency to externalise his feelings ('act out') with the result that he exasperates his teachers and other adults caring for him. Likewise his behaviour in the wider community will reflect a dynamic interaction between him, his personality and the culture of his peers, and other social pressures and influences.

It can be argued that logical, and maybe even effective, interventions could be provided to every level in this hierarchy, each in its own way designed to tackle dysfunction in that system but also, as a consequence, having an impact in the other systems.

Systemic interventions

Genes and biology

The authors in this book only consider interventions in the last three of these interlocking systems. However, in recent years there have been significant advances in knowledge of the importance of genetics, epigenetics and neurobiology and development of the attachment process (see Fonagy and colleagues and Music in Holmes & Farnfield 2014).

Intra-personal systems

Graham Music in Chapter 2 discusses in detail one-to-one psychotherapeutic work with very distressed and disturbed (as well as disturbing to others) children and teenagers. His emphasis is on work with the child alone in the context of his therapeutic relationship with her. That is not to say no assistance will have been given to her parents and carers, either through supportive sessions or perhaps personal therapy with other professionals and colleagues. In these intense sessions Music is working with children and teenagers perhaps too disturbed to function in family therapy sessions. However, as Music describes, his work has a positive impact on the families in which these children live.

Jeremy Holmes in Chapter 3 also considers therapeutic interventions in the intra-psychic or individual attachment system of adults, in the context of their roles as parents. However, he clearly acknowledges the interaction with the dyadic system of parent and child and the parent's position from their perspective of caring for a difficult child.

Holmes also discusses the consequences for a child who is being parented by an adult with their own marked emotional and psychiatric difficulties consequent upon their own attachment insecurity, and who might have been diagnosed as suffering from a borderline personality disorder (BPD). He considers the impact of the adult's fluctuating emotional state on their child's development and the possibility of indirectly assisting the child through psychotherapeutic work with her parent(s) (see also Fonagy and colleagues in Holmes & Farnfield 2014).

Holmes also touches on mentalisation-based therapy (MBT), a development of classical psychoanalysis by Peter Fonagy and his colleagues, which has a close association with attachment theory. MBT was initially developed to treat adults diagnosed as having a borderline personality disorder, although its use has now been widened to many other populations. It has, unlike many schools of psychotherapy, a significant evidence basis for its efficacy (Bateman & Fonagy 2004; Allen & Fonagy 2006; Allen 2013).

Individual psychotherapy with parents can thus be seen as an indirect way of assisting, or at least trying to protect, the emotional development of their children.

Inter-personal systems

The authors of Chapters 2 and 3 acknowledge that their patients exist in wider family and social systems, albeit their focus is on the individual. There are, however, numerous well-known and well-documented attachment-informed interventions specifically developed to work in multi-person contexts.

Chimera in Chapter 4 considers systemic family therapy, looking both at how family therapists might use attachment theory to inform their work and giving case examples of how an understanding of attachment theory and the assessment of attachment strategies used by individuals in the family can be used to inform the treatment. The assessment of attachment in individuals and families is the subject of Dallos in Farnfield and Holmes (2014).

Juffer and her colleagues in Chapter 5 discuss a formal attachment-based treatment Video-feedback Intervention to promote Positive Parenting (VIPP) which aims to improve both the quality of caregiving (parenting) and the security of children's attachment (see also Appendix 1.1). There is a growing body of evidence for the effectiveness of this type of intervention and a summary of some of the others is given in the appendix.

Hughes in Chapter 6 discusses the complexity of therapeutic work with children and teens suffering from attachment trauma and introduces his attachment-informed Dyadic Developmental Psychotherapy (DDP). DDP includes a basic therapeutic stance that is characterised by playfulness, acceptance, curiosity and empathy (PACE) together with close involvement of the child's parent or carer. As Hughes indicates this is a population known to be hard to successfully engage in therapy, resembling those young people Music discusses in Chapter 2 in the context of individual psychotherapy.

Social and cultural systems

The subsequent chapters in this book consider how attachment theory can inform interventions in the wider social systems.

Arnold in Chapter 7 highlights the importance of cultural and personal history on the formation of an individual's personality and emotional state and considers, through case examples, the impact of culture, loss and trauma on those who have moved to new countries to live. Attachment is strongly influenced by culture and context and Arnold highlights the need to allow clients time and space to tell their story, and the importance of culture and ethnicity in therapy with recent migrants and refugees.

Harris, as a lawyer, considers in Chapter 8 the importance of attachment theory and assessments to the legal process necessary to remove children, an intervention of last resort, from their birth families. She points to the importance of appropriate skills and supervision together with transparency about the process if attachment is to be assessed by social workers prior to the initiation of court proceedings. Proper attachment-based assessments should assist in establishing the needs of families and allow the professionals involved with them to form a view about which interventions are most likely to help the family.

Kaniuk, in Chapter 9, describes how society responds when attempts to address issues in the intra- and inter-personal systems are deemed to have failed to protect the child's safety or development. In these circumstances society (through its 'agents' local authorities and social workers) may have instigated processes to remove a child from their birth family with the aim of providing better care in a foster family or through adoption.

Finally Howe, in Chapter 10, discusses the uses and abuses of attachment theory in the context of social work practice and argues that the strength of the social work profession lies in knowing clients over time. In spite of the increasing bureaucratic nature of local authority social work, attachment thinking emphasises that it is essentially a relationship-based activity which is applicable across the life span. Howe's chapter draws together themes, such as mentalising, which run through those by the other contributors.

The assessment of attachment: an overview

The assessment of attachment is the subject of a companion book to this volume (Farnfield & Holmes 2014).

Formal assessments of attachment can provide very useful information that can be used in planning interventions designed to assist families and their children, examples of which form the subject of this book.

These insights can also be used in considering the level of risk parents might pose to their children's emotional development. At this stage, when other interventions have been tried, the level of professional concern might have reached the point where legal proceedings have been instigated to protect the child. For discussions of how to use assessments of attachment in forensic settings see Main *et al.* (2011) or Crittenden *et al.* (2013).

A range of validated procedures is now available for all developmental stages and they fall broadly into two groups: observation and representational measures. An important question that a formal assessment might assist in answering is, 'What can attachment theory and assessment tell us that will be useful in choosing and designing treatment?' The main procedures will now be given a brief introduction with this question in mind.

Observation

For children under 3 years the only way of assessing their attachment to a particular parent or carer is by observation. For this it is necessary to induce just enough stress for attachment-seeking behaviour to be activated, which is why the Strange Situation procedure (SSP) is so effective. The basic procedure can be used with children aged 10 months to around 4 or 5 years of age although the level of stress reduces significantly for many children after 4 years. An alternative is the Attachment-Q set which involves the observer (parent or professional) rating aspects of the child's behaviour according to statements on a series of cards (Waters *et al.* 1995). The SSP is the gold standard with regard to a child's attachment to a specific person but gives weak information regarding the caregiving behaviour of the parent.

Parental behaviour is better assessed using a play-based procedure such as the CARE-Index (Crittenden 1979–2005, 2005) or indeed using knowledge from such a procedure and observing (ideally with a video-record to assist analysis and client feedback) the parent(s) and child(ren) in naturally occurring settings for at least an hour.

Representational measures

From about 3 years of age children can tell stories about attachment-related events using a few simple props and the help of an attentive adult. Narrative story stems are typically used up until age 7 or 8 but have been tried with children as old as 12. By the age of 6 or 7 years formal interviews with children are possible. For example, the Child Attachment Interview (Shmueli-Goetz *et al.* 2008) and Can You Tell Me? (Farnfield in press), both developed from a milestone in attachment research, the Adult Attachment Interview (AAI) (George *et al.* 1985; Main & Goldwyn 1984).

Representational measures move assessment from behaviour to how people think about their behaviour. Whereas the information from the SSP is somewhat limited (the child's strategy shorn of much of the context), procedures like story stems and the AAI open a window onto the internal world of attachment, trauma and loss and are extremely valuable in calibrating interventions which are person-specific (Steele & Steele 2008a; Steele *et al.* 2007; Crittenden & Landini 2011).

The other very useful extension to representational assessments are interviews about caregiving; specifically the adult's perceptions of themselves, their child, and their relationship (Slade 2005, 2007; Zeanah *et al.* 1994; Grey 2010). Added to observations of the parent's behaviour with their child these interviews tell us a lot about why people do what they do. Taken together, in terms of a comprehensive assessment of parenting, we have crucial information on different aspects of attachment and caregiving which can be tested against each other to aid in formulating a workable intervention plan (Kozlowska *et al.* 2012a, 2012b, 2013; Farnfield 2008).

The selection of treatment

Attachment research orientates practitioners towards formulation rather than diagnosis and prescription; that is, a bridge from assessment to intervention which makes sense of how the presenting problems can be understood in the context of the person or family's history, what needs to be changed and how this will be achieved (Zeanah 2007; Crittenden & Landini 2011). Of particular importance is the function of attachment in self-protection. Hence a key question for any planned intervention is what will help the person, couple, family, wider group or society feel safer than they do at present?

The question of how attachment strategies can inform the direction and/or choice of treatment is complex and imperfectly understood (Slade 2008). Even though the majority of psychotherapy clients are insecurely attached (Dozier *et al.* 2008) insecure attachment is not an illness (after all, 40–50% of the non-clinical population are found to be 'insecure' on assessment) and correspondence between particular disorders and attachment strategy are, in the main, difficult to uncover (Van IJzendoorn & Bakermans-Kranenberg 2008).

Crittenden has argued that treatments should be selected according to the client's attachment strategies. For example, adults or children in Type A learned as a child to inhibit the expression of feelings they experienced as being forbidden by adults, in particular anger and the desire for comfort (having had the experience as infants that openly expressed emotions do not bring them closer to those who care for them). For them, interventions that encourage them to express these feelings in a safe environment and, for school-age children, to generate information from their own perspective not that of other people, may be beneficial. Conversely, treatments such as cognitive behaviour therapy (CBT) may actually reinforce the use of maladaptive cognition-based attachment strategies (Crittenden, personal communication).

For adults or children in Type C the opposite may be the case. As children they learned that freely expressed emotion will, eventually, bring them closer to their 'secure base' as their need for comfort is at last recognised. However, such behaviour might not always make them easy to live with or, indeed, to teach (Geddes 2006; Bomber 2007, 2011). Such individuals should be encouraged to regulate their display of anger or desire for comfort and focus on the perspective of others (Crittenden *et al.* 2001; Crittenden 1992).

At risk of over-simplification this would indicate cognitive-behavioural therapies would be beneficial for those in Type C but counter indicated for children in

Type A who might do better with expressive, creative arts-based approaches such as play therapy or psychodrama. This is broadly in line with observations by Daniel (2006, 2009) on the implications of narrative coherence for therapy.

Two major reviews of adult attachment and psychopathology found some qualified support for the hypothesis that internalising disorders, for example borderline personality disorder (see Bateman & Fonagy 2004) are linked with preoccupied states of mind and externalising disorders (for example, anti social personality disorder) with dismissive states of mind on the AAI (Van IJzendoorn & Bakermans-Kranenberg 2008; Dozier *et al.* 2008). However, rather than looking for correspondence between the two dimensions (as in an attempt to construct a marrying of attachment behaviour with the American Psychiatric Association Diagnostic and Statistical Manuel 5 (DSM 5) (2013)) it might be more useful to see them in terms of four categories with which 'to describe the complex reality of clinical patients with comorbid features' (Van IJzendoorn & Bakermans-Kranenberg 2008: 89).

On the other hand, the hypothesised relation between internalising-preoccupied and externalising-dismissing has been challenged by Crittenden and Landini (2011) who note that Crittenden and Ainsworth (1989) had proposed the opposite relationship.

Treatment by memory systems

A significant part of the work on the AAI has been the analysis of the speaker's state of mind regarding their childhood attachment in terms of 'memory systems'. These refer to a variety of ways in which information from past experience, in respect of attachment-based experiences, is processed regarding safety, danger and sexual opportunity in the present.

Memory can either be implicit and unconscious or explicit and thus available for conscious reflection. It can also be cognitive or affective.

The Main and Goldwyn AAI focuses on three memory systems – semantic, episodic and working memory – and the DMM-AAI adds three more: procedural, imaged and connotative language. People in Type B secure have fuller access to all systems and are able to integrate them into current thinking and behaviour whereas people in Types A and C omit or distort information in various ways (see Farnfield & Stokowy 2014).

To extend the simple example above, cognitive-based techniques which affect semantic and episodic memory are likely to show little efficacy with people in Type A but will help those in Type C. Family sculpting might benefit children in Type A, because it draws attention to their affective state, but be of limited value with children in Type C for whom explicit verbal semantic memory needs attention over nonverbal forms of communication (see Crittenden *et al.* 2001: Table 18.1; for a detailed example from a DMM-AAI see Crittenden & Landini 2011: Chapter 14). To put it another way, people may benefit from therapeutic assistance to access and use attachment-relevant information that is not part of their habitual repertoire. Such a process should allow them access to both Type A and Type C strategies, and as a consequence they move (integrate and reorganise) towards the balanced Type B. We would stress that such a shift may be 'earned' by other life events such as a powerful and rewarding close relationship.

Attachment-based interventions – what is the evidence?

This section offers a brief overview of some of the interventions that are attachment-based; i.e. they can provide empirical evidence regarding their effectiveness in changing attachment or caregiving behaviour or representations of the same. The focus is on interventions based on the validated assessments of attachment and caregiving (covered in Farnfield & Holmes 2014) and excludes self-report measures and also interventions designed to treat Reactive Attachment Disorder (RAD) in children.

Individual therapy for children

Based on the premise that attachment strategies function to protect the self, attempting to change a child's strategy without removing or modifying the danger seems counterproductive or could even be dangerous. Parents and other caregivers should ideally be involved in the intervention. If the caregiving environment can be modified, attention can then be given to helping the child adapt her strategy to the new conditions (Crittenden *et al.* 2001). Mentalisation-based child therapy 'can succeed only if important adults can be involved' (Verheugt-Pleiter 2008: 48) and the general effectiveness of play therapy may be increased when it also involves parents (Bratton *et al.* 2005).

This is doubly relevant in the light of research indicating that parents of children with clinical problems are, themselves, likely to be troubled people whose AAIs are significantly more likely to be rated insecure and unresolved compared with the non-clinical population (Van IJzendoorn & Bakermans-Kranenberg 2008; Crittenden & Landini 2009, reported in Crittenden & Landini 2011)

However, not all parents or carers are amenable to joining in the treatment process with their child and some young people become too anxious and disturbed in family therapy sessions. In such situations individual treatment might be a good, or the only, alternative. While individual child therapies are effective for a broad range of presenting problems (Weisz & Kazdin 2010), this enquiry made no advances on previous reviews which found no systematic evaluations, using validated measures, of the impact of direct interventions on children's attachment (Weisz & Kazdin 2010; Carr 2009; Becker-Weidman 2006; Prior & Glaser 2006; Tarren-Sweeney 2013; Benedict & Schofield 2010; Zilberstein 2013). Rather than increasing attachment security the appropriate aim of individual child therapy might be to improve mentalising (Verheugt-Pleiter *et al.* 2008).

Given the disruption to the functioning of attachment strategies attributed to unresolved trauma (Allen *et al.* 2008) an important role for child therapies might be treating post-traumatic stress disorder (PTSD) in children. A variety of treatments are available with a strong cognitive-behavioural basis. For example, trauma-focused CBT has been the subject of seven randomised control trials (Cohen *et al.* 2010). Where possible it employs a joint child–parent approach and is reported to be the most researched and best validated in terms of evidenced-based practice for treatment of child PTSD (Kliethermes *et al.* 2013; Cohen 2005; Scheeringa *et al.* 2011; Deblinger *et al.* 2012); see also Parent–Child Interaction Therapy which provides parents with behaviour modification skills (Urquisa & Timmer 2013).

One approach that clearly includes attachment and trauma in its remit is Eye Movement Desensitisation and Reprocessing therapy (EMDR). Reports regarding a reduction in trauma symptoms in children using EMDR in individual and group settings are positive (Marcus *et al.* 1997; Lee *et al.* 2002; Wesselmann 2012). See Allen (2013) for a review of EMDR with adults.

Individual therapy for adults

While there are a number of treatments called 'attachment therapies' for children this has not been the case with therapies for adults. On the whole, adult therapists have adapted aspects of their technique without radically changing their therapeutic orientation or devising new therapies (Obegi & Berant 2009).

Although therapy can improve attachment security in clients, choosing the right therapy for the right psycho-social problems requires more investigation (see Berant & Obegi 2009 for a review; also Jacobvitz 2008; Levy *et al.* 2006) and, as with parent–child interventions (below), it appears unrealistic to expect that people with complex problems will quickly reorganise into a secure attachment status. Put another way, while attachment informs many therapeutic modalities, treating attachment per se may be unrealistic and in some cases undesirable (Fonagy & Bateman 2006) as the intensity of the therapeutic relationship might, in itself, cause the patient excessive distress and instability.

Among the studies looking at treatment and outcome in terms of attachment security are the following: Fonagy *et al.* 1996; Levy *et al.* 2006; Strauss *et al.* 2011; Tasca *et al.* 2007; see also Daniel 2006 for an excellent review.

Mentalisation- based treatments (MBT)

Rather than a new therapeutic modality Allen, Fonagy and Bateman propose MBT is 'the *least novel* therapeutic approach imaginable, simply because it revolves around a fundamental human capacity – indeed, the capacity that makes us human' (2008: 6, their italics). Their approach to mentalising as good therapeutic technique is laid out in Allen *et al.* (2008: Table 6.1).

Mentalising is not to be equated with security of attachment even if the two are associated. Secure attachment enables high order mentalising whereas insecure attachment and, critically attachment trauma (typically abuse by an attachment figure in childhood) distorts the capacity to mentalise. Attachment is about relationships and self-protective strategies, whereas mentalising refers to information processing and the capacity to be aware of the mental processes of another person. An improvement in the capacity to mentalise should improve affect regulation and inter-personal relationships but Fonagy and colleagues note the mentalising of some people in therapy is actually destabilised by a too intense attachment relationship with the therapist (Fonagy & Bateman 2006; Luyten & Fonagy 2014).

Family systems

Coan (2008) notes the paucity of systemic compared with individualised interventions to help people manage affect regulation and that the systemic approaches may be both more efficient and cost effective.

An attachment-based family therapy (ABFT) has been developed by Diamond and colleagues (2002, 2010) who found a decrease in attachment-related anxiety (measured on a self-report scale) in a small group of adolescents (Diamond *et al.* 2012). Mentalisation-based family therapy is also used with families, children and adolescents or adults in groups (SMART; Fearon *et al.* 2006).

Parent–child interventions

Consistent with the emphasis on the importance of children developing secure attachments from the start of their life, parent–child interventions dominate the field of attachment-based interventions. Evaluation studies have generated an ongoing debate with regard to whether services should aim to change parental sensitivity (what parents do) or parents' perceptions of the relationship they have with their child (representation) or both. There is also a debate as to whether shorter interventions are more effective than longer ones – 'less is more'.

The means by which attachment is 'transmitted' from parent to child is imperfectly understood. In particular, parental sensitivity (what parents do in response to their children's behavioural signals) appears to play a relatively small part (de Wolff & Van IJzendoorn 1997) whereas a more potent mediator may be reflective functioning (how and what parents think when their child is anxious or distressed) (Slade 2005) which, in turn, is reflected in their behaviour.

With regard to child maltreatment, abusing parents were frequently abused when children themselves and are invariably (in AAI terms) unresolved regarding early losses and traumas. Bad things in childhood tend to come back and haunt parents when confronted with stressful situations involving their own children. This was highlighted many years ago by Fraiberg and colleagues' (1975) classic work on 'ghosts in the nursery', and is nicely captured in the phrase 'shark music' used by the Circle of Security programme (Appendix 1.1). Like a seaside scene in a movie, walking with one's child can feel relaxed and sunny but play the shark music (the ghosts of abuse and abandonment from the parent's past) and the scene instantly changes to one of fear and dread (Zanetti *et al.* 2011).

A growing number of attachment-based interventions focus on taming the ghosts and sharks in parents' minds by using parent–child psychotherapy, while others focus on improving parent/maternal sensitivity. Current evidence strongly supports the inclusion of video feedback involving the parent and child doing something together, rather than parent education using films that feature strangers (Berlin *et al.* 2008; Zeanah *et al.* 2011; Zilberstein 2013). Meta-analyses indicate interventions promoting parent sensitivity do better than those aimed at representation (mental models of caregiving) in increasing attachment security in children, and parent sensitivity is easier to change than child attachment (see Chapter 5).

A summary of some of the attachment-based parent–child interventions is given in Appendix 1.1. The inclusion criteria meant that some established interventions which are well validated in domains other than attachment were omitted on the grounds that they do not appear to have published empirical evidence for changes in attachment security and/or parent sensitivity/representation using validated procedures. For example, Theraplay (Jernberg & Booth 1999). The effectiveness of Video Interactive Guidance (VIG; Kennedy *et al.* 2010, 2011) in improving parent sensitivity has been supported by small studies in the UK and Holland (Robertson & Kennedy 2009; Velderman *et al.* 2013) with larger studies in preparation (Kennedy, personal communication). Another widely used intervention is the Incredible Years parent training programme (Webster-Stratton 1984) which is based on social learning theory and does not target child attachment per se. A recent study showed that Incredible Years with antisocial children aged 4–6 years did have a significant and positive impact on parent focused behaviour (sensitivity) but not on dyadic behaviour (mutuality), nor on security of child attachment as assessed by the MCAST codings for narrative story stems (O'Connor *et al.* 2013).

Adoption and fostering

The most drastic intervention is the removal of a child from her parents into permanent substitute care. Not surprisingly Lindhiem and Dozier found that foster parent commitment to the child was a strong influence on placement stability. They also found the number of children a foster carer had previously cared for was negatively correlated with commitment to the current child, and that the younger the child at the start of fostering the more committed were the carers (Lindhiem & Dozier 2007).

The attachment strategy of foster and adoptive parents can be assessed using the AAI and current attachment relationships by using the Attachment Style Interview (ASI) (Bifulco *et al.* 2008). Dozier and colleagues, using the Main and Goldwyn AAI, found a significant correlation between autonomous (secure) foster mothers and foster children assessed as secure on the SSP, whereas non-autonomous foster parents had a disproportionate number of children rated disorganised (Dozier *et al.* 2001). Hodges and colleagues' longitudinal study of adopted children and their parents showed all the children made progress in terms of increasing positive representations of attachment themes using the narrative story stem procedure, but those whose adoptive parents were secure on the AAI also showed a decline in negative themes, suggesting resolution of trauma (Steele *et al.* 2003; see also a study by Beijersbergen *et al.* 2012). These results indicated that children benefitted from being placed with alternative carers who were found to be secure on an AAI assessment.

Using the AAI, different studies have come up with different estimates regarding the distribution of attachment patterns in relatively small samples of foster and adoptive parents. For example, Dozier and colleagues found attachment among foster carers did not differ from non-clinical populations (Dozier *et al.* 2001). However, the Coram-Anna Freud study (Steele *et al.* 2008; see also Kaniuk in Chapter 9 of this volume) found more of the interviews of adoptive mothers were rated secure than expected, but the opposite was true for adoptive fathers.

A study using the DMM-AAI of prospective adoptive parents found only 7 per cent AAIs were rated balanced-secure and that mothers who already had a child of their own were significantly more likely to be in the range secure/normatively insecure (most often in Type A2 in the DMM) whereas for fathers who already had a child the opposite was the case (Farnfield 2012).

One conclusion to be drawn is that when it comes to predicting outcomes for children placed for fostering or adoption, the attachment security of their future carers matters. Another is that not all substitute parents will be secure regarding attachment, and assessments of attachment (AAI or ASI) will deepen our understanding regarding how previous experience influences their current parenting; information which in turn can be clinically useful in interventions to support their tasks as new carers or parents. See, for example, Attachment and Biobehavioral Catch-up with foster parents (Appendix 1.1 and Bick & Dozier 2008).

Life story work

Life story work is a tool widely used to help young fostered children develop a self-story of their life experiences but despite its popularity there appears to be no good empirical evidence as to its effectiveness with regard to either attachment security, placement stability or indeed any other relevant dimension. This approach is likely applied in various ways but in a study of fostered and adopted school years children Quinton and colleagues noted that: 'it is possible that the premises on which the work is currently based are wrong' (Quinton *et al.* 1998: 89). Cook-Cottone and Black (2007) reported a dearth of empirical evidence although Macaskill found that 'good quality' life story work had helped adopted and long-term fostered children start to grapple with their own family history, including abuse (Macaskill 2002).

The process and measurement of change

Not surprisingly, the best outcomes of therapy are achieved with securely attached clients but they do not represent the majority who receive treatment (Slade 2008; Berant & Obegi 2009). However, regarding the latter group, a study by Fonagy and colleagues found dismissing adults (in Type A) may do better in psychotherapy than those in other patterns (Fonagy *et al.* 1996). Dismissing patients have shown fewer ruptures in the therapeutic alliance than preoccupied patients (in Type C) patients (Eames & Roth 2000). Projections of childhood experience onto the therapist (transference) also vary according to attachment pattern (Bradley *et al.* 2005).

Changing our behaviour is always threatening. Self-protective strategies function because they help us feel safe, i.e. it is the strategy not safety itself which elicits a sense of security. The process of therapy can itself be challenging. For example, interventions which lead the attention of dismissing children towards possible attachment figures and preoccupied children away from their attachment figures will provoke anxiety (Main 1995: 452).

In adulthood the AAIs of people who have reorganised from insecure childhood attachments (A or C) towards Type B balance or autonomy (security) are referred to as 'earned B' to distinguish them from 'naive B' AAIs of people who have always been secure.

It seems unlikely that anyone shifts into secure attachment without bringing some of their past experience with them. Children who have been abused or neglected do not make magical transitions into secure attachment with adoptive parents. Rather they add new strategies (which meet new environmental conditions) but retain the old ones (which were functional to their survival in the past and may be needed again) (Hodges *et al.* 2005; Lieberman *et al.* 1991). The earlier attachment strategies remain as a 'default' position to which the individual may return when under increasing stress with the associated, albeit often short-lived, recurrence of old patterns of behaviour.

There is also a question as to whether current attachment assessments such as narrative stems and the AAI are sufficiently finely calibrated to pick up changes within strategies (Hodges *et al.* 2005; Slade 2008). And is change in attachment strategy feasible or even desirable? Jacobvitz, for example, notes that in some cases 'The AAI might be used to identify and to help adults at risk *work around* rather than *work through* their problems' (Jacobvitz 2008: 474, her italics).

The therapist as an attachment figure

Bowlby saw the therapist as a temporary attachment figure with a role that is 'analogous to that of a mother who provides her child with a secure base from which to explore the world' (Bowlby 1988/2005: 159). The primacy of the therapeutic relationship as a secure base is central to many therapeutic modalities in which the therapist, like the ideal mother, learns to attune, mentalise and contain their client's anxieties while providing a safe space for reflection. If parent–infant interaction is a meeting of minds so is the therapeutic relationship. Harris in Chapter 8 considers this process in the complex relationship between a lawyer and their client.

A number of issues flow from this. According to some authors what most counts towards success in psychotherapy is the nature of the relationship between therapist and client (Beutler 1991; Orlinsky *et al.* 1994). For example: 'By virtue of promoting the patient's mentalizing capacity, the therapist's mentalizing capacity, rather than any particular techniques, will determine the success of the treatment' (Allen *et al.* 2008: 222).

There are measurable differences in the impact of therapist attachment pattern on that of the patient or client (Tyrell *et al.* 1999; Petrowski *et al.* 2013) and, not surprisingly, secure attachment of the therapist increases the effectiveness of the treatment (Slade 2008). As with foster and adoptive parents, research on how secure therapists are compared to the general population has produced mixed results (Lambruschi *et al.* 2008, cited in Crittenden & Landini 2011; Tyrrell *et al.* 1999; Diamond *et al.* 2003).

This strongly suggests that attachment strategy and mentalising should be a central component of therapeutic trainings (Steele & Steele 2008b).

While the metaphor of the therapist as parent works fairly well with adults it is inherently problematic when working with children who have actual parents or alternative carers with whom they have, or are developing, an ongoing attachment.

Although many child therapists do refer to the therapist as an attachment figure (e.g. Benedict 2006; Becker-Weidman & Hughes 2008), others see their role in terms such as an 'identification model' who is not a parent substitute and must 'not become caught up in a real relationship' (Verheugt-Pleiter 2008: 50–51). It would be interesting to investigate how these two types of relationship are experienced from the child's perspective.

Conclusion

The influence of attachment theory and research on treatment and intervention is huge and it has not been possible in this chapter to do justice to the range of activity in the field. One conclusion that can be drawn is that attachment behaviour involves interrelated social systems in which the attachment strategies of we, the professionals, play an important part. A second conclusion is that while many interventions are informed by attachment thinking the number that have evidence-based data on their effectiveness in changing attachment behaviour is much smaller. Does this matter? Perhaps not, but with a long caveat! Attachment is not a theory of everything and there are occasions when we may be better leaving the self-protective strategies of our clients alone. This also means that when we really are claiming that our intervention improves attachment security we should be careful to evidence it.

Appendix 1.1

Parent–child attachment-based interventions

Searches were conducted using the databases PsycInfo, PsycArticles and Psyc-Books together with the California Evidence-Based Clearinghouse for Child Welfare.

Video-feedback Intervention to promote Positive Parenting (VIPP)

The model by Juffer, Bakermans-Kranenburg and Van IJzendoorn in Chapter 5 of this volume promotes the idea that 'less is more', i.e. interventions become less effective after 16 sessions. They also conclude that focusing on parental sensitivity rather than representation is more productive in terms of promoting secure attachment in children. VIPP is a home-based parent–child intervention using video feedback of the subjects. It was piloted with adoptive families then rolled out with other groups, and appears effective with the 'mid range' of family problems rather than those with multiple risks. They note that: 'A definite conclusion about the effectiveness of VIPP for enhancing attachment security cannot be drawn yet' (p. 93; see Moss *et al.* 2011 for positive effects of VIPP on child attachment security).

A critique of 'less is more' with regard to the challenge of improving attachment security in multi-risk families has been mounted by Egeland and colleagues (2000), raising the question as to whether improving attachment security of children in such families is a feasible goal, at least in the short term (Ziv 2005). Regarding sensitivity, Moran and colleagues found that mothers who were traumatised (unresolved/disorientated on the Main and Goldwyn AAI) were unable to benefit from an otherwise successful 'less is more' intervention programme (Moran *et al.* 2008).

However, intensive long-term 'more is better' approaches also appear to have mixed results with regard to child attachment security.

The Steps Towards Effective, Enjoyable Parenting (STEEP)

This programme (Egeland & Erickson 2004) included bi-weekly home visits starting in the second trimester of pregnancy and continuing until the child's first birthday, for the evaluation study, and at least until the second birthday overall. Once the baby was born the programme used video feedback and mothers attended bi-weekly group sessions. STEEP made a positive impact on maternal sensitivity but there was no significant difference in the quality of infant–mother attachment in the intervention group when compared with controls (Egeland & Erickson 2004). That said, the comprehensive UCLA programme (see below) has produced improvements in child security (for discussion see Spieker *et al.* 2005 on the US Early Head Start programme).

Infant or Child–Parent Psychotherapy (CPP)

In CPP the presence of the baby is a crucial part of understanding how the ghosts in the mother's past intrude into present time without necessarily making them explicit. Versatility and flexibility of psychotherapeutic technique are hallmarks of this approach; what Fraiberg and colleagues termed 'psychotherapy in the kitchen' (Fraiberg *et al.* 1975: 394; see also Fraiberg 1982; Lieberman & Zeanah 1999).

In the initial study Lieberman and colleagues used a pre/post SSP to assess the effectiveness of parent–infant psychotherapy and found significant improvements in the attachment of the intervention group compared with randomised controls, but this did not hold when using the Q-sort with observed toddler behaviour in the home (Lieberman *et al.* 1991). Since then a number of studies have reported significant improvement in children's attachment security assessed by the SSP (Berlin *et al.* 2008) and with children in kinship and foster care (Van Horn *et al.* 2011).

Infant–Parent Psychotherapy

Cicchetti and colleagues found that Infant–Parent Psychotherapy or a Psychoeducational Parenting Intervention significantly improved attachment security (using the SSP) in maltreated infants compared with not only controls but also a fourth group of non-maltreated infants from low-income families (Cicchetti *et al.* 2006).

Toth and colleagues used the SSP with toddlers (average age 20 months) as a pre/post measure of attachment to assess the effectiveness of toddler–parent psychotherapy with mothers diagnosed with a major depressive disorder. Followed up at 36 months the intervention group showed a substantial increase in attachment security compared with randomised controls or a community group of toddlers with non-depressed mothers (Toth *et al.* 2006). An earlier study used narrative story stems to evaluate preschool–parent psychotherapy (PPP) with maltreated children and found the attachment representations of the PPP group showed a greater decline in both maladaptive maternal representations and negative self-representations than either a group who received psychoeducational home visiting or standard community services (Toth *et al.* 2002).

The Circle of Security

This intervention uses small group treatment of five to six parents/carers in a 20-week programme with a pre/post SSP to follow changes in the child's attachment. Results with both advantaged and high-risk dyads (the children were toddlers or preschool age) showed a significant move in child attachment from disorganised to organised insecure (avoidant or resistant) or secure (Hoffman *et al.* 2006). This approach involves both video feedback and what can be construed as mentalisation-based therapy (MBT) with parents. The study did not have a comparison non-intervention group.

Watch, Wait and Wonder (WWW)

The WWW approach involves mother getting down on the floor with her infant and the therapist encouraging her to follow the infant's lead. The second part involves a 20-minute session in which the mother explores her observations with the therapist. Although links may be made with her past experience the focus is on observation and following the infant's lead. The SSP was used as one of a series of pre/post measures with infants aged 10 to 30 months. When compared with more traditional mother–infant psychodynamic psychotherapy (PPT) attachment security improved in both groups, with positive changes coming earlier in a six-month follow up for the WWW than the PPT groups (Cohen *et al.* 2002).

University of California at Los Angeles (UCLA) Family Development Project

This project used a mixture of home visiting, parent groups and advocacy with mothers at social risk (excluding drug use and psychiatric treatment for DSM-IV axis 1 diagnosis) (Heinicke *et al.* 1999, 2006; also Heinicke & Levine 2008). Infant attachment assessed by the SSP at 14 months showed significantly more secure children in the intervention group compared with random selected controls; in fact 77 per cent of the intervention children were assessed as secure compared with 52 per cent of the controls (Heinicke *et al.* 1999). The mothers whose state of mind regarding attachment was assessed as secure, using the Main and Goldwyn AAI before their child was born, were more involved in the intervention and showed better outcomes overall.

Sunderland Infant Programme

This programme used the DMM CARE-Index as a screening tool to assign mother–infant dyads to low-, medium- and high-risk groups with all groups offered video feedback and the high-risk group parent–infant psychotherapy. At the 12-month follow up the dyads again completed a CARE-Index and the children the DMM-SSP. Results showed significant improvement in security of attachment of the intervention group compared with a non-randomised comparison group who did not receive the intervention (Svanberg *et al.* 2010).

Attachment and Biobehavioral Catch-up (ABC)

The ABC was developed by Dozier and colleagues (2005) as a brief home visiting programme for foster parents and foster children. It uses video feedback and attends to a foster carer's state of mind as assessed by the AAI and their This Is My Baby interview (TIMB) which assesses commitment to the child, which in turn predicts durability of placements.[1] Intervention children showed more typical levels of the 'stress hormone' cortisol than controls and were not significantly different from a third group who had never been in care (Dozier *et al.* 2006, 2008).

Bernard and colleagues (Bernard *et al.* 2012) used the ABC with parents at risk of neglecting their young children. It was evaluated using the SSP with 120 children aged between 11 and 31 months. Children in the ABC intervention showed significantly lower rates of disorganised attachment (32%) and higher rates of secure attachment (52%) relative to the randomised control intervention (57% and 33%, respectively).

Note

1 TIMB promises to be a simple, easy to use tool: see Dozier *et al.* 2007: Appendix 4: 1.

References

Ainsworth, M.D., Blehar, M.C., Waters, E. & Wall, S. (1978) *Patterns of Attachment: A Psychological Study of the Strange Situation*, Hillsdale, NJ: Erlbaum.

Ainsworth, M.S. & Bowlby, J. (1991) 'An ethological approach to personality development', *American Psychologist*, 46(4): 333–341.

Allen, J.G. (2013) *Restoring Mentalizing in Attachment Relationships: Treating Trauma with Plain Old Therapy*, Washington, DC: American Psychiatric Publishing.

Allen, J.G. & Fonagy, P. (eds) (2006) *Handbook of Mentalization-Based Treatment*, Chichester: John Wiley & Sons.

Allen, J.G., Fonagy, P. & Bateman, J.G. (2008) *Mentalizing in Clinical Practice*, Washington, DC: American Psychiatric Publishing Inc.

American Psychiatric Association (2013) *Diagnostic and Statistical Manual of Mental Disorders, 5th Edition*, Arlington, VA: American Psychiatric Association.

BAAF (British Agencies of Adoption and Fostering) (2006) *Position Statement 4: Attachment Disorders, Their Assessment and Intervention/Treatment*, London: BAAF.

Bateman, A. & Fonagy, P. (2004) *Psychotherapy for Borderline Personality Disorder: Mentalization-Based Treatment*, Oxford: Oxford University Press.

Bateman, A. & Fonagy, P. (2008) '8-year follow up of patients treated for borderline personality disorder: mentalization-based treatments versus treatment as usual', *American Journal of Psychiatry*, 165: 631–638.

Becker-Weidman, A. (2006) 'Treatment for children with trauma-attachment disorders: Dyadic Developmental Psychotherapy', *Child and Adolescent Social Work Journal*, 23(2): 147–171.

Becker-Weidman, A. & Hughes, D. (2008) 'Dyadic Developmental Psychotherapy: an evidence-based treatment for children with complex trauma and disorders of attachment', *Child and Family Social Work*, 13: 329–337.

Beijersbergen, M.D., Juffer, F., Bakermans-Kranenburg, M.J. & Van IJzendoorn, M.H. (2012) 'Remaining or becoming secure: Parental sensitive support predicts attachment continuity from infancy to adolescence in a longitudinal adoption study', *Developmental Psychology*, 48(5): 1277–1282.

Benedict, H.E. (2006) 'Object relations play therapy: Applications to attachment problems and relational trauma', in C.E. Schaefer & H.G. Kaduson (eds), *Contemporary Play Therapy: Theory, Research and Practice* (pp. 3–27), New York: The Guilford Press.

Benedict, H.E. & Schofield, D. (2010) 'Play therapy for insecurely attached preschool children', in C.E. Schaefer (ed.), *Play Therapy for Preschool Children* (pp. 47–66), Washington, DC: American Psychological Association.

Berant, E. & Obegi, J.H. (2009) 'Attachment-informed psychotherapy research with adults', in J.H. Obegi & E. Berant (eds), *Attachment Theory and Research in Clinical Work with Adults* (pp. 461–489), New York: The Guilford Press.

Berlin, L.J., Zeanah, C.H. & Lieberman, A.F. (2008) 'Prevention and intervention programs for supporting early attachment security', in J. Cassidy & P.R. Shaver (eds), *Handbook of Attachment: Theory, Research, and Clinical Applications* (pp. 745–761). New York: The Guilford Press.

Bernard, K., Dozier, M., Bick, J., Lewis-Morrarty, E., Lindhiem, O. & Carlson, E. (2012) 'Enhancing attachment organization among maltreated children: Results of a randomized clinical trial', *Child Development*, 83(2): 623–636.

Beutler, L.E. (1991) 'Have all won and must all have prizes? Revisiting Luborsky *et al.*'s verdict', *Journal of Consulting and Clinical Psychology*, 59: 226–232.

Bick, J. & Dozier, M. (2008) 'Helping foster parents change: The role of parental state of mind', in H. Steele & M. Steele (eds), *Clinical Applications of the Adult Attachment Interview* (pp. 452–470), New York: The Guilford Press.

Bifulco, A., Jacobs, C., Bunn, A., Thomas, G. & Irving, K. (2008) 'The Attachment Style Interview (ASI): A support-based adult assessment tool for adoption and fostering practice', *Adoption & Fostering*, 32: 33–45.

Bomber, L.M. (2007) *Inside I'm Hurting: Practical Strategies for Supporting Children with Attachment Difficulties in Schools*, London: Worth Publishing.

Bomber, L.M. (2011) *What About Me? Inclusive Strategies to Support Pupils with Attachment Difficulties Make It Through the School Day*, London: Worth Publishing.

Bowlby, J. (1953) *Child Care and the Growth of Love*, London: Penguin Books.

Bowlby, J. (1973/1985) *Attachment and Loss, Vol. 2: Separation: Anxiety and Anger*, London: Hogarth Press and Institute of Psycho-Analysis.

Bowlby, J. (1979/2005) *The Making and Breaking of Affectional Bonds*, Abingdon, UK: Routledge.

Bowlby, J. (1988/2005) A Secure Base: Clinical applications of attachment theory, London: Routledge.

Bradley, R., Heim, A.K. & Westen, D. (2005) 'Transference patterns in the psychotherapy of personality disorders: Empirical investigation', *British Journal of Psychiatry*, 186(4): 342–349.

Bratton, S., Ray, D., Rhine, T. & Jones, L. (2005) 'The efficacy of play therapy with children: A meta-analytic review of treatment outcomes', *Professional Psychology: Research and Practice*, 36: 376–390.

Bretherton, I. (2005) 'In pursuit of the internal working model construct and its relevance to attachment relationships', in K.E. Grossman, K. Grossman & E. Waters (eds), *Attachment for Infancy to Adulthood: The Major Longitudinal Studies* (pp. 13–47), New York: The Guilford Press.

Carr, A. (2009) 'The effectiveness of family therapy and systemic interventions for child-focused problems', *Journal of Family Therapy*, 31: 3–45.

Chaffin, M., Hanson, R., Saunders, B.E., Nichols, T., Barnett, D., Zeanah, C. *et al.* (2006) 'Report of the APSAC Task Force on attachment therapy, Reactive Attachment Disorder, and attachment problems', *Child Maltreatment*, 11(1): 76–89.

Cicchetti, D., Rogosch, F.A. & Toth, S.L. (2006) 'Fostering secure attachment in infants in maltreating families through preventive interventions', *Development and Psychopathology*, 18(3): 623–649.

Coan, J.A. (2008) 'Towards a neuroscience of attachment', in J. Cassidy & P.R. Shaver (eds), *Handbook of Attachment: Theory, Research, and Clinical Applications* (pp. 241–265), New York: The Guilford Press.

Cohen, J. (2005) 'Treating traumatized children: Current status and future directions', in E. Cardeña & K. Croyle (eds), *Acute Reactions to Trauma and Psychotherapy: A Multidisciplinary and International Perspective* (pp. 109–121), New York: Haworth Press.

Cohen, J.A., Mannarino, A.P. & Deblinger, E. (2010) 'Trauma-focused cognitive-behavioral therapy for traumatized children', in J.R. Weisz & A.E. Kazdin (eds), *Evidence-based Psychotherapies for Children and Adolescents*, 2nd edition (pp. 295–311), New York: The Guilford Press.

Cohen, N.J., Lojkasek, M., Muir, E., Muir, R. & Parker, C.J. (2002) 'Six-month follow-up of two mother–infant psychotherapies: Convergence of therapeutic outcomes', *Infant Mental Health Journal*, 23(4): 361–380.

Cook-Cottone, C. & Black, M. (2007) 'A model for life-story work: Facilitating the construction of personal narrative for foster children', *Child and Adolescent Mental Health*, 12(4): 193–195.

Crittenden, P.M. (1979–2005) *CARE-Index. Infants. Coding Manual*, unpublished manuscript, Miami, FL.

Crittenden, P.M. (1985) 'Social networks, quality of childrearing, and child development', *Child Development*, 56: 1299–1313.

Crittenden, P.M. (1988–2011) *The Pre-school Assessment of Attachment: Coding Manual*, unpublished manuscript, Miami, FL.

Crittenden, P.M. (1992) 'Treatment of anxious attachment in infancy and the preschool years', *Development and Psychopathology*, 4: 575–602.

Crittenden, P.M. (1995) 'Attachment and psychopathology', in S. Goldberg, R. Muir & J. Kerr (eds), *Attachment Theory: Social, Developmental and Clinical Perspectives* (pp. 367–406), New York: The Analytic Press.

Crittenden, P.M. (1995–2008) *School-aged Assessment of attachment. Coding Manual Using the Dynamic-Maturational Method*, unpublished manuscript.

Crittenden, P.M. (2005) *CARE-Index. Toddlers. Coding Manual*, unpublished manuscript, Miami, FL.

Crittenden, P.M. (2006) 'A Dynamic-Maturational Model of Attachment', *Australian and New Zealand Journal of Family Therapy*, 27(2): 105–115.

Crittenden, P.M. & Ainsworth, M.D.S. (1989) 'Child maltreatment and attachment theory', in D. Cicchetti & V. Carlson (eds), *Handbook of Child Maltreatment* (pp. 432–463), New York: Cambridge University Press.

Crittenden, P.M. & Landini, A. (2011) *The Adult Attachment Interview: Assessing Psychological and Interpersonal Strategies*, New York: W.W. Norton & Co.

Crittenden, P.M., Landini, A. & Claussen, A.H. (2001) 'A dynamic-maturational approach to treatment of maltreated children', in J.N. Hughes, A.M. La Greca & J.C. Conoley (eds), *Handbook of Psychological Services for Children and Adolescents* (pp. 373–398), New York: Oxford University Press.

Crittenden, P.M., Kozlowska, K. & Landini, A. (2010) 'Assessing attachment in school-age children', *Clinical Child Psychology and Psychiatry*, 15(2): 185–208.

Crittenden, P.M., Farnfield, S., Landini, A. & Grey, B. (2013) 'Assessing attachment for family court decision-making: A forensic protocol for empirically-based evidence regarding attachment', *Journal of Forensic Practice*, 15(4): 237–248.

Daniel, S.I.F. (2006) 'Adult attachment patterns and individual psychotherapy: A review', *Clinical Psychology Review*, 26: 968–984.

Daniel, S.I.F. (2009) 'The developmental roots of narrative expression in therapy: Contributions from attachment theory and research', *Psychotherapy Theory, Research, Practice, Training*, 46(3): 301–316.

Deblinger, E., Pollio, E. & Neubauer, F. (2012) 'Trauma-related symptoms in children and adolescents', in J.G. Beck & D.M. Sloan (eds), *The Oxford Handbook of Traumatic Stress Disorders* (pp. 473–490), New York: Oxford University Press.

De Wolff, M. & Van IJzendoorn, M.H. (1997) 'Sensitivity and attachment: A meta-analysis on parental antecedents of infant attachment', *Child Development*, 68(4): 571–591.

Diamond, D., Stovall-McClough, C., Clarkin, J.F. & Levy, K.N. (2003) 'Patient–therapist attachment in the treatment of borderline personality disorder', *Bulletin of the Menninger Clinic*, 67(3): 227–259.

Diamond, G.M., Diamond, G.S., Levy, S., Closs, C., Lapido, T. & Siqueland, L. (2012) 'Attachment-based family therapy for suicidal lesbian, gay, and bisexual adolescents: A treatment development study and open trial with preliminary findings', *Psychotherapy*, 49(1): 62–71.

Diamond, G.S., Reis, B.F., Diamond, G.M., Siqueland, L. & Isaacs, L. (2002) 'Attachment-based family therapy for depressed adolescents: A treatment development study', *Journal of the American Academy of Child and Adolescent Psychiatry*, 41: 1190–1196.

Diamond, G.S., Wintersteen, M.B., Brown, G.K., Diamond, G.M., Gallop, R., Shelef, K., & Levy, S. (2010) 'Attachment-based family therapy for adolescents with suicidal ideation: A randomized controlled trial', *Journal of the American Academy of Child and Adolescent Psychiatry*, 49: 122–131.

Dozier, M., Stovall, K.C., Albus, K.E. & Bates, B. (2001) 'Attachment for infants in foster care: The role of caregiver state of mind', *Child Development*, 72: 1467–1477.

Dozier, M., Lindhiem, O. & Ackerman, J.P. (2005) 'Attachment and Biobehavioral Catch-Up: An intervention targeting empirically identified needs of foster infants', in L.J. Berlin, Y. Ziv, L. Amaya-Jackson & M.T. Greenberg (eds), *Enhancing Early Attachments: Theory, Research, Intervention and Policy* (pp. 178–194), New York: The Guilford Press.

Dozier, M., Peloso, E., Lindhiem, O., Gordon, M.K., Manni, M., Sepulveda, S. & Ackerman, J. (2006) 'Developing evidence-based interventions for foster children: An example of a randomized clinical trial with infants and toddlers', *Journal of Social Issues*, 62(4): 767–785.

Dozier, M., Grasso, D., Lindhiem, O. & Lewis, E. (2007) 'The role of caregiver commitment in foster care: Insights from the This is My Baby Interview', in D. Oppenheim & D.F. Goldsmith (eds), *Attachment Theory in Clinical Work with Children: Bridging the Gap Between Research and Practice* (pp. 90–108), New York: The Guilford Press.

Dozier, M., Stovall-McClough, K.C. & Albus, K.E. (2008) 'Attachment and psychopathology in adulthood', in J. Cassidy & P.R. Shaver (eds), *Handbook of Attachment: Theory, Research, and Clinical Applications* (pp. 718–744), New York: The Guilford Press.

Eames, V. & Roth, A. (2000) 'Patient attachment orientation and the early working alliance: A study of patient and therapist reports of alliance quality and ruptures', *Psychotherapy Research*, 10(4): 421–434.

Egeland, B. & Erickson, M.F. (2004) 'Lessons from STEEP: Linking theory, research, and practice for the well-being of infants and parents', in A.J. Sameroff, S.C. McDonough & K.L. Rosenblum (eds), *Treating Parent–Infant Relationship Problems: Strategies for Intervention* (pp. 213–242), New York: The Guilford Press.

Egeland, B., Weinfield, N.S., Bosquet, M. & Cheng, V.K. (2000) 'Remembering, repeating and working through: Lessons from attachment-based interventions', in J. Osofsky & H.E. Fitzgerald (eds), *WAIMH Handbook of Infant Mental: Vol 4. Infant Mental Health in Groups at High Risk* (pp. 35–89), New York: Wiley.

Farnfield, S. (2008) 'A theoretical model for the comprehensive assessment of parenting', *British Journal of Social Work*, 38(6): 1076–1099.

Farnfield, S. (2012) 'Bindung und Anpassung bei Ersatzeltern', in M. Stokowy & N. Sahhar (eds), *Bindung und Gefahr: Das Dynamische Reifungsmodell von Bindung und Anpassung* (pp. 163–186), Giessen: Psychosozial-Verlag.

Farnfield, S. (in press) 'Assessing attachment in the school years: The application of the Dynamic-Maturational Model of attachment to the coding of a Child Attachment Interview with community and looked after children', *Clinical Child Psychology and Psychiatry*.

Farnfield, S. & Holmes, P. (eds) (2014) *The Routledge Handbook of Attachment: Assessment*, London and New York: Routledge.

Farnfield, S. & Stokowy, M. (2014) 'The Dynamic-Maturational Model (DMM)', in P. Holmes & S. Farnfield (eds), *The Routledge Handbook of Attachment: Theory* (pp. 00–00), London and New York: Routledge.

Fearon, P., Target, M., Sargent, J., Williams, L.L., McGregor, J., Bleiberg, E. & Fonagy, P. (2006) 'Short-term mentalization and relational therapy (SMART): An integrative family therapy for children and adolescents', in J.G. Allen & P. Fonagy (eds), *Handbook of Mentalization-Based Treatment* (pp. 201–222), Chichester: John Wiley & Sons.

Fonagy, P. (2001) *Attachment Theory and Psychoanalysis*, New York: Other Press.

Fonagy, P. & Bateman, A.W. (2006) 'Progress in the treatment of borderline personality disorder', *British Journal of Psychiatry*, 188: 1–3.

Fonagy, P., Leigh, T., Steele, M., Steele, H., Kennedy, R., Mattoon, G. *et al.* (1996) 'The relation of attachment status, psychiatric classification, and response to psychotherapy', *Journal of Consulting and Clinical Psychology*, 64: 22–31.

Fonagy, P., Gergely, G., Jurist, E. & Target, M. (2004) *Affect Regulation, Mentalization and the Development of the Self*, New York: Other Press.

Fonagy, P., Twemlow, S.W., Vernberg, E.M., Mize Nelson, J., Dill, E.J., Little, T.D. & Sargent, J.E. (2009) 'A cluster randomized controlled trial of child-focused psychiatric consultation and a school systems-focused intervention to reduce aggression', *Journal of Child Psychology and Psychiatry*, 50: 607–616.

Fraiberg, S. (1982) 'Pathological defenses in infancy', *Psychoanalytic Quarterly*, 51: 612–635.

Fraiberg, S., Adelson, E. & Shapiro, V. (1975) 'Ghosts in the nursery: A psychoanalytic approach to the problems of impaired infant–mother relationships', *Journal of American Academy of Child Psychiatry*, 14: 387–421.

Geddes, H. (2006) *Attachment in the Classroom: The Links between Children's Early Experiences, Emotional Well-being and Performance in School*, London: Worth Publishing.

George, C., Kaplan, N. & Main, M. (1985) *Adult Attachment Interview Protocol* (2nd edition), unpublished manuscript, University of California at Berkeley.

Grey, B. (2010) 'The meaning of the child in parenting interviews: A comparative study using the Parent Development Interview and the CARE-Index', Poster and seminar presented to the 2nd Biannual Conference of the International Association for the Study of Attachment, Cambridge: August.

Heinicke, C.M. & Levine, M.S. (2008) 'The AAI anticipates the outcome of a relation-based early intervention', in H. Steele & M. Steele (eds), *Clinical Applications of the Adult Attachment Interview* (pp. 99–125), New York: The Guilford Press.

Heinicke, C.M., Fineman, N.R., Ruth, G., Recchia, S., Guthrie, D. & Rodning, C. (1999) 'Relationship based intervention with at-risk mothers: Outcome in the first year of life', *Infant Mental Health Journal*, 20: 349–374.

Heinicke, C.M., Goorsky, M., Levine, M., Ponce, V., Ruth, G., Silverman, M. & Sotelo, C. (2006) 'Pre-and postnatal antecedents of a home-visiting intervention and family developmental outcome', *Infant Mental Health Journal*, 27(1): 91–119.

Hodges, J., Steele, M., Hillman, S., Henderson, K. & Kaniuk, J. (2005) 'Change and continuity in mental representations of attachment after adoption', in D.M. Brodzinsky & J. Palacios (eds), *Psychological Issues in Adoption: Research and Practice* (pp. 93–116), Westport, CT: Praeger.

Hoffman, K.T., Marvin, R.S., Cooper, G. & Powell, B. (2006) 'Changing toddlers' and preschoolers' attachment classifications: The Circle of Security intervention', *Journal of Consulting and Clinical Psychology*, 74: 1017–1026.

Holmes, P. (1989) 'Wheels within wheels and systems within systems: The assessment process', *Children & Society*, 3(3), 237–254.

Holmes, P. (1992) *The Inner World Outside: Object Relations Theory and Psychodrama*, London and New York: Tavistock/Routledge.

Holmes, P. & Farnfield, S. (eds) (2014) *The Routledge Handbook of Attachment: Theory*, London and New York: Routledge.

Jacobvitz, R. (2008) 'Afterword: Reflections on clinical applications of the Adult Attachment Interview', in H. Steele & M. Steele (eds), *Clinical Applications of the Adult Attachment Interview* (pp. 471–486), New York: The Guilford Press.

Jernberg, A.M., & Booth, P.B. (1999) 'Theraplay: Helping parents and children build better relationships through attachment-based play (2nd edition), San Francisco, CA: Jossey-Bass.

Kennedy, H., Landor, M. & Todd, L. (2010) 'Video Interaction Guidance as a method to promote secure attachment', *Educational and Child Psychology*, 27(3): 59–72.

Kennedy, H., Landor, M. & Todd, L. (2011) *Video Interaction Guidance: A Relationship-Based Intervention to Promote Attunement, Empathy and Well-Being*, London: Jessica Kingsley Publishers.

Kliethermes, M., Nanney, R.W., Cohen, J.A. & Mannarino, A.P. (2013) 'Trauma-focused cognitive-behavioral therapy', in J.D. Ford & C.A. Courtois (eds), *Treating Complex Traumatic Stress Disorders in Children and Adolescents: Scientific Foundations and Therapeutic Models* (pp. 184–202), New York: The Guilford Press.

Kozlowska, K., Foley, S. & Savage, B. (2012a) 'Fabricated illness: Working within the family system to find a pathway to health', *Family Process*, 51(4): 570–587.

Kozlowska, K., English, M., Savage, B. & Chudleigh, C. (2012b) 'Multimodal rehabilitation: A mind-body, family-based intervention for children and adolescents impaired by medically unexplained symptoms. Part 1: The program', *The American Journal of Family Therapy*, 40(5): 399–419.

Kozlowska, K., English, M., Savage, B., Chudleigh, C., Davies, F., Paull, M., *et al.* (2013) 'Multimodal rehabilitation: A mind-body, family-based intervention for children and adolescents impaired by medically unexplained symptoms. Part 2: Case studies and outcomes', *The American Journal of Family Therapy*, 40(5): 212–231.

Lee, C., Gavriel, H., Drummond, P., Richards, J. & Greenwald, R. (2002) 'Treatment of PTSD: Stress inoculation training with prolonged exposure compared to EMDR', *Journal of Clinical Psychology*, 58: 1071–1089.

Levy, K.N., Meehan, K.B., Clarkin, J.F., Kernberg, O.F., Kelly, K.M., Reynoso, J.S. & Weber, M. (2006) 'Change in attachment patterns and reflective function in a randomized control trial of transference-focused psychotherapy for borderline personality disorder', *Journal of Consulting and Clinical Psychology*, 74(6): 1027–1040.

Lieberman, A.F. & Zeanah, C.H. (1999) 'Contributions of attachment theory to infant–parent psychotherapy and other interventions with infants and young children', in J. Cassidy & P.R. Shaver (eds), *Handbook of Attachment: Theory, Research, and Clinical Applications* (pp. 555–574), New York: The Guilford Press.

Lieberman, A.F., Weston, D.R. & Pawl, J.H. (1991) 'Preventive intervention and outcome with anxiously attached dyads', *Child Development*, 62: 199–209.

Lindhiem, O. & Dozier, M. (2007) 'Caregiver commitment to foster children: The role of child behavior', *Child Abuse & Neglect*, 31(4): 361–374.

Luyten, P. & Fonagy, P. (2014) 'Mentalising in attachment contexts', in P. Holmes & S. Farnfield (eds), *The Routledge Handbook of Attachment: Theory*, London and New York: Routledge.

Macaskill, C. (2002) *Safe Contact? Children in Permanent Placement and Contact with Their Birth Relatives*, Lyme Regis, Dorset: Russell House Publishing.

Main, M. (1995) 'Recent studies in attachment: Overview, with selected implications for clinical work', in S. Goldberg, R. Muir & J. Kerr (eds), *Attachment Theory: Social, Developmental, and Clinical Perspectives* (pp. 407–474), Hillsdale, NJ: The Analytic Press.

Main, M. & Goldwyn, R. (1984) *Adult Attachment Scoring & Classification System*, Unpublished manuscript, University of California at Berkeley.

Main, M. & Solomon, J. (1986) 'Discovery of a new, insecure-disorganized/disorientated attachment pattern', in M. Yogman and T. Brazelton (eds), *Affective Development in Infancy* (pp. 95–124), Norwood, Ablex.

Main, M., Hesse, E. & Hesse, S. (2011) 'Attachment theory and research: Overview with suggested applications to child custody', *Family Court Review*, Special issue: Special issue on attachment, separation, and divorce: Forging coherent understandings for family law, 49(3): 426–463.

Marcus, S.V., Marquis, P. & Saki, C. (1997) 'Controlled study of treatment of PTSD using EMDR in an HMO setting', *Psychotherapy*, 34: 307–315.

Marvin, R.S. (2003) 'Implications of attachment research for the field of family therapy', in P. Erdman & T. Caffery (eds), *Attachment and Family Systems: Conceptual, Empirical, and Therapeutic Relatedness* (pp. 3–27), Hove, UK: Brunner-Routledge.

Moran, G., Bailey, H.N., Gleason, K., DeOliveira, C.A. & Pederson, D.R. (2008) 'Exploring the mind behind unresolved attachment: Lessons from and of attachment-based interventions with infants and their traumatized mothers', in H. Steele & M. Steele (eds), *Clinical Applications of the Adult Attachment Interview* (pp. 371–398), New York: The Guilford Press.

Moss, E., Dubois-Comtois, K., Cyr, C., Tarabulsy, G.M., St-Laurent, D. & Bernier, A. (2011) 'Efficacy of a home visiting intervention aimed at improving maternal sensitivity, child attachment, and behavioral outcomes for maltreated children: A randomized control trial', *Development and Psychopathology*, 23: 195–210.

Obegi, J.H. & Berant, E. (2009) 'Introduction', in J.H. Obegi & E. Berant (eds), *Attachment

Theory and Research in Clinical Work with Adults (pp. 1–14), New York: The Guilford Press.

O'Connor, T.G., Matias, C., Futh, A., Tantam, G. & Scott, S. (2013) 'Social learning theory parenting intervention promotes attachment-based caregiving in young children: Randomized clinical trial', *Journal of Clinical Child and Adolescent Psychology: The Official Journal for the Society of Clinical Child and Adolescent Psychology, American Psychological Association, Division 53*, 42(3): 358–370.

Orlinsky, D.E., Grawe, K. & Parks, B.K. (1994) 'Process and outcome in psychotherapy: Noch einmal', in A.E. Bergin & L. Garfield (eds), *Handbook of Psychotherapy and Behavior Change*, 4th edition (pp. 270–376), New York: Wiley.

Petrowski, K., Pokorny, D., Nowacki, K. & Buchheim, A. (2013) 'The therapist's attachment representation and the patient's attachment to the therapist', *Psychotherapy Research*, 23(1): 25–34.

Prior, V. & Glaser, D. (2006) *Understanding Attachment and Attachment Disorders: Theory, Evidence and Practice*, London: Jessica Kingsley Publishers.

Quinton, D., Rushton, A., Dance, C. & Mayes, D. (1998) *Joining New Families: A Study of Adoption and Fostering in Middle Childhood*, Chichester: John Wiley & Sons.

Ray, D.C. (2006) 'Evidence-based play therapy', in C.E. Schaefer & H.G. Kaduson (eds), *Contemporary Play Therapy: Theory, Research, and Practice* (pp. 136–157), New York: The Guilford Press.

Robertson, M. & Kennedy, H. (2009) 'Relationship-based intervention for high risk families and their babies: Video Interaction Guidance – an international perspective', Seminar Association Infant Mental Health, Tavistock, London, 12 December.

Scheeringa, M.S., Weems, C.F., Cohen, J.A., Amaya-Jackson, L. & Guthrie, D. (2011) 'Trauma-focused cognitive-behavioral therapy for posttraumatic stress disorder in three-through six-year-old children: A randomized clinical trial', *Journal of Child Psychology and Psychiatry*, 52(8): 853–860.

Shmueli-Goetz, Y., Target, M., Fonagy, P. & Datta, A. (2008) 'The Child Attachment Interview: A psycho-metric study of reliability and discriminant validity', *Developmental Psychology*, 44: 939–995.

Slade, A. (1999) 'Attachment theory and research: Implications for the theory and practice of individual psychotherapy with adults', in J. Cassidy & P.R. Shaver (eds), *Handbook of Attachment: Theory, Research, and Clinical Applications* (pp. 575–594), New York: The Guilford Press.

Slade, A. (2005) 'Parental reflective functioning: An introduction', *Attachment & Human Development*, 7(3): 269–281.

Slade, A. (2008) 'The implications of attachment theory and research for adult psychotherapy: Research and clinical perspectives', in J. Cassidy & P.R. Shaver (eds), *Handbook of Attachment: Theory, Research, and Clinical Applications* (pp. 762–782), New York: The Guilford Press.

Slade, A., Bernbach, E., Grienenberger, J., Levy, D. & Locker, A. (2007) *Addendum to Reflective Functioning Scoring Manual for Use with the Parent Development Interview. Version 3.0*, New York: The City College and Graduate Center of the City University of New York.

Spieker, S., Nelson, D., DeKlyen, M. & Staerkel, F. (2005) 'Enhancing early attachments in the context of Early Head Start: Can programs emphasizing family support improve rates of secure infant-mother attachments in low-income families?', in L.J. Berlin, Y. Ziv, L. Amaya-Jackson & M.T. Greenberg (eds), *Enhancing Early Attachments:*

Theory, Research, Intervention, and Policy (pp. 250–275), New York: The Guilford Press.

Steele, H. & Steele, M. (eds) (2008a) *Clinical Applications of the Adult Attachment Interview*, New York: The Guilford Press.

Steele, H. & Steele, M. (2008b) 'Ten clinical uses of the Adult Attachment Interview', in H. Steele & M. Steele (eds), *Clinical Applications of the Adult Attachment Interview* (pp. 3–30), New York: The Guilford Press.

Steele, M., Hodges, J., Kaniuk, J., Hillman, S. & Henderson, K. (2003) 'Attachment representations and adoption: Associations between maternal states of mind and emotion narratives in previously maltreated children', *Journal of Child Psychotherapy*, 29: 187–205.

Steele, M., Hodges, J., Kaniuk, J., Steele, H., D'Agostino, D., Blom, I. *et al.* (2007) 'Intervening with maltreated children and their adoptive families: Identifying attachment-facilitative behaviours', in D. Oppenheim & D.F. Goldsmith (eds), *Attachment Theory in Clinical Work with Children: Bridging the Gap Between Research and Practice* (pp. 58–85), New York: The Guilford Press.

Steele, M., Hodges, J., Kaniuk, J., Steele, H., Hillman, S. & Asquith, K. (2008) 'Forecasting outcomes in previously maltreated children: The use of the AAI in a longitudinal adoption study', in H. Steele & M. Steele (eds), *Clinical Applications of the Adult Attachment Interview* (pp. 427–451), New York: The Guilford Press.

Strauss, B.M., Mestel, R. & Kirchmann, H.A. (2011) 'Changes of attachment status among women with personality disorders undergoing inpatient treatment', *Counselling and Psychotherapy Research*, 11(4): 275–283.

Svanberg, P.O., Mennet, L. & Spieker, S. (2010) 'Promoting secure attachment: A primary prevention practice model', *Clinical Child Psychology and Psychiatry*, 15(3): 363–378.

Tarren-Sweeney, M. (2013) 'Setting the bar higher: What information do we need to establish the effectiveness of mental health interventions for children with complex attachment- and trauma-related difficulties?' *Clinical Child Psychology and Psychiatry*, 18(1): 3–6.

Tasca, G., Balfour, L., Ritchie, K. & Bissada, H. (2007) 'Change in attachment anxiety is associated with improved depression among women with binge eating disorder', *Psychotherapy: Theory, Research, Practice, Training*, 44(4): 423–433.

Toth, S.L., Maughan, A., Manly, J.T., Spagnola, M. & Cicchetti, D. (2002) 'The relative efficacy of two interventions in altering maltreated preschool children's representational models: Implications for attachment theory', *Development and Psychopathology*, 14(4): 877–908.

Toth, S.L., Rogosch, F.A., Manly, J.T. & Cicchetti, D. (2006) 'The efficacy of toddler–parent psychotherapy to reorganize attachment in the young offspring of mothers with major depressive disorder: A randomized preventive trial', *Journal of Consulting and Clinical Psychology*, 74(6): 1006–1016.

Tyrrell, C.L., Dozier, M., Teague, G.B. & Fallot, R.D. (1999) 'Effective treatment relationships for persons with serious psychiatric disorders: The importance of attachment states of mind', *Journal of Consulting and Clinical Psychology*, 67(5): 725–733.

Urquiza, A.J. & Timmer, S. (2013) 'Parent-child Interaction Therapy', in J.D. Ford & C.A. Courtois (eds), *Treating Complex Traumatic Stress Disorders in Children and Adolescents: Scientific Foundations and Therapeutic Models* (pp. 315–328), New York: The Guilford Press.

Van Horn, P., Gray, L., Pettinelli, B. & Estassi, N. (2011) 'Child–parent psychotherapy with traumatized young children in kinship care: Adaptation of an evidence-based intervention', in J.D. Osofsky (ed.), *Clinical Work with Traumatized Young Children* (pp. 55–74), New York: The Guilford Press.

Van IJzendoorn, M.H. & Bakermans-Kranenburg, M.J. (2008) 'The distribution of adult attachment representations in clinical groups: A meta-analytic search for patterns of attachment in 105 AAI studies', in H. Steele & M. Steele (eds), *Clinical Applications of the Adult Attachment Interview* (pp. 69–96), New York: The Guilford Press.

Velderman, M.K., Pannebakker, F.D., Kennedy, K., Fukkink, R.G., de Wolff, M.S. & Reijneveld, S.A. (2013) 'The efficacy of short-term video feedback as a method to improve parental sensitivity in families at risk for child maltreatment', Society for Research in Child Development, Biennial Meeting, Seattle Washington, 18–20April.

Verheugt-Pleiter, A.J.E. (2008) 'Treatment strategy', in A.J.E. Verheugt-Pleiter, J. Zevalkink & M.G.J. Schmeets (eds), *Mentalizing in Child Therapy: Guidelines for Clinical Practitioners* (pp. 41–68), London: Karnac Books.

Verheugt-Pleiter, A.J.E., Zevalkink, J. & Schmeets, M.G.J. (eds) (2008) *Mentalizing in Child Therapy: Guidelines for Clinical Practitioners*, London: Karnac Books.

Waters, E., Vaughn, B., Posada, G. & Kondo-Ikemura, K. (eds) (1995) 'Caregiving, cultural, and cognitive perspectives on secure-base behavior and working models: New growing points of attachment theory and research', with Commentary by Christoph M. Heinicke and Inge Bretherton. *Monographs of the Society for Research in Child Development*, 60(2–3, Serial No. 244).

Webster-Stratton, C. (1984) 'Randomized trial of two parent-training programs for families with conduct-disordered children', *Journal of Consulting and Clinical Psychology*, 52: 666–678.

Weisz, J.R. & Kazdin, A.E. (Eds) (2010) *Evidence-Based Psychotherapies for Children and Adolescents*, 2nd edition, New York: The Guilford Press.

Wesselmann, D. (2012) 'EMDR as a treatment for improving attachment status in adults and children', *European Review of Applied Psychology*, 62(4): 223–230.

Zanetti, C.A., Powell, B., Cooper, G. & Hoffman, K. (2011) 'The Circle of Security intervention: Using the therapeutic relationship to ameliorate attachment security in disorganized dyads', in J. Solomon & C. George (eds), *Disorganized Attachment & Caregiving* (pp. 318–342), New York: The Guilford Press.

Zeanah, C. (2007) 'Constructing a relationship formulation for mother and child: Clinical application of the Working Model of the Child Interview', in D. Oppenheim & D.F. Goldsmith (eds), *Attachment Theory in Clinical Work with Children: Bridging the Gap Between Research and Practice* (pp. 3–30), New York: The Guilford Press.

Zeanah, C., Berlin, L. & Boris, N. (2011) 'Practitioner review: Clinical applications of attachment theory and research for infants and young children', *Journal of Child Psychology and Psychiatry*, 52(8): 819–833.

Zeanah, C.H., Benoit, D., Hirshberg, L., Barton, M.L. & Regan, C. (1994) 'Mothers' representations of their infants are concordant with infant attachment classifications', *Developmental Issues in Psychiatry and Psychology*, 1: 9–18.

Zilberstein, K. (2013) 'The use and limitations of attachment theory in child psychotherapy', *Psychotherapy*, pp. 1–11.

Ziv, Y. (2005) 'Attachment-based intervention programs: Implications for attachment theory and research', in L.J. Berlin, Y. Ziv, L. Amaya-Jackson & M.T. Greenberg (eds), *Enhancing Early Attachments: Theory, Research, Intervention, and Policy* (pp. 61–78), New York: The Guilford Press.

Chapter 2

Attachment theory and its uses in child psychotherapy

Graham Music

Introduction

In this chapter I explore some ways in which attachment theory can inform therapeutic work with children. Attachment theory is a hugely influential body of extremely rigorous research findings, maybe the most important set of findings in developmental psychology, and as a body of theory it can be extremely useful when thinking about therapeutic work. However, psychotherapy and attachment research are also separate domains of activity. While I think that we cannot do psychotherapy these days without an understanding of attachment, psychotherapy will always rely on a huge range of other ideas to inform clinical technique, while the main preoccupations of attachment researchers have been to understand developmental processes and not clinical change. In the main body of the chapter I will give several brief case vignettes to try to tease out some of the ways in which attachment theory can be useful in psychotherapy with children. Before this, I will mention some of the background to the interface between child psychotherapy and attachment theory.

First, though, in the hope that this will illustrate some of the ways in which attachment theory can imbue our understandings of clinical matters, I describe a typical few moments in a meeting of the clinical team of which I am a member at the Tavistock Clinic in London, which of course was where John Bowlby developed attachment theory. The team works exclusively with cases where there has been maltreatment of some kind, and where the child is adopted or in foster or kinship care.

Today's meeting is unusually testing, with normally thoughtful team members acting in a bristly manner towards each other about a case that has clearly got under our skin. The case is one where there are a range of serious worries.

> Martin, aged 9, was taken into care initially following the discovery of bruising, reports of violence in the home, serious drug use by mother, exposure to inappropriate videos and sexual acts, and a distinct possibility of sexual abuse. Martin was placed with a foster carer, but this carer was struggling to hold onto him, and it looked like the placement

was breaking down. In addition, two members of the family had come forward as potential carers, maternal grandmother as well as one of mother's sisters. The two have not spoken since a falling out over a decade ago.

Martin's Children's Guardian (a social worker appointed by the Court to protect the child's interests in Care Proceedings) has very clear views about what should happen (that he should be placed with grandmother) and social services have quite another idea of what is best for Martin. Conflict is endemic in this case and is spilling out everywhere.

Martin we know is hypervigilant and unable to relax or trust anyone, is very aggressive and everyone is worried about him. Although no formal attachment measures have been done, few would doubt that he has a disorganised attachment style. How could he not have? He has been exposed to shockingly frightening and inconsistent parenting, has had negligible attuned input and has had little choice but to be hyper-reactive, living in what one assumes is a constant state of high sympathetic nervous system arousal and little if any belief that adults can be trustworthy, kind or reflective.

While we heatedly discuss Martin, another colleague is tapping on the table restlessly and is desperate to talk about Sally, a 15-year-old girl in foster care.

Sally is clingy, anxious and needy, and her foster carer is finding her a burden. She has been cutting herself, recently took a minor overdose, and has been threatening once again to self-harm. Her mother had abused alcohol and was also inconsistent, at times providing good thoughtful care, and at others being neglectful and both emotionally and, often, physically absent. Sally had learnt to be very watchful of her mother's moods, carefully monitoring to see if her mother had been drinking or was about to become depressed, as that was the only way she could stay safe and retain proximity to her primary caregiver. When her mother suddenly would disappear Sally would become frantic with worry, and be unable to calm down. Nothing but the physical presence of a caregiver seemed to help her feel relaxed. Sally, one would surmise, had an underlying ambivalent attachment style. She constantly needed to make sure that the adults in her life were okay, as knowing this was how she tried to make herself feel safe. She took on caregiving in a rather parentified 'tend and befriend' way that could feel intrusive to others, but she also could make adults feel good. The team had heard about Sally many times before, and the truth was that people did not really want to hear about her today. The psychiatrist had assessed her for suicide risk on numerous occasions and was unlikely to take her seriously. In effect the team was today, like often, re-enacting an attachment pattern. Here Sally's needy and clingy self was being rejected. This time the person feeling for Sally was my finger tapping colleague who was working with her, and the person chairing the meeting and the rest of the team seemed to represent the wish to retreat from Sally's clinginess and not take her emotional state seriously.

True to the kind of re-enactments we often see, there is no time to discuss Sally as we have to think about new referrals. As we do each week, we hear about a range of cases that all seem urgent. Most of us have our heads lowered when we are asked if we have spaces to take cases. I find myself trying to find a good reason why one case should really be seen by another team.

This was of a severely learning disabled girl who had been extremely neglected, who was left to her own devices for much of her infancy and had severe developmental delay. While it is true that our learning disability service might well work effectively with her, what was also true was that I did not have space in my mind for this particular girl's problems. I had in effect shut her out. Again maybe this is not surprising. Afterwards I cannot even remember her name, but I would bet serious money on her having an avoidant attachment pattern.

These three cases in a brief period of a single team meeting are typical, in that nearly all the cases we see or hear about can have a helpful light shone on them from the perspective of attachment. However, for the psychotherapist of course attachment patterns are not just patterns of behaviour which are objects of study. They are very predictive of how children live their lives and interact with people close to them, they also have real, emotional impacts on the other people in children's lives, and these attachment patterns can offer vital clues about a child's needs and the best ways of interacting with, and responding to, them.

Child psychotherapy and attachment theory

One might intuitively assume that attachment theory and psychoanalytically informed therapeutic work with children would be perfect bedfellows, each influencing the other in helpful ways. In fact, though, these two disciplines have developed quite separately, with distinct ways of conceptualising the issues children present with, each using different languages and having their own understandings and preoccupations. Rather than a match made in heaven, this relationship was for a long time marked by mutual suspicion, rivalry and tension. The roots of this rift stretch right back to Bowlby's time. While, as is well known, Bowlby developed attachment theory at the Tavistock Clinic, what is maybe less known is that he also founded the Tavistock's child psychotherapy training. Yet, as has been documented carefully elsewhere, Bowlby's use of an overtly scientific and empirical paradigm was not well received by his Tavistock psychoanalytic colleagues. Psychoanalytic psychotherapy has always been preoccupied with inner worlds, the unconscious, fantasy, defences and processes such as projection, and in the early days there was less room for conventional scientific methods, for research or experimentation. Maybe more importantly, the more behavioural orientation of early attachment theory was particularly anathema to psychoanalytic therapists, who wanted to focus on 'deeper' and unconscious forces.

Early attachment theory, well before Main's Adult Attachment Interview (AAI) (Main and Goldwyn 1995), paid little heed to thoughts and fantasies, and although Bowlby did have a concept of internal working models, these were viewed as a rather concrete internalisation of real parental relationships, a somewhat crude and blunted version of the more elaborated and sophisticated forms of fantasies one saw in children's play, and the complex internal relationships being interrogated by child and adult psychotherapists.

In the following decades, attachment theory and child psychotherapy tended to follow diverse paths. Attachment theory became one of the more rigorous and best researched bodies of thought about how children develop. Later, subtle ways of understanding representational worlds, such as AAIs for adults and story-stem research with children (Hodges et al. 2003), allowed a rapprochement between a focus on behaviours and inner world of representations. Despite hugely influencing whole areas of policy and practice, whether in childcare, adoption, assessing families or organising nurseries, attachment theory is first and foremost a body of research, and not a way of intervening. In the decades that attachment theory was developing, psychoanalytically informed child psychotherapy ploughed an equally auspicious furrow, pushing the boundaries of the kind of cases that could be seen for therapy, beginning to work with some of the most troubled children in society (Boston and Szur 1990), extending its field of practice to children who have been in the care system (Kenrick et al. 2006), to autistic children (Alvarez and Reid 1999) and those who have suffered all manner of other forms of psychological and emotional deprivation (Alvarez 2012).

In the meantime the world of developmental science was being turned upside down. Building on the early work of Sander (2007), Stern (1985) and Brazelton and Cramer (1991) we have seen an extraordinarily swift expansion in related fields. For example, work in neurobiology (Schore 2012), fine-grained research about maternal depression (Murray and Cooper 1999) or how infant minds grow (Reddy 2008) and the biological systems linked with this (Panksepp 2007). Overall knowledge from the field of developmental psychology has grown exponentially (cf. Music 2010).

Some of the most important findings have been made by skilled clinicians who have also undertaken careful research into early infancy and its effects, thus making careful links between research and clinical practice (Tronick 2007; Beebe and Lachmann 2002). Mentalisation (Fonagy *et al.* 2004) also linked therapeutic practice and developmental findings. Yet, despite this, few therapists have until recently seriously taken the research ideas of attachment theory directly into their therapeutic theory and practice. There are a few exceptions, such as Jeremy Holmes in adult psychotherapy (Holmes 2001) and Juliet Hopkins in child psychotherapy (Hopkins 1990), and although there have been others, this group has been surprisingly sparse.

On the other hand, there has been a whole gamut of forms of therapy that claim to be based on attachment theory and which often endorse practices which few attachment researchers would countenance, indeed often based on ideas that such researchers would barely recognise.

The most controversial examples are the various forms of both holding and regression therapies (Simmonds 2007). Such therapies have often been viewed as part of a worrying fringe movement, one that those seriously interested in attachment theory want to distance themselves from (Prior and Glaser 2006). There have also been some well researched brief interventions which have attachment theory at their core (Marvin *et al.* 2002; Juffer *et al.* 2008), and these have mainly tended to be brief, structured interventions with young mothers and their infants, focusing on enhancing parental sensitivity and facilitating more secure attachment styles.

Thus, on the one hand we have a rigorous body of attachment research findings being developed in research laboratories, and on the other hand we see therapeutic practice which often is working to principles very similar to attachment theory but is seemingly making little direct use of the ideas. Increasingly child psychotherapists have been influenced by the new developmental findings, such as the now inescapable knowledge that babies are interpersonal and reciprocal from birth (Bråten 2006), that they imitate and learn from their first minutes (Meltzoff 2007), that they respond to rhythm and prosody (Trevarthen 2004) and that relational templates are taking root in the first months of life (Beebe and Lachmann 2002), in the form of procedural memories.

Alvarez (1992), for example, had adapted and transformed her psychoanalytic child therapy technique due to the influence of such findings, and we see other work influenced by similar ideas (Green 2003), while Greenspan (2008) has always espoused a more developmental approach. Yet when closely examined, these therapists are not explicitly using attachment theory, although its ideas are often taken for granted. Rather, they are influenced by other areas of infancy research, such as how we come to understand other minds, how empathy develops, how we internalise expectations of relationships, how trauma might affect the nervous system, and people's hormonal cocktails.

The reasons for this might in part be that attachment theory as a body of scientific research on its own could never be a whole theory about therapeutic work. The term 'attachment' of course can be used more loosely, to describe people's relationship styles, or why parents are important, and in that looser sense attachment is and has always been central to therapeutic work. Therapy has always focused fundamentally on the ways in which people negotiate intimate relationships, the transference relationship with the therapist being one important example.

An excellent example of such an approach is Mills' work on Attachment Pathology (Mills 2005). Attachment theory in its more rigorous research variants has a more back-seat role in terms of psychotherapy practice, alongside related fields such as neurobiology, infancy research, the science of play or new understandings of how memories and expectations of relationships form. Attachment makes a hugely important contribution to therapeutic practice, but it will always only be part of the story. I will now introduce some clinical issues and case examples to try to develop these ideas more.

Clinical cases

Trevor

While I am sitting anxiously, about to meet Trevor, who I see weekly for psychotherapy, I notice my heart is beating fast, my stomach is tight and my breathing seems to go barely lower than my neck. I have all the symptoms of sympathetic nervous system arousal (Porges 2011) even before Trevor arrives, and in his presence I often find that I am bracing myself for something bad to happen. I had had an anxious jolt as I thought about him on my way into work, and now I am remembering last week's session, the toys flying close to my head, the fact that I confiscated the scissors just in time, how Trevor managed to force his way into another staff-room on his way to his therapy, inevitably the room of a very eminent colleague who I assumed glared disapprovingly at me. In some weeks the sessions have become so difficult that I have had to stop them and take him back to the waiting room. He has also been known to run down the stairs and out into the street, to let off fire extinguishers and deliberately flood the toilets. The reception and ancillary staff all know Trevor well.

Trevor has been the victim of domestic abuse; his mother was a prostitute and her partner a violent man, dealing in drugs, sex and fear. He was taken into care at two years old, and has already had a string of foster placements. Trevor had no further contact with his mother after he was taken into care, as his mother had never turned up for contact meetings. He was placed for adoption but no one came forward for him and now, at six, he is in the process of being approved for long-term foster care. Much as the neuroscience would predict, he is a hypervigilant, rarely still boy, who expects danger everywhere, and with whom one must be cautious, not moving too fast, not varying anything too quickly. He was a bit of a whirlwind anyway but has been in a tumultuous mood since he was told he will not be staying with his current carers. They, in fact, feel too old to give him the ongoing care he needs. At the point of referral he was already at serious risk of exclusion from school. He was violent with other children, had few friends, was often a bully in the playground, and he struggled to concentrate or to learn. He had a statement of educational needs with 18 hours a week of one-to-one support, but still the school were unclear about whether they could hold onto him.

In the initial assessment I found Trevor was wary and charming with an edge of potential threat about him. He seemed unable to play symbolically and said that the toys in the box were 'for girls'. As I have found so often with such boys, an inordinate amount of time was spent playing football. In our football games he always wanted to win and he made sure he did so. He would score a goal, clench his fist in triumph, yelp triumphantly and look disdainfully in my direction. He would often coax me into believing that he would let me have a tiny moment of glory, suggesting I might be able to score one meagre goal to his hatful, but he always at the last moment quashed my hopes and left me feeling tricked, betrayed and stupid. He was projecting something of his own horrible experience into me and took malicious delight in this. It felt better of course for me to be the victim, and his world primarily consisted of victims or perpetrators. I thought he was on the cusp of hoping that I (as projected into) could somehow make sense of the experiences he was trying to get rid of, being tricked, abused, manipulated; however, he was also on the cusp of becoming addicted to the 'secondary gain' of the pleasure in the power and violence.

He had enough understanding of my thoughts and feelings to work out how to trick me, but this is very different from real empathy. For him, other people were not there to be liked or to be interested in, but were a means or an obstacle to his end.

Interestingly, when psychopathic adults watch people's faces or actions, their brains (Deeley *et al.* 2006; Hein and Singer 2008), show different patterns of activation from those of the general population. They display less capacity for empathy and less ability to understand the emotions of others or awareness of their own feelings. I suspect that Trevor's brain might show similar abnormal neuronal activation. Indeed his potential for cruelty was at times chilling.

We know that securely attached children generally have high empathy, get on well with peers and are able to be reflective and flexible. Not so disorganised boys like Trevor. As so often happens with children like Trevor, his language was delayed and certainly he had little emotional vocabulary. He also had little capacity to reflect on his life, barely any autobiographical capacity (he could not imagine himself into a future and had no real stories about his life up until now) and, like many such children, he lacked a capacity for symbolic play. At the same time he could barely ever be still, was very vigilant and reactive and was always getting into trouble. It is easy to see how he might be given diagnoses of Autistic Spectrum Disorder (ASD), Attention Deficit Disorder (ADHD) and Conduct Disorder, and too often maltreated children are wrongly diagnosed (see DeJong 2010) as psychiatric classifications rarely capture the complexity of these children's problems (see Gutjahr in *The Routledge Handbook of Attachment: Theory* (Holmes and Farnfield 2014)).

In my work with Trevor I found that I had to address him at a very basic level (Alvarez 2012), trying to name emotions, but with feeling ('That made you very very cross!'). I would try to resist the deadening pull of constant football and when we played, try at least to expand on the characters. Didier Drogba and John Terry were his heroes, ruthless and triumphant figures with whom he identified. It was possible to momentarily wonder about the feelings of these alpha-male footballing protagonists, or about their character traits, which he would allow briefly before stating, 'Can we play properly now?' Moments of thought could be only occasionally allowed into the sessions. When he did not like the fact that I scored he might say, 'No, I was not ready', and at best I could just about talk about how upsetting and annoying it was when things did not go his way. Much of the play felt dead and sterile, interspersed with sadistic attacks and sudden outbursts which could be frightening.

Today in the room he speedily takes a toy, a female doll about the age of his carer, and makes to destroy it. I take a step back, aware of the possibility of an eruption but knowing I must steel myself, and take a huge deep breath, and say loudly but calmly, 'Why on earth should you believe anyone cares, it's just not fair'. He continues to tear at the doll, but less wildly, half glancing at me. I say, 'Of course you sometimes want to lash out and don't know why', but I realise I have made a mistake, and he glares with menace. For kids like Trevor just the word 'you' can feel accusatory and persecutory. I take a step back, remember to try to re-find my body, take a deep breath and then begin to talk aloud, with feeling, as if to myself. 'Sometimes we can have huge jumbly feelings inside and we want to just explode, they can seem to come from nowhere'. He is still glaring, but there is a sense of a lowering of the temperature. At a stretch one might think of this as attunement; I was certainly trying to reflect back to him something of his own experience, but sufficiently digested that he might take it in (Bion 1962b). I breathe again and watch, and I notice him watch me, and surprisingly, he takes a deeper breath himself. He reaches back into the toy box and takes out some vehicles, including the ambulance. I think that I have reached and re-found a slightly trusting part of him, and he has remembered that rescuers, in the form of the ambulance, exist. It is not always that way, and rarely lasts long at this stage.

In a session some six months later, partly out of frustration but also maybe with a little hope that some potential shift was occurring, I began to get toy animals out myself, in a rather desperate hope that he would start to play a bit. In one session, I got out a baby pig and said, 'Oh here is a little pig'. The other toys included a crocodile and he took this, taped its mouth with Sellotape and in just a few seconds the protection afforded to the other animals by the tape had been rendered useless. A series of killings of large and small animals took place, gleefully and triumphantly. Chilling as this was, it allowed me to talk about feelings and what was happening, which in turn enabled him to continue playing, albeit for only a few minutes. By this time he was in a Pupil Referral Unit, excluded from his mainstream school. He had begun to be able to talk a little more, to explain some tiny things to me when asked, but his speech remained rudimentary. He said, 'There is this boy', as if I would know who he meant. I asked, 'Yes Trevor, this boy . . .', and he said, 'Food all over his face'. The start of a meaningful story perhaps, but a very minimal one. Small moments of hope were creeping in. In one session he was about to take a shot at goal and he momentarily hesitated. Normally I would have missed the moment but this time I asked where his mind was. He looked surprised that I asked, and then said, 'I was thinking about my old school'. Maybe there was a sign here of the tiniest beginnings of a thinker who could think thoughts (Bion 1962a). I said, 'Wow Trevor, you really are having thoughts, and we can get to know your thoughts'.

This led in a few sentences to how he wished he was still at his old school and how, 'I think about it lots of the time'. He had never had the kind of attuned attention (Stern 1985) that forms the basis of a developing sense of self in relation to others (Beebe and Lachmann 2002).

These changes were fairly slight. He was still extremely challenging at school and at home and people remained worried about him. A few weeks later there were hopeful moments when he talked about how 'bad' he had been (probably told to do so by his carer). I was able to be slightly playful with him and with his help we gave a name to this 'Cross Trevor', and I tried to guess what 'Cross Trevor' was feeling when he got so angry in a recent incident. He said, 'You sound funny' but seemed visibly to relax, I think at the idea that 'Cross Trevor' might not be all of him. At the same time I saw some tiny examples of him being less reactive. The end of his pencil kept breaking, something that would have made him very angry previously, but this time he said, 'Okay I can do it' as he again sharpened it. Some belief that things could come right was forming, and some idea that he need not be overwhelmed. I said, 'Well it is not so bad, that's a new Trevor, not Cross Trevor', and he said, 'No that's Boy Trevor' and a new character had formed. 'Boy Trevor' was to play a role in our therapy for the remaining time. Boy Trevor grew out of a sense of self-developing, and a belief that he could have some control over his life, that mismatches and ruptures in relational moments (Tronick 2007) were repairable and not disastrous.

A few weeks later in the midst of a football game he turned the light on and I observed a slight flicker of interest and asked him what he noticed and he said, 'The colour'. I said, 'Isn't that amazing, the room seems to change colour when you turn the light on'. He did it again and looked at me and then said, 'The room goes sort of pink'. I said, 'Yes the whole room seems to change, and what is so-oo interesting is that Trevor, you noticed it'. I thought this was the nearest he had been to aesthetic appreciation (Meltzer et al. 1988). He looked pleased, did it again and said, 'It makes a sound'. I said, 'Wow yes, you have noticed the sound it makes when you turn the light on', as I cocked my ear dramatically, and he did it again. Then he said, 'It's like a star', which I repeated and said how interesting it was when we noticed things. I think this is the kind of early attuned input that most lucky babies receive, but not children like Trevor who so often manifest a wide array of serious developmental deficits. Interestingly at the end of this session, for the first time ever, he 'helped' me to put away his things into the box, maybe not the most altruistic gesture ever but another tiny change. Similarly school and home had both spotted examples of increased thoughtfulness, such as offering to help clean something up that was spilt at home.

Trevor like all children is unique, but also shares many similarities with others who develop disorganised attachment patterns. All attachment patterns are adaptive, including the disorganised pattern. In fact these children can be highly organised, and are perpetually on high alert in case of danger. They can look like they have no strategy but their responses make sense, given their environment. Trevor was also typical in other ways. He had a low threshold for frustration, poorly developed abilities to self-regulate, and a hypervigilant and very easily aroused sympathetic nervous system. Like many with disorganised attachments, he could flip from being very controlled and rigid to extremely chaotic behaviour. My single hour a week was hard work, but I had it easy compared to others, with the luxury in that hour of only concentrating on him. I do not have 30 other kids to teach, or the washing up to do at home, or umpteen other kids on my social work caseload and reports to write. In my hour a week with Trevor I saw my role as trying to find a small oasis of calm, a place of safety in the room and in himself, which we might build and grow. This is the window of tolerance that Ogden describes (2006), a window that for such children is often very narrow. For Trevor it takes little to flip out of this window of tolerance into very tense, angry states, sometimes also frightened ones. It is hard to believe that I or anyone else can really be trusted or thoughtful. However, as this window slowly became more of a trusted place, some narrative and reflection also became possible, and he in fact became more likeable as he began to be able to concentrate a bit, and even be a little more empathic. He began, while in this window, to show signs that we often see in secure attachment, such as empathy, curiosity, confidence, trust in others, belief that he could be cared for, interest in others and even enjoyment. These remained very shaky and rudimentary but were coming alive as real potentials.

Lucas

After Trevor, I see nine-year-old Lucas. Lucas was born into a family with parents who were distant and could not bear emotions. Neighbours reported him being strapped in a baby stroller for hours, left to his own devices, rarely picked up, having baby bottles shoved in his mouth and being given little stimulation or interpersonal contact. It is fascinating that my body, mind and feelings are completely different with him, compared to Trevor, as if I am another person. While I wait for him I note myself feeling deadened and distracted. I know I take longer to answer the receptionist's phone, that I am not looking forward to seeing him, and I feel wooden in my body as I go to collect him. I predict correctly the ensuing ritual, where he will be sitting, his posture, his looks, his words, and how the start of the session will go. I steel myself in a different way with Lucas than with Trevor, to help bring some aliveness and hope. It took me a while until I could admit to myself that I found him dull. My guilt was lessened when I learnt just how others such as his teachers, and more worryingly, his parents, felt about him. His adoptive parents have another child, a daughter who has a more ambivalent attachment pattern, who was traumatised and who acts out dramatically, and who claims most of their attention. He is rather too 'easy' and in some ways they are relieved when Lucas is up in his room playing play station and reading Argos catalogues. This is rather like his teachers, who are glad there is a boy sitting quietly at the back of the class not causing trouble, even if he is not learning. They are not drawn to him, and in fact few people are, and he has few friends. He does not easily elicit worry or concern or interest. He is in many ways typical of many of the neglected children we work with, who can so easily continue to be neglected as they get older, because they do not inspire interest, or concern, or enjoyment.

Both Lucas and Trevor affect all those around them in very different ways, but each affects us profoundly. We need to be affected by them to know them, as well as having tools to understand the meaning of their behaviours. I think only in this way can we hold them in our minds. Lucas is typical of many with avoidant attachment styles. He had been brought to therapy but certainly did not think he had a problem. To his parents he was a mystery and they felt disconcerted that they could make so little contact with him. They were warm and affectionate people but received little back from him, and found themselves becoming hurt and angry, or withdrawing. He evoked frustration and hopelessness in them, feelings I soon understood too. At school, too, he was seen as a little odd and something of a loner. He was described, sometimes to his face, as 'lazy' and 'stubborn'. Sessions were dull, and he would sit, stare, look compliantly, and then hesitantly tell me what he was going to do that day. Each session was neatly divided up: he might start by saying, 'I will talk about my dreams for three minutes, things at home for four minutes, play a game of hangman for five minutes, talk about worries for four minutes'.

Attachment patterns are of course adaptive and Lucas had adapted to a very bleak world. Unfortunately he did not really believe that another, more lively, human or emotional world existed. I found myself at quite a loss as to how I might ever have any impact on him and his detached attachment style. What I have learnt from working with such children is that one has to carefully watch the feeling stirred up in the therapist, what we call our countertransference, maybe of boredom, irritation or drifting away. Being bored, watching the clock, mentally writing shopping lists, these are all useful sources of information but when we indulge in them then that is an enactment or acting-in (Aron 2001). On one occasion when I was in a kind of half-alive torpor I managed to concentrate hard on what he seemed to be experiencing, and surprisingly found myself feeling some sympathy. I am fairly sure in response to a change in my feeling tone, he looked up and smiled, a small moment to cherish, one from which some genuine relating followed; for once there was a smile which seemed real, not compliant. At such moments when I spoke I know my voice had more urgency, but also genuineness, I was 'calling him back', 'reclaiming' (Alvarez 1992) him, and he could respond.

Slowly he seemed to slightly loosen up, as I found a way to empathise and feel my way into his world, and as a result I realised I could find myself liking him. Then I could be more actively challenging of him in a way that he would not feel as critical and judgemental. Sometimes my attempts to engage him were all too clearly expressions of my frustration, and then my less than sympathetic tone precluded real contact. When my attempts to reach him had urgency but not frustration, and challenged him warmly, then real contact was made. When as I leaned forward slightly I said, 'Huh, when you turn away like that it is like I am too much for you, and you forget I can be someone you can talk to', he looked up and his tone changed. These small changes nearly always seemed to result from immersing myself in an aspect of his being that I found almost unbearable, but that it helped to know. As he bounced his leg, I bounced mine in response and he looked up at me and awkwardly smiled.

There was maybe the beginning of 'reciprocity' (Brazelton and Cramer 1991) as he stopped jigging his leg, and I did too, he then looked up again, jigged and waited for me to respond. Here developed an ordinary rhythmic to-and-fro that most babies engage in with their parents, but which Lucas had lacked. He was developing the beginnings of a capacity for conversation in which eventually slightly more difficult feelings could be processed. It made no sense to him when I talked, as I did too much, of breaks between sessions, or of holidays. However, when in a game I enacted being suddenly stopped in my tracks and expressed frustration, he seemed to enjoy this. He looked awkward, then laughed, and in the next session he did a slightly wooden version of the same thing, showing a capacity for both introjections and for 'deferred imitation' (Meltzoff 1988). He had also become slightly humorous, which as we know is always a hopeful sign. He had begun to be interested in what I was making of him, starting to believe that I had a story in my mind about him, the kind of story that securely attached kids take for granted that their parents have about them.

As Lucas began to seem more lively in his play I sometimes saw rather disturbing and sickly scenes being enacted, such as horrible deaths and torture. Animal and human toys were lined up, hurt and killed. If I interpreted this in a way that revealed any hint of disapproval his play ground to a halt. When I realised what was happening, I could stay with the play more, and it at times did turn into a sickening frenzy of death and destruction, although still expressed in his rather wooden and slightly deadened way.

As horrible as it could seem, there was some 'wanting', some 'desire', in his play which needed encouraging. Sometimes when something frozen begins to thaw out, what replaces it might be traits that we find abhorrent. In the cases I have seen, tolerating this has been a stepping stone in development, rather than the unleashing of psychopathic monsters. What such kids lack, as well of course as the belief that other people can be interested and responsive, is that life can be richer and that vitality and interest can be enjoyable and not anxiety provoking. Beatrice Beebe found that many such children, as mere four-month-old babies, could not look at their mothers when they smiled at them, they had their heads 'cocked for escape' and self-soothed (Beebe and Lachmann 2002). Gently showing that the relational world is safe, and even pleasurable, is a big part of working with avoidant children.

In time he began to show some initiative, and a sense of agency, but maybe more importantly, seemingly the beginnings of fun. Fun and positive emotions are neglected in the psychoanalytic literature (Music 2009), but for children like Lucas who have not been really enjoyed, they are crucial. Alvarez (1992) suggested that while the child who jumps on the chair and shouts 'I am king of the castle' might be being defensive, for some children this act might be the first experience of feeling strong and confident, and they need this to be validated. I had to be very careful with Lucas to try to ensure that the tiny signs of hope and self-belief were noticed and mirrored. I am quite sure that I often felt so dulled in his company that I completely missed them. Slowly, though, his communications became slightly louder, firmer and clearer, as if he was beginning to believe that there were other people who could be interested in him. In his attempts to make things with the therapy toys, he seemed to have developed more determination and began to try harder, to not give up so easily, and he developed confidence that he could make things happen. Often when he tried to do something, like build a tower, and he seemed to be failing, he would quickly give up. I would then begin to actively encourage him ('yes you can do it, no need to give up, wow, you are doing well'). He was rather like the children of depressed mothers that Murray (1992) or Field and colleagues (2006) studied, who tend to be passive, with little sense of agency or self-belief.

Old attachment templates never disappear, but new ones can slowly grow and I think this was happening with Lucas. His parents also became more relaxed. It was not just because Lucas was changing, but also that we had helped them to understand Lucas, to make sense of why he was as he was, to link this with his past. This allowed them to feel sympathy and warmth towards him and less self-blaming. Therapy was of course only part of the story. Playing a lot with his more demanding adoptive sister also had quite an effect, I am sure. One really positive sign was that he was invited to a couple of parties, which had not happened before, and suggested that he was entering the world of peer relationships in a new way. I still certainly felt bored at times, and frustrated, and my heart never raced like it did with Trevor. However, some aliveness was definitely forming.

Grace

Later I looking forward to seeing 16-year-old Grace; she was an easy person to be with after Lucas and Trevor. She smiled at me slightly nervously in the waiting room, looked at me longer than usual and followed me to the room. She was very careful to ensure that she left enough space when someone else came along the corridor in the opposite direction, looked down and smiled awkwardly. In the room she sat with her body half turned away and half turned towards me and she asked me, 'How are you?' This was not the first time she had done this, but today it was as if she had something on her mind. I asked, 'How come you are wondering this today?' She replied, 'I thought you looked tired'. She provided me with a classic psychoanalytic dilemma. I in fact was tired, as I had been working away all weekend and had had no time off. As relational analysts have pointed out (Aron 2001), often patients know something about us before we know it about ourselves, and then it is not helpful to just bat back their questions or be evasive. I find this to be commonly the case with people who have ambivalent attachment styles. Rather like Sally who I mentioned in the introduction, Grace had learnt to monitor the important adults in her life very carefully. She was brought up as an only child by a single mother who was very needy and often depressed. Grace had felt responsible for her mother's moods, something it seems her mother encouraged. Her mother could also be subject to angry outbursts which, as a child, Grace had found very frightening. Often when I have a serious expression on my face she can suddenly look very worried. Her ambivalent attachment style was an extraordinarily nuanced adaptation to her early environment, but our early presuppositions about relationships are hard to unlearn.

Grace was doing well academically and also had a lot of friends at school. Yet she often felt very alone. Her friends relied on her a lot and she had developed an adeptness at using 'tend and befriend' ways of keeping people at ease and making sure that they were not too upset. Yet she reported often feeling terribly rejected and hurt. A typical example was when she was not invited to a party of a friend and was mortified. She could not stop thinking about this for weeks, it went round and around in her head. She even, somewhat masochistically, found herself walking down the road where the party was being held. Such desperation was not uncommon. Following a split up from a brief relationship she would haunt the areas where she thought her former boyfriend might be, hoping to bump into him 'accidentally'. In therapy I found that breaks were particularly tough and she would often get tearful just before. She was of course far too polite to protest, and indeed she was in many ways the perfect client. She always arrived exactly on time, almost never even a minute early or late, and on the rare occasion that she was about three minutes late she apologised profusely.

Her comment about me being tired challenged me. She obviously had accurately picked up something about me. I decided to say that yes, I probably was a bit more tired than usual. Rather than asking her how she felt about that, I decided to remark on just how very good she was at picking up my feelings, as she was with other people too. It seemed, I said, to be like a basic survival response, as if the world would feel terribly unsafe if she did not know. She looked relieved and lent back into the chair, a bit more relaxed. I said how hard it seemed to believe that I might still have her in my mind even if I was a bit tired. I said that she really believed that if she did not look after me, or whoever she was with, she would be rejected or dismissed or just be dropped from our minds. She began to cry. She had often cried, but in a rather desperate way. This time the crying was deep, from the pit of her belly. Afterwards she looked brighter in her face, more at ease, and she began to talk about memories of her childhood. I had heard some of what she talked about before, but even though some of the content was the same, there was a slightly new feel to it, one that had been creeping into the sessions in recent weeks. She felt angry and aggrieved that she had wasted so much of her childhood looking after her mother and being fearful of what would happen if she did not. The anger seemed to suggest a new sense of self-worth starting to form. It need not be her lot in life, she was beginning to believe, to always be the one who looked after others.

She still had to look carefully at me after this, check I was with her, that she was not being too much. These patterns take a long time to change. Slowly though she began to trust that she could relax a bit, take the guard down. My main clue that this was genuine came when I noticed that I felt more at ease, which was linked to not being monitored quite so much. In effect a new template of emotional relating was beginning to develop in Grace. It was not going to replace the old ones of course, but could slowly and steadily take root and begin to grow. Silences began to occur in our sessions, in the way that Winnicott described, a sense that one could be alone in another's presence (Winnicott 1958). This, of course, is what one sees in a secure attachment relationship. Children feel free to leave their caregiver and go off and play, knowing that, when needed, there will be someone there for them. This was not what Grace had initially learnt to believe about the world.

Such changes were slow and incremental, with many backward steps. Luckily we had time and Grace came for several years. One session just after a summer break I expected her to come in quiet and contrite, as she often would, checking that I was okay, monitoring my mood. Instead she barely glanced at me and told me in no uncertain terms that she was very angry that I had gone away at this time. She knew, she said, that her feelings were irrational but she had needed me. In the past this might have been said in a forlorn self-pitying way at most. However, this was a first, an expression of anger, albeit of a very tentative kind. Winnicott again had something to say about such moments (Winnicott 1971). He understood that children needed to know that the full force of their emotions could be received by another, who could bear and survive these feelings, whether of distress or particularly of rage and hatred. Only this allowed children to feel genuinely separate from the other. Children with ambivalent attachments rarely feel this but hopefully with Grace it was beginning. She was getting interested in herself as a feelingful person with hopes and dreams, whom others might take seriously. She could begin to believe that others might be there for her when needed, that she did not have to constantly monitor them, that she could sometimes forget about them, and that her life might be lived from an inner sense of trust and belief, again much as we are likely to see in securely attached people.

Summary

Each of these cases, and indeed probably all of the cases seen in our team, can be thought about in attachment terms. Attachment theory of course does not explain everything about these children. We need to understand in addition many other things to work with such children, such as the power of pernicious introjects, forms of transference and countertransference, the ways defences form and are maintained, the power of resistance to change, and of course the whole complex world of therapeutic technique, of what and how to say things, how to be with clients, when to challenge, when to be empathic, what kind of feeling tone to adopt, and so much more. However, attachment theory does help to make sense of the kinds of relational patterns that children have developed, and gives us an understanding of why such entrenched ways of relating have developed. Child psychotherapy works primarily and fundamentally with relationship templates as they manifest themselves in the consulting room, as well as in other areas of a child's life.

As will already have been gathered from these examples, attachment theory can really help to make sense of a child's expectations of relationship, what Daniel Stern called RIGs or Representations of Interactions Generalized (Stern 1985), what Bowlby described as internal working models (Bowlby 1969), but this understanding is by no means mainly cognitive or abstract. Child psychotherapy works with such patterns as they become alive in the therapy room, and in our relationships with these children. If our understanding is to be helpful, it has to be of an emotional kind. When therapy is going well we are able to make emotional sense of the kinds of feelings and ideas that we find are affecting us while we are with a child; we can remain open and curious about the ways in which we find ourselves prodded into acting in certain ways in a child's presence (Sandler 1993), and we can process rather than act on the thoughts and feelings that are evoked in us. The child psychotherapy consulting room, as I see it, is a kind of crucible for psychological, indeed psychobiological, enactments that need to be born, processed, internally modulated and helpfully used in the service of the child's development (Bion 1962b). Like with metal or glass, in the heat of the therapeutic relationship opportunities arise for new patterns to be forged, new relational shapes to be experimented with, and new hopes and beliefs about attachment, intimacy and trust, to come alive and take a solid form. Of course the old templates remain, but they hopefully slowly diminish in power. Our attachment styles are interpersonal and our relationship styles are learnt with real people. Just as a child might have a secure relationship with one parent and an insecure one with another, new, secure relationship representations can grow from within a therapeutic relationship to become internalised as structured aspects of the personality. I hope this was happening with Trevor, Lucas and Grace.

References

Alvarez, A. (1992) *Live company* (London: Routledge)

Alvarez, A. (2012) *The thinking heart: Three levels of psychoanalytic therapy with disturbed children* (Oxford: Routledge)

Alvarez, A. and Reid, S. (1999) *Autism and personality: Findings from the Tavistock Autism Workshop* (London: Routledge)

Aron, L. (2001) *A meeting of minds: Mutuality in psychoanalysis* (New York: Analytic Press)

Beebe, B. and Lachmann, F. M. (2002) *Infant research and adult treatment: Co-constructing interactions* (New York: Analytic Press)

Bion, W. R. (1962a) A theory of thinking, *Melanie Klein today: Developments in theory and practice* 1: 178–86

Bion, W. R. (1962b) *Learning from experience* (London: Heinemann)

Boston, M. and Szur, R. (1990) *Psychotherapy with severely deprived children* (Stylus Publishing, LLC)

Bowlby, J. (1969) *Attachment and loss. Vol. 1, Attachment* (London: Hogarth)

Bråten, S. (2006) *Intersubjective communication and emotion in early ontogeny* (Cambridge: Cambridge University Press)

Brazelton, T. B. and Cramer, B. G. (1991) *The earliest relationship: Parents, infants, and the drama of early attachment* (London: Karnac Books)

Deeley, Q., Daly, E., Surguladzes, S., Tunstall, N., Mezey, G., Beer, D. *et al.* (2006) Facial emotion processing in criminal psychopathy: Preliminary functional magnetic resonance imaging study, *The British Journal of Psychiatry* 189: 533

DeJong, M. (2010) Some reflections on the use of psychiatric diagnosis in the looked after or 'in care' child population, *Clinical Child Psychology and Psychiatry* 15: 589–99

Field, T., Diego, M. and Hernandez-Reif, M. (2006) Prenatal depression effects on the fetus and newborn: A review, *Infant Behavior and Development* 29: 445–55

Fonagy, P., Gyorgy, G., Jurist, E. L. and Target, M. (2004) *Affect regulation, mentalization, and the development of the self* (London: Karnac Books)

Green, V. (2003) *Emotional development in psychoanalysis, attachment theory and neuroscience: Creating connections* (London: Routledge)

Greenspan, S. I. (2008) A dynamic developmental model of mental health and mental illness. In A. Fogel, B. J. King and S. G. Shanker (eds), *Human development in the twenty-first century: Visionary ideas from systems scientists* (pp. 157–75) (Cambridge: Cambridge University Press)

Hein, G. and Singer, T. (2008) I feel how you feel but not always: The empathic brain and its modulation, *Current Opinion in Neurobiology* 18: 153–8

Hodges, J., Steele, M., Hillman, S. and Henderson, K. (2003) Mental representations and defences in severely maltreated children: A story stem battery and rating system for clinical assessment and research applications. In R. N. Emde, D. P. Wolf and D. Oppenheim (eds), *Revealing the inner worlds of young children: The MacArthur Stem Battery and Parent–Child Narratives* (pp. 240–67) (Oxford: Oxford University Press)

Holmes, J. (2001) *The search for the secure base: Attachment theory and psychotherapy* (London: Routledge)

Holmes, P. and Farnfield, S. (eds) (2014) *The Routledge handbook of attachment: Theory* (London and New York: Routledge)

Hopkins, J. (1990) The observed infant of attachment theory, *British Journal of Psychotherapy* 6: 460–70

Juffer, F., Bakermans-Kranenburg, M. J. and Van IJzendoorn, M. H. (2008) *Promoting positive parenting: An attachment-based intervention* (New York: Taylor & Francis Group)

Kenrick, J., Lindsey, C. and Tollemache, L. (2006) *Creating new families: Therapeutic approaches to fostering, adoption, and kinship care* (London: Karnac Books)

Main, M. and Goldwyn, R. (1995) Interview-based adult attachment classifications: Related to infant-mother and infant-father attachment, *Developmental Psychology* 19: 227–39

Marvin, R., Cooper, G., Hoffman, K. and Powell, B. (2002) The Circle of Security project: Attachment-based intervention with caregiver-pre-school child dyads, *Attachment & Human Development* 4: 107–24

Meltzer, D., Williams, M. H. and Trust, R. H. (1988) *The apprehension of beauty: The role of aesthetic conflict in development, violence and art* (Clunie Press for Roland Harris Trust)

Meltzoff, A. N. (1988) Infant imitation and memory: Nine-month-olds in immediate and deferred tests, *Child Development* 59: 217–25

Meltzoff, A. N. (2007) 'Like me': A foundation for social cognition, *Developmental Science* 10: 126–34

Mills, J. (2005) *Treating attachment pathology* (New York: Jason Aronson)

Murray, L. (1992) The impact of postnatal depression on infant development, *Journal of Child Psychology and Psychiatry* 33: 543–61

Murray, L. and Cooper, P. (1999) *Postpartum depression and child development* (New York: Guilford Press)

Music, G. (2009) What has psychoanalysis got to do with happiness? Reclaiming the positive in psychoanalytic psychotherapy, *British Journal of Psychotherapy* 25: 435–55

Music, G. (2010) *Nurturing natures: Attachment and children's emotional, social and brain development* (London: Psychology Press)

Ogden, P. (2006) *Trauma and the body: A sensorimotor approach to psychotherapy* (W. W. Norton & Co.)

Panksepp, J. (2007) Can PLAY diminish ADHD and facilitate the construction of the social brain? *Journal of the Canadian Academy of Child and Adolescent Psychiatry* 16: 57–66

Porges, S. W. (2011) *The polyvagal theory: Neurophysiological foundations of emotions, attachment, communication, and self-regulation* (New York: W. W. Norton)

Prior, V. and Glaser, D. (2006) *Understanding attachment and attachment disorders: Theory, evidence and practice* (London and Philadelphia: Jessica Kingsley Publishers)

Reddy, V. (2008) *How infants know minds* (Harvard: Harvard University Press)

Sander, L. (2007) *Living systems, evolving consciousness, and the emerging person: A selection of papers from the life work of Louis Sander* (London: Routledge)

Sandler, J. (1993) On communication from patient to analyst: Not everything is projective identification, *International Journal of Psycho-Analysis* 74: 1097–107

Schore, A. N. (2012) *The science of the art of psychotherapy* (New York: W. W. Norton)

Simmonds, J. (2007) Holding children in mind or holding therapy: Developing an ethical position, *Clinical child psychology and psychiatry* 12: 243–51

Stern, D. N. (1985) *The interpersonal world of the infant* (New York: Basic Books)

Trevarthen, C. (2004) How infants learn how to mean. In M. Tokoro and L. Steels (eds), *A learning zone of one's own* (p. 39) (Amsterdam: IOS Press)

Tronick, E. (2007) *The neurobehavioral and social emotional development of infants and children* (New York: W. W. Norton)

Winnicott, D. W. (1958) The capacity to be alone, *International Journal of Psycho-Analysis* 39: 416–20

Winnicott, D. W. (1971) The use of an object and relating through identifications. In *Playing and Reality* (New York: Basic Books)

Chapter 3

Where the child is the concern

Working psychotherapeutically with parents

Jeremy Holmes

Parents are only as happy as their least happy child

(traditional saying)

Introduction

A fundamental postulate – perhaps *the* fundamental postulate – of attachment theory is that children, when threatened, tired, or sick, seek out an 'older, wiser' Secure Base for protection and succour (Bowlby 1971; Holmes 2013). Reciprocally, parents are programmed to respond to their infants' and children's distress with nurturing behaviours such as physical contact, hugging, comforting, warming, cleansing, and feeding.

In addition to this 'emergency' aspect of the attachment relationship, there is a 'non-emergency, ordinary' (Waters 2008) everyday aspect, in which the caregiver attends to the child's developmental needs by close attention, providing scaffolding and supporting the child's agency and independence. A crucial component in both is 'affect regulation' (Mikulincer *et al.* 2003) in that the child's distress is modulated by a variety of parental manoeuvres such as containment, soothing, distraction and/or stimulation, but also that positive affects are contained and modulated, and responded to with pleasure, thereby instilling the capacity for mutual fun and joyfulness. As development proceeds, these become internalised by the child, who learns both to manage her own feelings when she can, and to recruit others for help when needed. Authors such as Waters (2008) and Schore (2004) see both dimensions as integral to the attachment dynamic, although it can be argued that the inter-subjective developmental aspects of early relationships are distinct from the security-providing attachment component.

Staying with the 'emergency' vector, the sequence of stress/distress followed by soothing/recovery proceeds fractally throughout development, at micro and macro levels. In the early weeks and months of life, several times per day, there will be mini-stresses and disruptions to be contained, focused on and overcome. At a macro level, children can be expected to negotiate a series of developmental hurdles – separation and stress (parents away or ill; starting school; bullying; fears,

phobias and frightening experiences, etc.), as well as physical illnesses and injuries, usually self-limiting. The cycle of stress, mental or physical pain, soothing
and recovery, when things go well, fosters resilience, The developing child is
strengthened emotionally, with a growing sense that adversity can, with appropriate
help, be faced and overcome (Fonagy *et al.* 2004). A comparable maturation occurs
for parents, who gain confidence in their capacity to provide effective nurture
and support for their children, as, together, they face the quotidian vicissitudes
of family life.

Chronic illnesses, physical or mental, pose particular difficulties for both parents and children within this model. Unlike self-limiting illnesses or physical
trauma, there is often no clear recovery point. Rather than complete cure, optimal
outcomes are likely to be those of adjustment, acceptance, and courage in the face
of adversity. These considerations apply equally to ill parents and parents of ill
children.

Intergenerational transmission of attachment patterns

Most psychotherapeutic practice relies on hunches and heuristics, permeated by a
mild 'cult of personality', rather than established facts. In establishing the attachment paradigm, Bowlby's self-effacingness, and strict adherence to scientific principles of evidence and refutation, mitigated against both: one of the great strengths
of attachment theory is its empirical base, eschewing appeal to authority.

A significant breakthrough came in the 1990s when a number of researchers
found evidence of continuity between attachment patterns in the parental generation and their children in the next. The classic Fonagy, Steele and Steele (1991)
study measured attachment dispositions in a non-clinical sample of 'pregnant parents' using the Adult Attachment Interview (AAI); then, based on the Strange Situation procedure (SSP) (Mary Ainsworth's first formal measure of infant/mother
attachment) the resulting offspring were assigned attachment categories some
15 months later. For a detailed discussion of the Strange Situation assessment
measures see *The Routledge Handbook of Attachment: Theory* (Holmes & Farnfield 2014) or *The Routledge Handbook of Attachment: Assessment* (Farnfield &
Holmes 2014).

Parents whose narrative styles were 'free/autonomous' were statistically more
likely to have children who were securely attached, while those with dismissing
narrative styles tended to have children who were classified as insecure-avoidant
in the SSP.

This seminal study opened up two decades of study of how attachment patterns
might be transmitted from one generation to the next. The current view rests on the
prevailing gene × environment perspective. Given the inherent polymorphism of
the human genome, some children are relatively robust and can achieve a degree
of attachment security and psychological health notwithstanding adverse parenting styles or trauma. By contrast, infants with 'plasticity' genes are powerfully

affected by their parents' handling, for good or ill (Steele & Siever 2010). The ongoing parent–child dynamic has to be conceptualised in terms of a subtle set of self-maintaining developmental pathways to which genetic and environmental factors and the relationship itself contribute.

The early attachment literature saw the differences between secure and insecure children in terms of parental 'sensitivity' (Ainsworth 1973). Fonagy and co-workers now specify aspects of this quality under the rubric of 'mentalising' (Fonagy & Luyten 2009; Holmes 2010). Mentalising is a complex group of inter- and intra-personal skills which include the ability to: (a) view oneself and others as sentient beings with desires, projects and motivations, (b) reflect on one's own and others' motivations, and (c) understand how beliefs about self and others, because filtered through the mind, are inherently error-prone, and in need of negotiation and correction.

In the original Fonagy/Steele study, mothers able to mentalise (with high levels of 'reflexive function', as it was then called), even when their own upbringing had been troubled, tended to have secure offspring. Those without that capacity were more likely to have insecure children, especially if their own developmental history had been problematic. Parents who can see their children as separate sentient beings, who can differentiate their own feelings from those of the child, see the child in a developmental context, and recruit appropriate help when needed, are likely to be rated as 'sensitive' and therefore able to foster secure attachment in their care-providing practices.

Neuroscience techniques help to further illuminate these findings. In a recent study Strathearn *et al.* (2009) identify two features which differentiate secure from insecure mothers as measured on the AAI. When exposed in an fMRI setup to smiling or sad pictures of their infants' faces, brain patterns in the two groups were significantly different. Compared with their insecure counterparts, mothers with secure attachment dispositions showed increased activation of mesocortico-limbic reward brain regions on viewing their own infant's smiling face. They also showed an increased peripheral oxytocin response while interacting with their infants, which was correlated with activation of oxytocinergic and dopamine-associated reward processing regions of the brain (hypothalamus/pituitary and ventral striatum). Thus it might be said that secure mothers find interactions with their babies more rewarding than the insecure.

Even more remarkable was the finding that 'striking differences in brain activation were seen in response to their own infant's sad facial affect' (Strathearn *et al.* 2009: 2662). Securely attached mothers showed greater activation in reward processing regions of the brain, whereas 'insecure/dismissing' mothers showed increased activation of the anterior insula, a region associated with feelings of unfairness, pain, and disgust.

For securely attached mothers, infant cues (whether positive *or* negative) reinforce and motivate responsive maternal care. By contrast, insecure mothers, it seems, when exposed to negative cues in their infants, react with withdrawal and aversion when the expected positive feedback from their child is absent. This in turn evokes negative feelings in the mother, including disgust. This finding is consistent with the typical dampening-down of feeing seen in avoidant/deactivating children: to manifest separation distress runs the risk of further alienating the care-giver, and exposing the child to danger as parental Secure Base provision is withdrawn. In such sub-optimal care-giving environments affect suppression maintains proximity, and therefore a degree of safety, but at an emotional cost. This formulation is consistent with the finding that negativity is a more salient feature in insecurely attached children than in the securely attached (Belsky *et al.* 1996). But negative affect, although suppressed, remains subliminally present, adversely colouring the child's mental universe.

Insecure attachment in children is not itself problematic. At least 30 per cent of non-clinical populations demonstrate insecure attachment. This may, indeed, be an adaptive response to sub-optimal care-giving environments (which are of course widespread, and reflect prevailing social and political structures). It is important that professionals respect such resilience, and eschew as far as possible imposing their own 'middle class' social and ethical norms, both in research and clinical contexts.

However, the case of Disorganised attachment (labelled D in attachment theory), especially when combined with severe patterns of hyperactivating insecurity is somewhat different. Disorganisation is highly predictive of later psychological difficulties including poor peer adaption, disruption in school, and externalising and dissociative disorders in middle childhood and adolescence. It is these children who are most likely to come to the attention of educational, medical, social care, and criminal justice agencies (see Shemmings in Holmes & Farnfield 2014).

Disorganised attachment seen from the parent's perspective

Disorganised attachment as measured in the SSP between 12 and 18 months predicts psychopathology in later childhood and early adulthood (Van IJzendoorn *et al.* 1999). Lyons-Ruth has pioneered studies looking at the characteristics of mothers of D children, and on the basis of a number of 'communication errors', classifies them into two broad groups: frightened/withdrawn and hostile/intrusive (Lyons-Ruth *et al.* 1999). Both groups report significant amounts of childhood trauma in their own development, the withdrawn group more likely to have been sexually abused, the hostile group physically abused.

In the withdrawn group the mother appears unable to respond to her child's distress, leaving the infant to find some means of self-soothing, however uncoordinated – appearing dissociated, rocking, head banging, etc. In the hostile-intrusive pattern the mother typically attacks and blames the child for being distressed. 'You're only doing this to wind me up' would be a characteristic hostile-intrusive response to an infant's attachment-seeking behaviours. The relevance of this to later responses to chronic illness might be either a helpless 'giving up' on the part of the parent, or 'blaming the victim' where the child's illness is seen as self-inflicted, leading often to futile attempts to get the child to behave 'normally'. Neither the child's nor the parent's (herself often a victim of abusive or insensitive parenting) attachment needs are met in these self-defeating interactions.

Such dysfunctional patterns were originally conceptualised primarily from the child's point of view as 'fear without solution' (Main & Hesse 1990). The child is presented with an insoluble paradox, reminiscent of the supposed 'schizophreno-genic' 'double bind' (cf. Holmes 2010) in which the very person who would alleviate attachment arousal is also the source of the threat, and the child thus faces an unresolvable approach-avoidance dilemma.

Within the context of this chapter, Disorganised attachment needs also to be seen from the point of view of the parent. From this perspective, the care-giver herself feels either disempowered and helpless, or suffused with unassuaged rage. The parent's care-giving attachment dynamic is activated, but cannot be assuaged – the child remains unwell, despite the parent's best efforts at alleviation. The withdrawn 'given up' posture is an expression of helplessness in the face of an unresolvable situation; conversely the hostile-intrusive pattern can be seen in terms of a desperate parent, longing for diminution of attachment arousal, verbally (or sometimes physically) attacking the child in the hope that rage will somehow alleviate her unbearable feelings.

Further, children in Type D are typically found beyond infancy to be 'controlling', often with role-reversal between themselves and their parent (O'Connor et al. 2011). This can be understood from the child's point of view as a means of locating their own vulnerability in the other and thus feeling a measure of freedom from fear and mental pain. From the parent's perspective this can be disempowering, reinforcing feelings of helplessness and incompetence. An analogous pattern may exist with chronically ill children, for example with eating disorders or chronic fatigue syndrome (CFS), where parents may cow-tow and pander to their child's every need in the hope of recovery, but end up feeling baffled and frustrated.

Parents suffering from Borderline Personality Disorders

The discussion thus far has focused on children designated as Disorganised in the Strange Situation, the parental handling associated with that classification, the impact on the parent, and their long-term consequences for child mental health. In this section we will look at the converse: the implication for their children of mothers with mental health difficulties, especially Borderline Personality Disorder (BPD).

Murray and co-workers (Murray et al. 2011) have studied the implications of maternal depression on attachment patterns in children, showing that depressed mothers are more likely to have insecurely attached children, but that when the mood disorder is successfully treated, the child's attachment pattern often becomes secure. Personality Disorders are, by definition, more long-lasting than so-called 'Axis 1' illnesses such as depression. The implications for the child of being brought up by a mother suffering from BPD are thus highly significant.

From the point of view of parenting, important features of BPD include affective instability; an unstable sense of self; substance abuse; and episodes of deliberate self-harm. All of these are likely to compromise effective and sensitive parenting. Difficulties with mentalising are at the heart of the Fonagy-Bateman model of BPD (Fonagy & Luyten 2009), and their interventions are targeted around efforts to enhance it. If parental mentalising is the key to the fostering of secure attachment in children, then clearly the children of BPD-suffering parents will be at risk. A person's ability to help regulate their child's feelings is likely to be compromised if they themselves are subject to unstable moods, and their mentalising capacities deficient if they lack a secure sense of self which provides a vantage point from which to view their own needs and those of others, including their children. In addition parental intoxication and deliberate self-harm (DSH) are potentially traumatic for children. In the absence of a mentalising care-giver, such children will suffer not only from the trauma itself, but, given the absence of an affect-regulating parent, lack of someone with whom to process the feelings it engenders.

A number of studies have looked at the impact of BPD on developmental processes in sufferers' offspring. Feldman *et al.* (1995) confirmed clinical impressions that children aged 11–18 of BPD sufferers are at risk of psychopathology, showing more delinquency, aggression and depression than comparable offspring of non-BPD sufferers. Hobson and colleagues have studied the possible developmental antecedents of these clinical findings. Children of BPD mothers have high levels of Disorganised attachment at 18 months (Hobson *et al.* 2005). The origins of this are illuminated by studies which show that such mothers show more intrusiveness and insensitivity, are more likely to be withdrawn and fearful when their infants become distressed, and are limited in their capacity for reflexive functioning (i.e. mentalising) compared to children whose mothers are not so diagnosed (Crandell *et al.* 2003; Hobson *et al.* 2009). We see here the possible routes by which BPD may be transmitted from one generation to the next, and also the developmental difficulties that children of BPD mothers are likely to encounter.

Intervention studies

Interventions can be broadly classified under three headings. First, preventive measures aiming to reduce the likelihood of Disorganised attachment in the offspring of at-risk parents, whether due to low socio-economic status or physical or mental illness. Second, there are treatment programmes aimed at helping mothers once an 'at-risk' child is identified, especially with Disorganised attachment. Third, parents who are themselves ill, especially those with BPD, can be helped with the aim to improve not just their mental health but, indirectly, that of their children.

Integral to the attachment perspective is the hypothesis that infant security is causally linked to, rather than merely correlated with, parental sensitivity. If so, interventions to enhance parental sensitivity should increase security of attachment in their infants. In an early meta-analysis, Van IJzendoorn *et al.* (1999)

found that this was the case, but there were a number of paradoxical effects. First, short-term interventions appeared to be more effective than longer ones. Second, increasing parental sensitivity did not always impact on infant attachment security and, conversely, attachment security could be improved without changes in parents' sensitivity. Third, causal links, although demonstrable, were weak and did not account for the total variance.

Van IJzendoorn's group dub this the 'transmission gap'. Recent genetic findings mentioned above go some way to explain this – if only a proportion of target infants have 'plasticity genes' (see above), the overall impact of interventions will be thereby lessened (Bakermans-Kranenburg & Van IJzendoorn 2007). A subsequent review (Berlin *et al.* 2008) summarised a number of intervention programmes, varying from simple behavioural measures such as giving mothers a soft sling with which to carry their babies around, to more sophisticated and prolonged psychoanalytically informed programmes aiming to enhance mentalising. Their findings suggest that relatively brief, sensitivity-focused interventions in high-risk groups, where the base-line level of Disorganised attachment is greatest, show the most gains. However, the evidence for the benefits in terms of maternal sensitivity and child attachment security of long-term psychoanalytic child psychotherapy interventions is rather weak. The authors concede this may be due to the broad-spectrum impact of this approach, with general rather than specific benefits, and that there may be 'sleeper effects' which would reveal themselves with longer term follow-up.

Clinical implications

The studies summarised above are based mostly on attachment-informed interventions in the early years, and many are mother–infant, rather than parent-only programmes. In this section I shall comment from a research-informed clinical perspective on two types of problem: working with parents suffering from BPD, and working with parents of children suffering from chronic illnesses.

Both groups may benefit from a 'pedagogic' psycho-educational exposition of the attachment model. It can be a relief to hear that constant worry and inability not to think about an ill child is a normal biologically driven aspect of the attachment dynamic. One parent with an eating-disordered daughter confessed guiltily that while taking a deserved break away for a night in a health spa, she found that she had forgotten to think about her daughter for at least 10 minutes! Such guilty feelings are common in the bereaved; having an ill child could be seen as a species of bereavement, but one with no definite end-point. This is consistent with Bowlby's (1980) formulation of bereavement in terms of irreparable separation. Equally BPD parents can be helped with the thought that some of their feelings of fear and helplessness when confronted with a needy child are normal responses, not signs of intrinsic inadequacy or madness.

Another aspect is the attachment view that attachment behaviour and exploration are mutually incompatible (Holmes 2010). As a result, parents who are chronically aroused with worry about their children, may find it difficult to 'accept' – i.e. to think about and experiment with – the help that is being offered, since their thoughts and feelings are so dominated by the search for, and seeming impossibility of finding, a solution to their child's difficulties. In one case, after apparently helpful sessions in which strategies for living with a depressed teenaged son were discussed, his mother would repeatedly, as she made for the door, blurt out: 'Well, *will* he get better or not? I want and need an answer – why won't you give me one?'

Bakermans-Kranenburg *et al.* (2005) see preventive interventions as having one or more of three objectives: enhancing parental sensitivity, improving attachment security in the IP (identified patient) child, and using the therapeutic relationship as a model for secure parent–child interaction. As mentioned, 'sensitivity' remains a somewhat mysterious capacity.

Ainsworth's early formulations focused on the rapidity and ease with which mothers responded to and assuaged their infants' distress. More recent approaches emphasise 'affect regulation' and 'mentalising', and the idea that to the extent that these are available in the parent–child relationship in infancy and early childhood, they become gradually internalised by the growing child.

Affect regulation entails the ability of the parent to identify a child's emotional states and to mobilise a regulatory appropriate response. A crucial aspect of 'mentalising' is the parent's ability to see her child not as an extension of herself and her own needs, but as an autonomous sentient being with his or her own projects, desires and wishes. Mentalising is thus contra-narcissistic, and implies the ability to find an internal vantage point from which to view and reflect on one's own and others' thoughts, emotions and actions.

If we postulate a 'parallel process' (a concept borrowed from the supervisor-therapist/therapist-patient constellation, cf. Holmes 2012) between therapist–parent and parent–child relationships, then the therapist's 'sensitivity' to the presenting parent will be a mutative ingredient in helping the parent to be more sensitive to her child. Therapists need to tune into and identify verbally parents' feelings, to contain and hold them, to acknowledge and soothe where appropriate. A further aspect entails including the parent's partner, if there is one. An ill child often drives a wedge into a family, prising couples apart. The needs of the other siblings are often overlooked. Working with the parent of the IP will also mean focusing on the couple relationship, and helping the parent to recruit her partner (usually the father) as a Secure Base to whom she can turn with her worries and troubles, and who will also take over when she herself is miserable or exhausted.

The neuroimaging data on the 'disgust' reaction on the part of the parent when failing to elicit an expected positive response from their child, contrast with secure mothers who can accommodate and encompass their children's unhappiness. In insecure relationships the parent might say something like, 'Look, I do everything for that child, drive him/her to school, supply his meals, bail him out when he's got no money, cook wash and clean – and all I get is sulks and monosyllables. It's intolerable! He's got to get his act together'. This might be a typical avoidant child–parent pattern; the child gets a degree of protection, but with diminished parental 'sensitivity'. The price paid is the suppression or diverting of distress, rather than its resolution, with both parent and child's affect unassuaged. All this goes on non-consciously: avoidant children show physiological evidence of arousal in the SSP as manifest by elevated cortisol levels, and tachycardia (Dozier & Rogers Kobak 1992) although outwardly they appear equable.

Therapeutic work informed by this would concentrate: (a) on the therapist acknowledging and accepting parents' worry, misery, and 'disgust', (b) helping the parent similarly to 'name and contain' their children's difficult feelings. A typical interaction with, say, an eating-disordered teenager might be:

Child: I hate myself, I'm fat, fat, fat . . .
Parent: You're NOT fat – you're thin! If you just put on some weight you'll stop feeling so bad about yourself".

An attachment-guided alternative response (which could be tried out in role-play) might be:

Parent: It sounds like you're feeling really terrible and unhappy today . . . shall we have a look at those diet websites together and see if we can work something out? . . .

An interesting finding that emerged from the Bakermans-Kranenberg *et al.* (2005) meta-analysis was that video-feedback was particularly effective in enhancing both maternal sensitivity and infant security. Observing oneself on video is inherently mentalising, if the latter is viewed as the 'ability to see oneself from the outside and others from the inside' (Holmes 2012). Since arousal is inimical to mentalising, the stressed parents of ill children are often too agitated to be able to reflect on the impact they are having on the child, let alone the past traumas the child's illness may be activating from their own childhood.

Quietly observing oneself on video, however painful it might be, provides such an opportunity for observation and learning. In one-to-one therapy, 'role-play' with a therapist can work in similar ways. The therapist might move from conventional dialogue into role-plays in which the therapist alternates between enacting the parent's role, with the mother 'being' the child, and vice versa. The same scenario can be repeatedly played this way, with participants alternating: playing it 'as it was', and then with a different hoped-for outcome. It is important, however, to observe the dictum that when working with parents, a therapist should never make them feel that he or she makes a better job of being a parent than they do.[1]

A final point comes not from attachment research but from a systemic-psychoanalytic perspective. It concerns the 'location' of the presenting problem. A systemic point of view sees the family as a system, with individual members playing parts in a drama where the target dysfunction is the family itself, rather than the individuals who make it up (cf. Lock *et al.* 2010).

This is consistent with the psychoanalytic notion of 'projective identification', in which feelings, conflicts and desires may be transferred unconsciously from one member of an intimate system to another, typically in the Kleinian model from baby to mother, but equally, and especially when problematic, vice versa. Seen this way, 'badness', and especially negative affect, is no longer located in any one individual, but in the system as a whole. Thus when a patient refers to the needs of her children – for instance is worried about 'child care' for her baby – it is a useful heuristic to think that it is the patient's 'inner child' that needs therapeutic attention. Working with parents of ill children, part of the therapeutic task is to help the parent grasp and identify her own un-met childhood needs, manifest in her child as she perceives him.

Conclusion

According to maestro (a degree of 'cult of personality' is admissible!) Daniel Barenboim (Barenboim & Said 2004) 'music' arises at the intersection of two axes: vertical, instantaneous and harmonic; horizontal, temporal and melodic/rhythmic. Comparably, families have their own music. At any given moment there are harmonies and discords whose overtones reverberate throughout the system. At the same time family members are bound together in an ongoing story or 'script' (Byng-Hall 1999) which is transmitted and modified from generation to generation. Both melody and harmony have attachment overtones.

Early psychoanalytic theorising tended to see the developmental process in terms of two generations – the IP, and his or her parents. Fraiberg's (1980) 'ghosts in the nursery' acknowledged that at any clinical situation a minimum of three generations are involved – the patient, the patient's parents, the parents' parents, and if the patient is a parent, their children. Lacan (Leupnitz 2009) similarly shows how at the moment of birth, a child has a pre-assigned 'place' in the family and parental system/psyche, and that the child, and his or her difficulties, must be seen as a link in a family chain stretching back into the past and forwards into the future.

Therapists tend to be highly attuned to these self-perpetuating patterns of pathology, but sometimes miss an opposing trend – the inherent self-righting capacity of both individuals and families. A parental generation plagued by abuse might, by the third generation, be once more on a more secure track. The key to this self-rightingness is the capacity of parents to mentalise their own difficulties, and thus to hold them in check as they work for the best for the next generation. It is the task of the science and art of psychotherapy, and especially the mentalising approach based in the attachment paradigm, to foster this self-righting process, and to study those conditions that make it more, or less, likely to be achieved.

Note

1 The author often gets round this by comparing watching an 'action replay' of a missed open goal in football on the television – easy to get it right from the comfort of one's armchair; equally easy to miss in the real-life heat of the moment.

References

Ainsworth, M. (1973) The development of mother–infant attachment. In *Review of Child Development Research Vol. 3* (Eds B. Caldwell & H. Ricciuti), pp. 1–49. Chicago: University of Chicago Press.

Bakermans-Kranenburg, M. & Van IJzendoorn, M. (2007) Genetic vulnerability of differential susceptibility in child development: the case of attachment. *Journal of Child Psychology and Psychiatry* 48: 1160–1173.

Bakermans-Kranenburg, M., Van IJzendoorn, M. & Juffer, F. (2005) Disorganised attachment, infant attachment and preventive interventions: a review and meta-analysis. *Infant Mental Health Journal* 26: 191–216.

Barenboim, D. & Said, E. (2004) *Parallels and Paradoxes: Explorations in Music.* London: Bloomsbury.

Belsky, J., Spritz, B. & Crnic, K. (1996) Infant attachment security and affective-cognitive information processing at aged 3. *Psychological Science*, 7: 111–114.

Berlin, L., Zeahnah, C. & Lieberman, A. (2008) Prevention and intervention programs for supporting early attachment security. In *Handbook of Attachment* (Eds J. Cassidy & P. R. Shaver) 2nd edition, pp. 745–761. New York: Guilford.

Bowlby, J. (1971) *Attachment.* London: Penguin.

Bowlby, J. (1980) *Loss and Bereavement.* London: Penguin.

Byng-Hall, J. (1999) Family couple therapy: towards greater security. In *Handbook of Attachment* (Eds J. Cassidy & P. R. Shaver) 1st edition, pp. 625–645. New York: Guilford.

Crandell, L. E., Patrick, M. P. H. & Hobson, R. P. (2003) 'Still-face' interactions between mothers with Borderline Personality Disorder and their 2-month-old infants. *British Journal of Psychiatry* 183: 239–247.

Dozier, M. & Rogers Kobak, R. (1992) Psychophysiology in Attachment Interviews: converging evidence for deactivating strategies. *Child Development* 63: 1473–1480.

Farnfield, S. & Holmes, P. (eds) (2014) *The Routledge Handbook of Attachment: Assessment.* London and New York: Routledge.

Feldman, R. B., Zelkowitz, P., Weiss, M., Vogel, J., Heyman, M. & Paris, J. (1995) A comparison of the families of mothers with borderline and nonborderline personality disorders. *Comprehensive Psychiatry* 36(2): 157–163.

Fonagy, P. & Luyten, P. (2009) A developmental mentalisation-based approach to the understanding and treatment of Borderline Personality Disorder. *Development and Psychopathology* 21: 1355–1381.

Fonagy, P., Steele, H. & Steele, M. (1991) Maternal representations of attachment during pregnancy predict the organization of infant–mother attachment at one year of age. *Child Development* 62: 891–905.

Fonagy, P., Steele, M., Steele, H., Higgitt, A. & Target, M. (2004) The theory and practice of resilience. *Journal of Child Psychology and Psychiatry* 35: 231–257.

Fraiberg, S. (1980) *Clinical Studies in Infant Mental Health.* New York: Basic Books.

Hobson, R. P., Patrick, M., Crandell, L., Garcia-Perez, R. & Lee, A. (2005) Personal relatedness and attachment in infants of mothers with Borderline Personality Disorder. *Development and Psychopathology* 17: 329–347.

Hobson, P., Patrick, M., Honson, J. *et al.* (2009) How mothers with Borderline Personality Disorder relate to their year-old infants. *British Journal of Psychiatry* 195: 325–330.

Holmes, J. (2010) *Exploring in Security.* London: Routledge.

Holmes, J. (2011) Superego: an attachment perspective. *International Journal of Psychoanalysis* 92: 1221–1240.

Holmes, J. (2012) *Storr's The Art of Psychotherapy* (3rd Edition). London: Hodder.

Holmes, J. (2013) *John Bowlby and Attachment Theory* (2nd Edition). London: Routledge.

Holmes, P. & Farnfield, S. (eds) (2014) *The Routledge Handbook of Attachment: Theory*. London and New York: Routledge.

Lear, J. (2003) *Therapeutic Action: An Earnest Plea for Irony*. London: Karnac.

Leupnitz, A. (2009) Thinking in the space between Winnicott and Lacan. *International Journal of Psychoanalysis* 90: 957–981.

Lock, M., Le Grange, D., Agras, S., Move, A., Bryson, S. & Booil, J. (2010) Randomized clinical trial comparing family-based treatment with adolescent-focused individual therapy for adolescents with anorexia nervosa. *Archives of General Psychiatry* 67: 1025–1032.

Lyons-Ruth, K., Bronfman, E. & Parsons, E. (1999) Maternal frightened, frightening, or atypical behaviour and disorganised infant behaviour patterns. *Monographs of the Society for Research in Child Development* 64: 67–209.

Main, M. & Hesse, E. (1990) Parents' unresolved traumatic experiences are related to infant disorganised attachment status: is frightened and/or frightening parental behaviour the linking mechanism? In *Attachment in the Preschool Years* (Eds M. Greenberg, D. Cicchetti & M. Cummings), pp. 161–182. Chicago: University of Chicago Press.

Mikulincer, M., Shaver, P. & Pereg, D. (2003) Attachment theory and affect regulation: the dynamics, development and cognitive consequences of attachment-related strategies. *Motivation and Emotion* 27: 77–102.

Murray, L., Arteche, A., Fearon, P., Haligan, S., Goodyear, I. & Cooper, P. (2011) Maternal postnatal depression and the development of depression in their offspring up to 16 years of age. *Journal of the American Academy of Child and Adolescent Psychiatry* 50: 460–470.

O'Connor, E., Bureau, J.-F., McCartney, K. & Lyons-Ruth, K. (2011) Risks and outcomes associated with disorganised/controlling patterns of attachment at age three years in the National Institute of Child Health and Human Development study of early child care and youth development. *Infant Mental Health Journal* 32: 450–472.

Steele, H. & Siever, L. (2010) An attachment perspective on Borderline Personality Disorder: advances in gene-environment considerations. *Current Psychiatry Reports* 12: 61–67.

Strathearn, L., Fonagy, P., Amico, J. & Montague, P. (2009) Adult Attachment predicts maternal brain and oxytocin response to infant cues. *Neuropsychopharmacology* 34: 2655–2666.

Van IJzendoorn, M., Schuengel, C. & Bakermans-Kranenburg, M. (1999) Disorganised attachment in early childhood: meta-analysis of precursors, concomitants, and sequelae. *Development and Psychopathology* 11: 225–249.

Waters, E. (2008) Live long and prosper: attachment and evolution. Available online at http://www.psychology.sunysb.edu/attachment/gallery/live_long/live_long.html

Chapter 4

The marriage of attachment theory and systemic family therapy practice

An invitation to join the wedding party

Chip Chimera

Introduction

Family therapists work with the family group, subsystems within it and individual members of the family. Families come to therapy for many reasons, however it is this writer's clinical experience, spanning over 20 years, that at the heart of most family problems lie attachment dilemmas. Working with the family system, whether the whole or parts, allows attachment issues to be explored in a way that honours each person's attachment experience and attachment truth. Opportunities for change can be discovered and new, more satisfying ways of relating can be tried. Systemic practice gives specific attention to the influence of relationships on other relationships within the family and the wider network. In what follows two case examples will illustrate the use of attachment as a focus in family therapy together with the theoretical connections.

For many years there has been a passionate affair between some quarters of systemic family therapy and attachment theory. John Byng-Hall (1995) and more latterly Arlene Vetere and Rudi Dallos (Dallos 2006; Dallos and Vetere 2009) in particular have done much to join the two theories into a coherent practice.

This chapter examines how attachment theory can be used within the many models and approaches contained within systemic family therapy that are in current practice in Britain and the wider world. It proposes that it is not necessary to have a separate and distinct form of 'attachment family therapy' but that the ideas can be used across the board in systemic practice from whatever orientation a systemic therapist adopts.

It aims to show that by orienting themselves to attachment issues, those working with families who present with a variety of clinical problems can use the whole array of systemic approaches effectively. At the same time those using primarily an attachment-based approach can benefit from the integration of systemic theories and techniques.

Like all good marriages there are times when compromise is essential.

How attachment enhances a systemic approach

Attachment theory invites us to look at how meaning and affect are arranged in the family. It gives a structure within which the expression of feelings and the ways relationships are enacted make sense. Many family therapists will have a 'hidden history' with attachment, having come across it in other trainings and finding an acquaintance with the ideas more or less useful.

Attachment researchers from Bowlby onwards have made careful and repeated observations. Theory and assessment is deduced from observations, not from report. This is very useful for practitioners who work with families together in parts and wholes.

Observation rather than report has also been at the heart of family therapy models throughout the development of family therapy practice (Minuchin and Fishman 1981; Cecchin 1987; Andersen 1987). Changes to theory and practice have been introduced based on these observations and the therapists' own interaction with families.

The use of recording equipment, a key feature of family therapy clinical training, makes it possible to analyse interactions in retrospect. Therapists in training work as part of a team with a number of people and a live supervisor behind a one-way mirror. This teamwork makes it possible to have the benefit of multiple lenses of observation. What each team member brings to the observation enables an understanding of how their personal attachment styles and strategies affect what they see. Hence the social constructionist maxim that what you see depends on how you look at it (Burr 1995) has particular resonance for therapists in developing therapeutic self-reflexivity. This refers to the therapist's knowledge of their own history and emotional responses which is put into action in the therapy room and brought to supervision. An appreciation of personal attachment experiences, strategies and style is essential for developing a therapeutic approach of one's own. This understanding of our own inner working models is crucial in helping to create a secure base for the family in therapy. The core concepts of mutual influence and relational reflexivity (Burnham 2005) allow us to observe the family relationships and simultaneously experience how our own attachment system is being activated.

While close observation is possible for family therapists the uniqueness of each family and the different issues brought for therapy make the laboratory conditions set up by Ainsworth (Ainsworth and Bell 1970) in her meticulous infant research projects impossible, both practically and ethically. Unlike Ainsworth and her colleagues, systemic therapists consider themselves as part of the system that is under observation. We consciously work intensively with the family dynamics in the room. Relationships, including attachment strategies, are played out before us.

Coming to therapy is in itself a stress-inducing activity. Therefore, the attachment system is activated by the act of coming into the therapy room in most cases. Trying to understand the situation and not jump to 'premature certainty' (Mason 1993) helps us to slow down, observe carefully and allow relationships to unfold.

Attachment as a systems sensitive model of individual development

Systemic theory does not provide a model of individual development per se. Becoming a Systemic Psychotherapist, like other psychotherapy trainings, involves undertaking an advanced qualification, achieved by most practitioners after they have qualified in a previous related profession, such as psychiatry, psychology, social work or teaching. It is generally expected that knowledge of child development is gained in these previous professional trainings, and therefore no overarching system of human development is taught on most family therapy qualifying courses.

However, family therapists do have ideas about *family* development and life cycle (Carter and McGoldrick 1989). These are well documented and have been broadened and revised over the years to take into account the wide diversity of family forms. With the influence of social constructionist ideas the notion of a normative model of family life is considered unhelpful. The criteria for adequate family functioning includes the notion that children are able to grow and develop in a way that meets their needs and fulfils their potential, giving consideration to the context in which the family is situated. It is recognised that a wide variety of family forms may have specific challenges but nevertheless fit the bill of raising children to maturity in order to reproduce successfully.

'Staying safe and reproducing constitute the basic biological imperatives of any species' (Crittenden 2008: 11). Anthropological studies have identified some 1,200 different past and present cultures (Van IJzendoorn and Sagi 1995: 731). In the cultures that have been studied attachment has been shown to be normative, i.e. existing in all cultures, though the ways in which attachment needs are met may vary.

Attachment offers a model of development which transcends culture and family form in that it can be understood by exploring how safety and comfort are achieved (or not). Unlike previous models of psychological development, which posit that persons become 'stuck' at certain points, attachment reflects a trajectory of continuous development with opportunities along the way for readjustment, realignment or taking a different path and a new trajectory. The Dynamic-Maturational Model of Attachment (DMM) (Crittenden 2008) in particular emphasises this. Bowlby writes:

Attachment theory emphasises:

(a) the primary status and biological function of intimate emotional bonds between individuals, the making and maintaining of which are postulated to be controlled by a cybernetic system situated within the central nervous system, utilizing working models of self and attachment figure in relationship with each other

(b) the powerful influence on a child's development of the ways he is treated by his parents, especially his mother-figure, and

(c) that present knowledge of infant and child development requires that a theory of developmental pathways should replace theories that invoke specific phases of development in which it is held a person may become fixated and/or to which he may regress.

(Bowlby 1988: 135–6)

Thus the model of individual development inherent in attachment theory is fundamentally in tune with systemic principles: what the child/person brings from their history and experience interacts with their present context to create their reality.

At one time the popular understanding of attachment theory was that once attachment was 'set' at about a year or 18 months of age, it formed a deterministic path on which the person would relate to the world and important relationships within it for the rest of their life. Bowlby never said this was the case. Quite the contrary, he stressed that patterns of attachment persist where interactions between the child and the attachment figures persist. Where nothing changes, patterns remain the same. Where the interaction changes for the better, there are opportunities for repair and a different developmental pathway may be taken. Longitudinal studies have shown that patterns of attachment persist, *unless something happens to change them.* '[E]stablished patterns of adaptation may be transformed by new experiences while, at the same time, new experiences are framed by, interpreted within, and even in part created by prior history of adaptation. Bowlby's was a dynamic view of development' (Sroufe 2005: 350). They can change for better or worse, depending on the person's life experiences and interaction with their context. Therapy is one important interaction that can influence attachment strategies.

I remember well a parent and child who attended a day assessment and treatment unit I worked in some years ago.

Janet, the mother, had been adopted from a Barnardo's institution in her late infancy. She felt 'lucky to be chosen' and grateful to her adoptive parents, who had died some years earlier. This story of gratitude is one that was often given to children who were rescued from institutions by well-meaning adopters who received little ongoing support. She never expressed curiosity about her family of origin. When she married in her teens she did reasonably well with her first two children who were boys. There was some involvement with social services due to delinquency when they became adolescent. However, it was minor and there was never a threat to remove the boys. Her husband was a good provider but a somewhat distant father, as was a common cultural expectation of the time.

Janet's last child, who arrived a few years behind the boys, was a little girl and the relationship was always difficult. Maggie was a fussy baby, never very rewarding. She was clingy as a toddler and showed aggression to her mother and siblings. School age did not bring change: she was aggressive to other children and demanded a great deal of teacher time. She was excluded from school as a six year old. There were questions of neglect by her mother who was by now openly rejecting. I remember their first day at the centre. Meeting them on the doorstep I was introduced to Maggie, then seven, as 'this is the little bitch.'

They attended for six months, somewhat longer than usual. The day involved school in the morning for the children while the parents attended groups and individual therapy. In the afternoon there were family activities and family therapy. During this time Janet was chal- lenged to re-examine her beliefs about her daughter and the narrative of her own childhood. In deconstructing her experience a different story emerged of her adoptive parents treating her harshly and being punitive to her at the least provocation. She was frequently unfavour- ably compared to males in the family and was acceptable only when she showed 'gratitude'. Being able to examine some of these experiences and begin to come to terms with them in the safe and containing envi- ronment of the centre where she was valued and encouraged, enabled her to change her position in relation to Maggie. She would often com- ment on how tiring the day was, and that she could not understand it because she 'hadn't done much'. She could not recognise the very difficult psychological restructuring she was undertaking as work.

The result however was dramatic. Maggie returned to school and at six month follow up was doing fine, catching up on lost learning time and getting along reasonably well with her peers. There were some blips but the parents responded well and appropriately to these. Jan- et's parting words were 'thank you for giving me my daughter back', even then not appreciating that it was she herself who had done the work to repair the relationship.

No formal assessments of attachment were undertaken, however the following hypothesis can be made.

Janet was using avoidant (A) strategies. These had been helpful to her in her childhood where she was unable to express her negative feelings for fear of punishment, and had to concentrate on pleasing the attachment figures in order to avoid rejection. She focused on being a good girl. Her pre-adoption circumstances are not known though it can be assumed that there were times when she felt very unsafe, and very likely experienced abandonment.

As a young adult she chose a partner who was also avoidant of intimacy, i.e. who also adopted A strategies. The expression of strong negative feelings and emotions was not in his repertoire and he used withdrawal rather than confrontation to manage any difficulties in the relationship. This strategy seemed to work for the couple. Janet adopted a role as mother in which expectations of the children's behaviour took priority over comfort and affection, a replicative script (Byng-Hall 1995), though she was by no means an unemotional mother. This worked adequately with her boys (though they had some difficulty in adolescence) but giving birth to a daughter seemed to trigger her own unmet needs and as she did not know how to be with a girl infant, she used her avoidant strategies to keep the unwanted emotions at bay. The child's calls for attention were experienced by her mother as excessive and unreasonable. The father was not equipped to help her understand this, leaving responsibility for parenting to the mother, a traditional gender role. This led to further feelings of inadequacy and failure on the part of the mother who then increased her efforts to get Maggie to conform to her expectations of behaviour.

For her part the child, experiencing a distant and misattuned parent, had to rely on her own emotional state to try to get needs for safety and security met. Her alternating coy and controlling behaviours (C strategies) were not understood by her mother as a need but seen through her mother's experience as naughty and in need of punishment; hence the dance of misattuned attachment began and escalated. The more her mother applied strict rules and expectations accompanied by punishment, the more Janet felt misunderstood, abandoned and rejected. She began to believe the story of herself as a bad child. Her behaviour deteriorated as she had no other strategies, and problems were soon to be located within her.

Here systemic ideas of symmetrical escalation, applying more of a failed attempted solution (Watzlawick et al. 1974), repetitive scripts (Byng-Hall 1995), and Narrative therapy (White 1988) were integrated with attachment ideas to help address the underlying relationship problems which were understood as being both between and within the mother and child.

Crittenden (2008) has shown how attachment strategies, i.e. the person's tool-kit for keeping safe, develop across the life cycle. She augments Bowlby's and Ainsworth's original ideas of developmental pathways and shows how these are related to both the child's maturational processes and the contexts in which they find themselves. She identifies five stages of maturation: infancy, pre-school, school age, adolescence and adulthood. Within each stage specific maturational processes are available to the child to help maintain safety and connection to a protective figure. In the above vignette the child's maturational stage made higher and more behaviourally challenging ambivalent (C) strategies available to her which could not be ignored. Fortunately they were able to be dealt with therapeutically: the escalation was stopped so that reattunement of the mother and child could be attempted.

Using attachment as a systemic lens

Jeremy Holmes (Holmes 2001: 6) identifies six domains of attachment theory. Each of these can be utilised from a systemic perspective. The six domains are:

- Secure base,
- Exploration and enjoyment,
- Protest and anger: rupture and repair, differs across the spectrum,
- Loss,
- Inner working models, and
- Reflexive functioning.

A systemic perspective allows these to be explored with families in a safe and non-blaming way. Any and all models of systemic family therapy can be utilised to explore these areas and most overlap to greater or lesser extent.

Using a structural approach (Minuchin 1974; Minuchin and Fishman 1981) the attachment domains can be explored in the way decisions are made, boundaries are organised and the priority given to child care needs. Together with how roles are allocated and power is negotiated, both overtly and covertly, a picture can be built of how the family is organised. Do they pull together in the face of danger or become blaming and chaotic? Of particular interest are role reversals and care and control battles, both of which can be understood more fully using an attachment approach. These issues are often enacted in the therapy room, particularly with younger children. Emphasising and reinforcing rules and boundaries which increase safety and hence the ability to explore, express feelings, manage loss and have positive and optimistic expectations of relationships are all attachment interventions undertaken from a structural perspective.

Strategic approaches focus on how the family is organised around the problem and how the problem organises the family. For instance where attachment strategies in a child of either helplessness or control (ambivalent type C strategies:

Crittenden 2008) are being used, one would look at how other parts of the system respond. What does the main attachment figure do in response, how does that response ripple through the rest of the system?

For example, where parents have separated and a child is refusing to see one parent, one might look at how the child's strategies are functioning to keep the main care-taker close and at the same time maintain a high level of anxiety in the system. The intervention would be to help the family understand the child's anxieties in a different way and experiment with different approaches to help the child overcome them. Strategic approaches consider whether the problem may be a failed solution to a worse problem. The use of specific attachment assessments such as the Adult Attachment Interview (Crittenden and Landini 2011) or the School Age Assessment of Attachment (Crittenden 2008) give insight into the person's internal world and the way they employ attachment strategies.

In both structural and strategic approaches the concept of triangulation (Bowen 1978; Fivaz-Despeursinge and Corboz-Warnery 1999) is useful in thinking about how attachment dilemmas are enacted in the family system. Triangulation is an ordinary process that occurs in all families. Most parents will have had the experience of a child asking for something (ice cream, new trainers, going out with a friend, etc.) being told 'no' and then going to another source of authority in the hope of a different answer. Where there is intense conflict between parents, triangulation of a child into the conflict is emotionally damaging. In damaging triangulation the child cannot have a free and unfettered relationship with either parent without having to consider the impact on their relationship with the other parent. In divorced and separated families this can become highly problematic and at its most extreme can result in the child cutting off contact with one parent in order to meet the (covert) needs of the other parent (Kelly and Johnson 2001).

These approaches focus on family rules and how the system organises around a problem. In particular it is thought that the problem may consciously or unconsciously fulfil a function in the system. The classic example of this is a child whose refusal to attend school arises from fear for the parent at home which cannot be directly expressed.

The strategies a parent developed in their own childhood will play a key role in how the next generation develops strategies. It is important to gain an understanding of how the two parents' family of origin experiences have come together in their family of procreation: another example of the impact of relationships on relationships. Often where parents are over-punitive, the problem may be defined by professionals as over-chastisement, a form of physical abuse. Using an attachment lens to focus on issues of safety, a more severe problem from which the over-chastising parent is trying to save the children may be revealed; for example, in the vignette cited below the father's over-chastisement was largely a measure of his deeper concern about his children's safety.

In applying attachment theory to family belief systems as in the Milan and post-Milan approaches, the family's beliefs around safety and security and the roles different family members are expected to play in relation to these are explored. Beliefs impel actions and how the family members situate themselves in relation to their beliefs will be an organising factor.

In the case of Janet and Maggie described above, the meaning of Maggie's aggression to her mother had to be changed from her being a mad, crazy and unlovable child who needed to be punished, to her being a lonely and frightened child who did not know how to connect with people and needed her mother's help. Such changes in orientation can be made in a context of therapy which is itself nested in a system of protection in which violence or punishment of any kind is not condoned.

These approaches focus on making beliefs more explicit. Such beliefs are often outside of consciousness: 'It's just the way we are.' When beliefs can be deconstructed and examined they can also be considered, modified and changed. Beliefs emanating from the attachment system might centre on how children should be raised, how danger should be faced, what is appropriate comfort to give and at what age this becomes inappropriate.

Experiential approaches will borrow from all of the above and try to elicit how thinking, feeling and doing are tied up together. Experiential approaches are based in action and will be concretely focused on identifying and strengthening family resources.

Similarly, using a Narrative orientation, the emergence and development of family stories of staying safe, overcoming danger, eliciting and receiving comfort and expectations of relationships can be explored. Developing new attachment stories that are coherent and integrate both cognition and affect is the therapeutic task. Making sense of experience in a way that has logic and contains feelings and facts without omissions or distortions will help the family and the individuals within it to integrate difficult experiences. They can then begin to move on from them in a way that allows experience to be assimilated into the family story, therefore reducing the likelihood of repetition. Transgenerational stories, family scripts (Byng-Hall 1995), can be edited and re-edited to fit with changing contexts and times.

Conversations about how safety is negotiated in the family will elicit stories which may be rich and well developed or thin and in need of expansion. The idea is that there are healthy stories in families that are undeveloped but exist in embryonic form (White and Epston 1990). Often these are stories of strength and overcoming adversity. Inviting a story about how the family stays safe and has done so in the past may elicit untold stories of strength and resilience and indicate paths for further development.

Obviously the foregoing is a very brief sketch and there is considerable overlap between systemic approaches.

The role of the therapist

Clearly, in each of the attachment domains cited above there is a key role in how the therapist orients him or herself in relationship to the family. The therapist's prime responsibility is to create a secure base for therapy. This promotes reflexive functioning – the ability to speak coherently about oneself and one's difficulties. There is a strong link between this and secure attachment and it is of crucial importance in family psychotherapy.

Emotion and action are central ideas in attachment-based family therapy. The therapist who can initiate constructive action in the therapy room, between all members of the family who are present, will increase the likelihood that positive attachments will be promoted.

The N family

The following case goes some way to illustrate the integration of systemic approaches using an attachment focus.

I was asked by the Court to undertake an independent assessment for rehabilitation of a family with three children who had been removed following the physical abuse of the two youngest boys.

The family consisted of the mother, Angela, the Father, Julius, an older daughter, Laura, 13, and two boys, Jeremy, aged 8, and James, aged 7. The family was Christian and from West Africa. Angela was born in England and returned to West Africa when she was 2. As a young adult she met Julius. They married and came to England where she completed her training as a nurse and the children were born.

Julius, while having no formal qualification was an intelligent and ambitious man who was motivated to provide for his family. He turned his hand to a number of jobs including working as a care assistant in residential care, a car mechanic and undertaking electrical repairs. Angela worked as a theatre sister on the night shift at a large London teaching hospital.

Both parents worked hard and the family were eventually able to move from their two-bedroom rented flat and start buying a three-bedroom house with a garden in East London.

One Saturday, a few weeks after the move, Julius returned home from work and found that the boys had taken the key to the back garden, which they were forbidden to enter and had gone outside. Worse, they had brought the garden hose into the house, turned it on and soaked a good deal of the carpet and furniture before they had been able to turn it off. Angela was in the house at the time; however, she was unaware of what the boys had done until it was too late to stop it.

The boys were in trouble and they knew it. Julius was angry that they had disobeyed him, had put themselves at risk and had damaged the new home. Some electric flex was close by from a repair job he had finished. He told the boys to hold out their hands and hit them each three times on the back of their hands. That was their punishment and they accepted it.

On Monday they went to school. There were very few black children in their area of London. Teachers noticed the marks and, there having been some previous concerns, an urgent child protection investigation was started. A medical examination revealed some further older marks on Jeremy's back which he could not explain. When asked, Jeremy confirmed that he was sometimes frightened of his father.

All three children were then placed in emergency foster care: the boys together and Laura separately. The parents were informed of this after school by the local authority social workers and the police who undertook the investigation.

My involvement started eight months later following contested care proceedings in which the parents sought the return of the children and the local authority sought care orders.

The psychiatrist who undertook the original assessment recommended family therapy with a view to rehabilitation. There were no identified mental health problems in either parent.

I started by seeing the different family members separately. Each assessment is different and whether it is started with a whole-family meeting or meeting with sub-groups or individuals is dependent on clinical judgement. There is no hard and fast rule. My decision to see members separately at first was based on my knowledge of the situation and my need to understand the individuals' perspectives and positions.

Each parent was interviewed regarding their histories of being parented, following the format of the Adult Attachment Interview (Crittenden and Landini 2011).

Although the resulting interview transcripts were not formally rated the interview in itself is a wonderful clinical tool for understanding and orienting to attachment issues. In my experience, this interview often helps parents to begin a reflective process on how their early experiences have impacted on the kind of parents they have become. However, taking a good clinical history of the person's experience of being parented with an attachment orientation, asking about comfort, care and especially about the person's perception of and response to danger, may also reveal significant attachment information on which to base attachment hypotheses.

The father's experiences were of growing up in a high status Christian family. He had a difficult relationship with his mother who was the power in the family. He found her mean spirited and they were not close. He was critical of the way she treated others. He was close to his father by whom he felt understood, loved and protected. At the same time he described his father as strict and somewhat rigid in applying rules. However, he remembered several incidents of warmth and gentleness from his father and genuine caring. He became tearful on several occasions in recalling these. He seemed to use the Adult Attachment Interview (AAI) to begin a reflective process on how his relationship with his father influenced him as a father.

Both boys were then interviewed in their foster home. They were unhappy in foster care and wanted to go home. They did, however, repeat that they were sometimes afraid of their father. Jeremy in particular said that his father could turn and be nice one minute, then angry.

Laura was seen separately and showed no ambivalence at all. While she liked the foster carers she was with she wanted to be home with her brothers and parents. She was not frightened of her father and was held in high esteem in the family. She missed the activities she did with her family, in particular singing in the church choir of which her father was the leader.

The first whole-family meeting was spent discussing issues of safety and danger. Stories were elicited about the many challenges the family faced by being culturally different in a predominantly white, working-class area of London. Family rules and norms for managing danger were discussed. The parental decision-making subsystem and how the family organised around problems and difficulties were also explored.

Towards the end of the first family session the following discussion took place.

I asked why the children were not allowed into the garden, a fairly obvious question which had not been addressed in the voluminous Court papers. Julius spoke about the context of living in their new neighbourhood in which a number of frightening things had happened. He recounted several stories of danger. Around the time they moved in, a child who lived down the street was abducted by two men with guns who fired a number of shots into the house where the boy was living. Thankfully no one was killed. At this point Laura started coughing and went out to get some water. Clearly anxiety was being awakened for all the children. James had been moving closer to their father during the conversation, and seemed to need physical contact. When Laura returned their father continued.

Chip: (*picking up where we left off*) So the police were putting a letter through everybody's letter box.

Julius: It said everybody should be very careful about their children. (pause) And the third one that scared me most, it happened to me; thank God it was me and not any of them (meaning the children). They were chasing somebody, the police were chasing somebody, I don't know what the person has done. And from the other side of the house this guy has been jumping the fence to each house and he jumped the fence and now hides at my garden. (*pause*) I don't know what happened; I was coming home from my day work.

(James climbed into his father's lap and was trying to interrupt him to join in the conversation. The father patted him on the leg and encouraged the physical connection while continuing the conversation. I noted the gentleness with which the father touched him and the reassuring way he put an arm around him, allowing James to seek comfort. Jeremy continued drawing on a low table in the centre of the room.)

Let me finish *(to James who clearly wanted to say something)*. As I open the door, the police, they ask me, they say 'Is there anyone in the house?' (*using an animated and challenging tone of voice*). I say 'No, there is nobody in my house.' I close the door again and as soon as I open the back door, I see this giant man and immediately I saw him, I don't know what to do. I was shivering because he has a big stick and I was shivering, seriously. By the time I got round to calling the police he jumped back round again to the other house (this was said in an animated and excited tone of voice).

Chip: Were the children there at the time?

Julius: Yes.

Angela: They were still at home then.

Julius: But they were not in the garden.

Chip: Thank goodness.

Angela: Inside.

Chip: (*Addressing the children*) Did you know what happened then?
               (This was followed with general noise, all the children talking at once, saying they did know about it.)

Julius: I explained to them that that's why I'm kind of strict with them. I say 'Listen.' I say to them 'Don't go to the garden without the supervision of any adults.'

Jeremy: That's why we can't go in the garden.

Comment

It was clear that although Jeremy had been more contained than James during the conversation, he had been listening intently. His reiteration of the family rule 'we can't go into the garden' was an indication of a Type 'A' orientation to attachment. That and James' ability to wait until his father had finished talking before talking more made me think of James as a child who wanted to be a good boy and follow the rules. Laura's response had been to go out of the room to lower her arousal level by getting a drink of water.

I noted that the father's language was animated, emotive and imaged – 'a big man' with the emphasis on 'big' and 'I was seriously shivering' for instance. He also spoke at times in the present tense, as if this was happening now and not in the past. This language led me to hypothesise that Julius' orientation to attachment was one in which he was more reliant on his gut feelings and instinct, than on pure logic. This was consistent with the emotional expression of his AAI narrative.

I then turned back to James who was still on his father's lap.

Chip:	What did you want to say to your Daddy, James?
James:	Daddy, you know that cat that keeps going over our fence from Nancy's? *(their neighbour).*
Julius:	Yeah, and *(picking up James' story and talking directly to me)* there's a cat that they are kind of . . . when you see them they look like a wild cat; you chase them and they will chase you.
	(I noted that the father was able to join with James in his concern about the cat, which was of a much lower order of danger than he had been describing. This seemed to join the family together. However James then tried to leave the room, whether this was because his arousal level was too high I never fully understood. The father brought him back to his lap and James accepted this without resistance.)
Chip:	We need to think about ending and finishing off the session now. What I'm hearing is that some very scary things have happened outside the home. *(General agreement to this from all family members.)* And that you were very concerned about the children's safety.
Jeremy:	Was there anything scary happening *inside* the house? *(This comment from Jeremy who had remained quietly drawing throughout the session in the middle of the room, came as a surprise to both parents and to me.)*
Both parents:	Sorry?
Jeremy:	*(repeating)* Was there anything scary happening inside the house?
Angela:	Let me ask you, has there been anything scary happening inside the house? *(Angela had been quiet in this part of the session until this moment. She leaned forward slightly in asking this question and her voice was challenging.)*

Jeremy:	No.
	(Shaking his head 'no', Jeremy seemed to realise the potential of his question in showing his parents in a bad light. His retraction was unconvincing.)
Julius repeats:	Has there been anything scary inside the house?
Jeremy:	No, has anything *happened* that is scary inside the house?

Comment

Jeremy, aged 8, seemed to find himself in a hole and kept digging. The atmosphere immediately changed from one of cooperation and the family joining together against outside threats, to one of being unbalanced and having to face the possibility of danger existing within the family. We were two minutes away from the end of the session and there was no possibility of exploring Jeremy's comment thoroughly. Several things happened simultaneously in my mind. I felt I had gone some way to engaging these parents in a process of reflection on their parenting and on the children's needs, particularly the father. I could see many strengths in the father's parenting that could be built upon and was eager to understand how events had developed. Therapy needed to be established as a safe base for all family members and myself as a temporary secure attachment figure who could be trusted. If this therapy was to be successful in establishing a containing environment that could hold the anxiety of all family members, I needed to take care of each person's need for safety. The future of the family staying together was dependent on the therapy being successful. I was mindful that the boys had told me the previous week that they were sometimes frightened of their father. It would have been inappropriate to put the child on the spot in this context to explain his statement. I had also met with the parents independently and formed the view that they had the capacity to care for their children with sensitivity to their needs. The children's identity and sense of self was clearly rooted in their family connections. Tentatively I took the following relational risk with the parents.

Chip:	I think there *have* been some scary things that have happened and that's why I think we are here, to talk about those scary things.
Julius:	What?
	(He seemed genuinely perplexed, which I understood, as until then our conversation in the session had been about him as a protective father.)
Chip:	Well, I think when they were hit it was scary. When you hit them. And even understanding that you were concerned about their safety and wanting to keep them *safe*, it was still frightening for them to be hit by you and I think I am right about that. But I know it's very hard for the children to say that. And one thing that we have to work on here is to talk about how you can keep them safe and also not make them scared of you at the same time, because being scared of you then wipes out your protectiveness. You know what I mean?

Julius: *(Nodding agreement)* By being too harsh we do not bring the safety that one is working towards.
(Both parents relax.)

Chip: *(Inwardly breathing a huge sigh of relief and being affirmed that this father was someone who could use the intervention – I was not yet sure of the mother.)*
I think the children know you want them to be safe, don't you?

All: Yes.
(All vigorously nodding, especially Jeremy.)

Chip: It's just that it's backfired and didn't work the way it was supposed to work.
(Julius agreed with this statement and the session ended on a cooperative and hopeful note.)

Julius' comments were consistent with his AAI in which he described his father as setting rules which must be obeyed without question but as having the children's welfare at the centre of his actions. I was able to strongly recommend working towards these children's return home. Subsequently I was joined by a colleague to continue the work. Over the next nine months – the children returning home after three months – we worked with the family to develop understanding of emotional states and for the parents to help the children with their fears and anxieties.

We created a circle of safety using the family drawings of strengths. These included the things they did together, such as singing, watching television and family outings, as well as what they were each good at such as cooking a particular meal for the family or achieving a certificate at school. At each session we offered the family the opportunity to add to their strengths. They were very good at drawing and it was something they enjoyed doing together.

We asked each person to make a list of their worries and used psychodramatic enactments to explore different, more positive, endings to stories of danger both inside and outside the home. These ranged over many issues and included the children's worries about the parents arguing in the home and Jeremy experiencing racial bullying at school. The enactments involved different members of the family taking the role of 'director' under our guidance and staging a reconstruction of worrying episodes of family life and working out a more satisfactory outcome in action. This family engaged readily in this work and over the months we saw positive changes and deeper emotional connections and understandings between family members. Many of the changes enacted in the sessions were incorporated into daily life.

At the end of the work we were able to present them with a book containing all of the strengths they had drawn, leaving blank pages for the ones to come.

Conclusion

An attachment orientation to family therapy allows affect and cognition to be examined in a way that can bring the covert and hidden family rules and behaviours out into the light. Creating a therapeutic base that is secure for all members of the family can help them to re-examine their positions and consider how change may be beneficial.

Attachment helps us to look below the surface and excavate meanings and beliefs as well as illuminating feelings of fear and anger which might be unknown to the family itself, or previously too unsafe to voice.

Attachment conversations are those conversations and activities that address safety and protection from danger, including comfort. Danger that comes from inside the family may be the most difficult to name. Many such conversations are possible depending on the systemic therapist's orientation. The premise here is that attachment and systemic ideas are mutually beneficial and complement each other to benefit the family.

Attachment theory and systemic family therapy have had a long and flirtatious courtship. Whether this ongoing relationship is a genuine love match or a marriage of convenience remains to be seen.

References

Ainsworth, M. D. S. and Bell, S. M. (1970) Attachment, exploration, and separation: illustrated by the behaviour of one-year-olds in a Strange Situation. *Child Development*, 41: 49–67.

Andersen, T. (1987) The reflecting team: dialogue and meta dialogue in clinical work. *Family Process*, 26(4): 415–428.

Bowlby, J. (1988) *A Secure Base*, London and New York: Routledge.

Bowen, M. (1978) *Family Therapy in Clinical Practice*, New York: Jason Aronson.

Burnham, J. (2005) 'Relational reflexivity: a tool for socially constructing therapeutic relationships', in C. Flaskas, B. Mason and A. Perlesz (eds) *The Space Between*, London: Karnac.

Burr, V. (1995) *An Introduction to Social Constructionism*, London: Routledge.

Byng-Hall, J. (1995) *Rewriting Family Scripts*, New York: Guilford Press.

Carter, B. and McGoldrick, M. (eds) (1989) *The Changing Family Life Cycle: a framework for family therapy*, 2nd ed., London: Allyn & Bacon.

Cecchin, G. (1987) Hypothesising, circularity and neutrality revisited: an invitation to curiosity, *Family Process*, 26: 405–413.

Crittenden, P. (2008) *Raising Parents: Attachment, parenting and child safety*, Devon: Willan Publishing.

Crittenden, P. and Landini, A. (2011) *Assessing Adult Attachment*, New York and London: W. W. Norton & Co.

Dallos, R. (2006) *Attachment Narrative Therapy*, Maidenhead: Open University Press.

Dallos, R. and Vetere, A. (2009) *Systemic Therapy and Attachment Narratives*, London: Routledge.

Fivaz-Despeursinge, E. and Corboz-Warnery, A. (1999) *The Primary Triangle: A developmental systems view of mothers, fathers and infants*, New York: Basic Books.

Holmes, J. (2001) *The Search for the Secure Base: Attachment theory and psychotherapy*, New York and London: Routledge.

Kelly, J. B. and Johnson, J. R. (2001) The alienated child: a reformulation of parental alienation syndrome, *Family Court Review*, 39: 249–266.

Mason, B. (1993) Towards positions of safe uncertainty, *Human Systems*, 4: 189–200.

Minuchin, S. (1974) *Families and Family Therapy*, London: Tavistock Publications.

Minuchin, S. and Fishman, C. (1981) *Family Therapy Techniques*, Cambridge, MA: Harvard University Press.

Sroufe, L. A. (2005) Attachment and development: a prospective, longitudinal study from birth to adulthood, *Attachment & Human Development*, 7(4): 349–367.

Van IJzendoorn, M. H. and Sagi, A. (1999) 'Cross-cultural patterns of attachment: universal and contextual dimensions', in J. Cassidy and P. R. Shaver (eds) *Handbook of Attachment: Theory, research and clinical applications*, New York and London: Guilford Press.

Watzlawick, P., Weakland, J. and Fisch, R. (1974) *Change: Principles of problem formation and problem resolution.* New York: W.W. Norton & Co.

White, M. (1988) The externalising of the problem and the re-authoring of lives and relationships, *Dulwich Centre Newsletter*, Summer 1988, reprinted in Selected Papers, Dulwich Centre Publications, 1991.

White, M. and Epston, D. (1990) *Narrative Means to Therapeutic Ends*, London and New York: W. W. Norton & Co.

Chapter 5

Attachment-based interventions

Sensitive parenting is the key to positive parent–child relationships

Femmie Juffer, Marian J. Bakermans-Kranenburg and Marinus H. van IJzendoorn

Introduction

In this chapter we present attachment-based parenting interventions from the perspectives of attachment theory and relevant empirical research. In a series of meta-analyses of the pertinent intervention studies we have tested how effective these interventions are and which features of the interventions contribute to their effectiveness.

Based on attachment theory and research, and after extensive experience, we have developed an intervention model with video feedback that was rigorously tested in various samples of parents and children at risk. We elaborate on how to use this attachment-based video-feedback intervention in practice to support sensitive parenting and positive parent–child interactions.

We focus here on attachment-based parenting interventions and we do not include parent behaviour-management interventions aimed at helping parents of children with severe behaviour problems or conduct disorders (e.g. Scott & O'Connor 2012; Webster-Stratton *et al.* 2004, 2011). We also do not address 'attachment therapy' and similar approaches such as 'holding' or 'trauma therapy' offered at numerous internet sites for parents of troubled children. Unfortunately, many so-called attachment therapies not only miss a solid theoretical foundation and empirical evidence-base, but they may even be harmful and dangerous for children (Chaffin *et al.* 2006; Pignotti & Mercer 2007).

Attachment security

The key is sensitive parenting

Departing from an evolutionary perspective and drawing on research that examined the effects of separations of (primate) infants from their parents (e.g. Harlow 1958), John Bowlby (1982) developed attachment theory. According to that theory, infants are biologically predisposed to use their parents as a haven of safety to provide comfort and protection when they are distressed, and as a secure base from which to explore the world (Waters & Cummings 2000). Securely attached children feel free to play and to express their positive and negative emotions because they trust their parents to support them whenever they need help.

However, not all children experience their parents as a haven of safety and a secure base. Mary Ainsworth (Ainsworth *et al.* 1978) observed that children vary in their attachment behaviour and she suggested that sensitive parenting might be the key to children's attachment security. Ainsworth defined parental sensitivity as the ability to accurately perceive and interpret the child's behavioural signals and to respond to these signals in a prompt and adequate way (Ainsworth *et al.* 1978). In Ainsworth's study, and replicated in many empirical studies and a meta-analysis (De Wolff & Van IJzendoorn 1997), children who had experienced insensitive parenting tended to develop insecure (avoidant or ambivalent) attachment relationships with their parent whereas children who had received sensitive care had a greater chance to become securely attached.

In a longitudinal adoption study we found that sensitive parenting not only matters for young children. Maternal sensitive support in early childhood and adolescence predicted continuity of secure attachment from 1 to 14 years, whereas less maternal sensitive support in early childhood but more maternal sensitive support in adolescence predicted children's change from insecurity in infancy to security in adolescence (Beijersbergen *et al.* 2012). We concluded that both early and later sensitive parenting are important for the continuity of attachment across the first 14 years of life. By using an adoption design, we ensured that no effect of parenting could be attributed to genetic transmission from adoptive parent to child.

To date, Ainsworth's concept of parental sensitivity has proven to be useful not only because it sheds light on the aetiology and continuity of the different patterns of secure and insecure attachment relationships but also because it offers an essential framework for the development of attachment-based interventions to support parents of young children. Later in this chapter we will present our video-feedback intervention and show how Ainsworth's concept of parental sensitivity has been translated and integrated in the intervention approach, structure, and themes.

While Ainsworth distinguished the categories of children's secure, insecure avoidant, and insecure ambivalent attachment, Mary Main added a fourth category: insecure-disorganised attachment (Main & Solomon 1990). Main and Hesse (1990) proposed that in stressful situations insecure-disorganised children want to seek comfort and protection from their parent while, at the same time, feeling frightened by the parent, which results in an irresolvable paradox. As a consequence the child may (momentarily) show bizarre or contradictory behaviours. They proposed that parents of disorganised children suffer from unresolved loss or trauma and parents' negative memories and fears may suddenly intrude into their consciousness and behaviour, resulting in frightening, frightened or dissociated behaviour toward their child (Main & Hesse 1990). Unresolved loss or trauma can also negatively affect the parent's ability to perceive the child's signals accurately and to respond in adequate ways, leading to (extreme) insensitivity. Frightening, disconnected and (extremely) insensitive parenting behaviours may thus be complementary to and only partially overlapping (in the lower range) with parental sensitivity. Frightening and disconnected parental behaviour was found to be related to disorganised attachment (Hesse & Main 2006; Madigan *et al.* 2006; Out *et al.* 2009; Schuengel *et al.* 1999), while in its turn disorganised attachment was associated with elevated risk for later child psychopathology (Van IJzendoorn *et al.* 1999).

Compared to insecure attachments, early secure attachment relationships have been associated with better social competence in both genetically related families (e.g. Sroufe *et al.* 2005; Thompson 2008) and genetically unrelated adoptive families (Jaffari-Bimmel *et al.* 2006), ruling out genetic confounding in the latter case. Further, a series of meta-analyses has shown that attachment insecurity predicts both more externalising and internalising behaviour problems in childhood and adolescence although effect sizes were modest (Fearon *et al.* 2010; Groh *et al.* 2012).

Because insecure and disorganised attachment can be seen as risk factors in the development of child psychopathology, both attachment security and the related concept of parental sensitivity are relevant for the clinical field, and for the development and evaluation of attachment-based interventions in at-risk and clinical families. In particular, parental sensitivity as the best-documented and evidence-based determinant of children's attachment security has been the focus of intervention efforts tested in multiple studies. But what do we know about the success and effectiveness of these efforts, and do we know which intervention methods and models work best? To find answers to these theoretically and clinically significant questions, we adopted a meta-analytic approach.

Meta-analyses of sensitivity and attachment interventions

Meta-analysis is one of the most useful tools to reach evidence-based conclusions about best intervention practices. With a meta-analytic approach, data from multiple studies can be synthesised and quantified, and solid conclusions can be drawn about essential features of effective attachment-based interventions, such as the duration or the focus of the intervention.

In a series of meta-analyses, we examined 70 published intervention studies with 88 interventions directed at either sensitivity or attachment or both (see Bakermans-Kranenburg *et al.* 2003, 2008a). All intervention studies reported observed parental sensitivity or children's attachment security, or both, as outcome measures. The intervention studies were not restricted to a specific population. Some samples consisted of low-risk families with typically developing infants, but studies with clinical and at-risk populations were included as well.

Parental sensitivity

Eighty-one studies (including 7,636 families) presented intervention effects on parental sensitivity; and the combined effect size (d, the standardised difference between the means of the intervention and control groups) was a moderately strong effect of 0.44 ($p < .001$). To estimate the combined effect size in the set of studies with the most adequate designs, randomised controlled trials were selected. In this set of 51 studies (including 6,282 participants), interventions were also significantly effective in enhancing parental sensitivity ($d = 0.33$).

The interventions appeared to be equally effective in at-risk or multiple risk samples (including, for example, families with low socio-economic status (SES) or adolescent mothers) and in low-risk families. The only difference was that interventions with clinically referred families were significantly more effective ($d = 0.46$) than interventions with other groups ($d = 0.31$) (Bakermans-Kranenburg *et al.* 2003).

Interventions with a relatively narrow focus, aiming at enhancing parental sensitivity through an interaction-focused approach, were found to be significantly more effective ($d = 0.45$) than broader interventions (such as interventions focusing on mental representations of attachment or on social support) ($d = 0.27$). Interventions with video feedback were more effective than interventions without this method. Interventions with fewer than five sessions were as effective as interventions with five to 16 sessions. Surprisingly, however, interventions with more than 16 sessions were less effective than interventions with a smaller number of sessions (*'Less is More'*; see Bakermans-Kranenburg *et al.* 2003). Short-term, interaction-focused interventions with video feedback thus appear most effective in improving sensitive parenting.

Attachment security

Twenty-nine intervention studies (involving 1,503 families) aimed at promoting children's attachment security (Bakermans-Kranenburg *et al.* 2003). The combined effect size for attachment security was modest but significant ($d = 0.19$). Twenty-three studies (including 1,255 families) presented randomised controlled trials resulting in a similar effect size ($d = 0.20$). The characteristics of the samples, such as low SES, clinical referrals, or the presence of multiple risk factors, did not result in differences in effect sizes between the studies. Attachment interventions were thus equally effective in low-risk and high-risk families and in clinical and nonclinical families.

Interventions focusing on parental sensitivity were significantly more effective in fostering secure attachment than interventions targeting other aspects such as representational interventions or social support. In fact, only sensitivity-focused interventions showed a significant combined effect size on attachment ($d = 0.39$). Most importantly, those interventions that were most effective in enhancing parental sensitivity ($d > 0.40$) were also most effective in enhancing children's attachment security ($d = 0.45$; Bakermans-Kranenburg *et al.* 2003).

Attachment theory and empirical research (see the meta-analysis of De Wolff & Van IJzendoorn 1997) already had predicted and confirmed the correlational association between sensitive parenting and children's attachment security. From the meta-analytical findings on attachment-based interventions (Bakermans-Kranenburg *et al.* 2003) we can extend the findings from correlational to causal relations and conclude that sensitive parenting is, indeed, the key to (changes in) attachment security in children. In fact, the meta-analytic study of randomised experiments in this field is the most conclusive evidence for a causal relation between parental sensitivity and infant attachment security to date.

Disorganised attachment

In another meta-analysis, we examined 15 attachment-based intervention studies (including 842 families) that reported on children's insecure-disorganised attachment as an outcome measure (see Bakermans-Kranenburg *et al.* 2005, 2008a). The combined effect size of these studies was not significant, $d = 0.05$. However, the five interventions focusing on parental sensitivity only were most effective; they were significantly more effective in reducing attachment disorganisation ($d = 0.26$) than other interventions not focusing on sensitive parenting ($d = -0.08$). This finding is intriguing as disorganised attachment has been associated with frightening and atypical parenting (see above) instead of parental sensitivity which is the focus of attachment-based interventions studied in the meta-analysis.

Concluding, our meta-analyses showed that interventions can significantly enhance parental sensitivity and children's attachment security, but attachment security to a lesser extent than sensitivity (the same conclusion was reached in a previous meta-analysis including a much smaller number of studies; see Van IJzendoorn *et al.* 1995). Most importantly, our findings showed that specific characteristics distinguished more effective interventions from less effective interventions. In particular, brief interventions with a focus on sensitive parenting behaviour appeared to be most successful in decreasing parents' insensitivity as well as children's attachment insecurity and disorganisation.

The Leiden parenting programmes: VIPP and VIPP-SD

Supporting sensitive parenting

Based on insights from attachment theory and building on the knowledge from our meta-analytic studies, we developed an intervention aiming at promoting sensitive parenting and positive parent–child interactions: Video-feedback Intervention to promote Positive Parenting (VIPP). Essential outcomes of the meta-analyses of attachment-based interventions (Bakermans-Kranenburg *et al.* 2003) were integrated in the VIPP model: as a result we designed a short-term, home-based intervention directed at sensitive parenting behaviour by utilising video feedback, and we tested the VIPP in a series of randomised controlled trials.

Parental sensitivity, as the key to positive parent–child interactions and relationships, was translated and integrated in the intervention approach, structure and themes of the VIPP. The main objective of the VIPP is to promote the parent's sensitivity by showing and reinforcing moments of sensitive parenting of the parent herself in video fragments. The structure of the VIPP intervention closely follows the components of Ainsworth's concept of sensitivity by paying attention in the first and second home visit to teaching parents how to *accurately perceive and interpret their child's signals,* and in the third and fourth session by reinforcing and promoting parents' efforts to *respond to their child's signals in prompt and adequate ways.* The themes of the home visits are adapted to this structure so that learning and practising observational skills are paramount in the first two intervention visits (e.g. by 'speaking for the child', see below) while highlighting and encouraging sensitive reactions are the main focus of the third and fourth sessions (e.g. reinforcing 'sensitivity chains', see below). In cases where there are more booster sessions, all themes are combined and repeated.

Development of VIPP

A first attempt to enhance parental sensitivity through an attachment-based video-taped model of sensitive parenting, featuring strangers, appeared to be ineffective (Lambermon & Van IJzendoorn 1989). A problem with videotaped model behaviour is that parents might not identify with the specific model of a parent–child dyad on the videotape. Parents apparently need a mirror of their own daily interactions with their child to change their behaviour. Based on attachment theory (Ainsworth *et al.* 1978; Bowlby 1982), a first version of our video-feedback intervention programme was developed in a study of families with early-adopted children (Juffer 1993). The intervention, consisting of three home sessions implemented in the child's first year of life, appeared to be successful in promoting maternal sensitivity, secure infant–mother attachment, and the prevention of disorganised attachment (Juffer *et al.* 2005, 2008a). On the basis of these outcomes a nationwide and government subsidised adoption aftercare service was started and, since the year 2000, Dutch parents can ask for this service for each newly adopted child, including special-needs or older-placed children and sibling placements.

The first version of this video-feedback intervention was extended to other types of families and then also to toddlers and preschoolers into the current VIPP (Juffer *et al.* 2008b, 2009), consisting of four to six sessions, organised into structured stages according to a detailed protocol. Another extension of the VIPP programme was developed and tested a few years later, with an additional component aimed at enhancing adequate discipline (VIPP-SD: VIPP with an additional focus on Sensitive Discipline; Juffer *et al.* 2008b; Mesman *et al.* 2008; Van Zeijl *et al.* 2006). The VIPP has been adapted for use with clinical groups (e.g. Stein *et al.* 2006), group care, and for fathers (see below).

The Leiden Centre for Child and Family Studies offers regular training courses on how to use VIPP and VIPP-SD in practice (www.leidenattachmentresearch-program.eu/vipp).

How to use attachment-based interventions

Illustrations from the VIPP programmes

How can attachment-based interventions be used in practice? What kind of themes and techniques are included and how are the parents involved in the intervention? We present illustrations and examples from the VIPP programmes in which parents are offered short-term, interaction-focused interventions aimed at enhancing sensitive parenting (VIPP) and adequate discipline (VIPP-SD). The programmes are standardised *and* individualised, meaning that the interveners work from a standard protocol (Juffer *et al*. 2008c) but attune the guidelines to the individual parent–child dyad. The VIPP programmes use videotaped interactions of the parent and child involved and video feedback: interveners watch and review the videotape together with the parent. The VIPP programmes are home-based and short-term: the interventions are implemented in the home in a modest number of sessions (usually six). Building a supporting relationship between the intervener and the parent (Bowlby 1988) is a crucial element of the intervention.

In the VIPP programmes, parent and child are videotaped during daily situations at their home (for example, playing together, bathing, mealtime) during brief episodes of 10 to 30 minutes. Parents are encouraged to react to their children the way they normally do. In the period between the home visit and the intervention session, the intervener reviews the videotape and prepares comments on the parent–child interaction as shown on the videotape. The intervener writes down these comments, directed by the guidelines of the protocol and screens the videotape for suitable fragments to connect the information in the guidelines to the video fragments, and this script serves as a guide for the video feedback in the intervention session. This script can be discussed in a review session with peer interveners or supervisors.

As an illustration, when the theme of exploration versus attachment behaviour (see Table 5.1) is to be discussed in the next intervention visit, the intervener searches for relevant fragments. Thus fragments of the child making eye contact or seeking physical proximity are used to illustrate the child's attachment behaviour, whereas fragments of the child's play behaviour are used to illustrate exploration. In the intervention the intervener connects the fragments to general messages described in the protocol. For example, while showing attachment and exploration fragments, the intervener explains that these behaviours ask for differential parental reactions: children's attachment signals should be met with prompt, adequate reactions, whereas parents should adopt a different role during children's play and share the child's activities without being intrusive or interfering. The intervener may also comment that play behaviour is important for children because they learn a lot from manipulating toys. At the same time, *playing together* provides children with an extra dimension compared to playing alone: their overtures are responded to, making them feel understood, and moments of joy can be shared (the intervener may say: 'A toy does not smile back, you do!').

Table 5.1 Sensitivity themes used in VIPP and additional sensitive discipline themes used in VIPP-SD

Session	Sensitivity	Sensitive discipline
1.	Exploration versus attachment behaviour (A)	Inductive discipline and distraction
2.	'Speaking for the child' (A)	Positive reinforcement
3.	Sensitivity chain (B)	Sensitive time-out
4.	Sharing emotions (B)	Empathy for the child
5.	Booster session (A and B)	Booster session
6.	Booster session (A and B)	Booster session

Note: (A) refers to the first part of Ainsworth *et al.*'s (1978) concept of sensitivity: accurately perceiving and interpreting the child's signals; (B) refers to the second part of Ainsworth's concept of sensitivity: prompt and adequate reactions to the child's emotional and behavioural signals. In the booster sessions all themes are combined.

During the next visit the videotape is shown to the parent, and the intervener reviews the videotape with her, discussing the selected fragments on the basis of the comments and script prepared before the session. Positive interaction moments shown on the videotape are always emphasised. Focusing on positive interactions serves the goal of showing the mother that she is able to act as a sensitive, competent parent: she should feel empowered by positive feedback rather than incompetent due to negative feedback. To focus the parent's attention on the positive moments, the videotape is stilled and the parent is shown a picture of a successful interaction or a happy child. By repeating positive fragments, reinforcing messages are enlarged and emphasised while negative moments are counterbalanced. In case of insensitive parental behaviour, the parent is encouraged to use more sensitive behaviours, preferably behaviours she displayed at other moments on the videotape, so that she is her own model of competent parenting. These 'corrective messages' are, however, postponed to the third or later intervention sessions (see below).

Video feedback provides the opportunity to focus on the child's videotaped behaviour, thereby stimulating the parent's reflective functioning, his or her observational skills and understanding of the child. It also enables positive reinforcement of the parent's moments of sensitive behaviour shown on the videotape. Video feedback thus enables the intervener to focus on both parts of Ainsworth's concept of sensitivity: accurately *perceiving* and *interpreting* child signals and adequately *responding* to them (Ainsworth *et al.* 1978).

VIPP

VIPP consists of four themes (see Table 5.1) that are elaborated successively during four home visits: (1) Exploration versus attachment behaviour: showing the difference between the child's contact-seeking behaviour and play, and explaining the differential responses needed from the parent, (2) 'Speaking for the child': promoting the accurate perception of children's (subtle) signals by verbalising their facial expressions and non-verbal cues shown on the videotape, (3) Sensitivity chain: explaining the relevance of prompt and adequate responding to the child's signals ('chain': child signal–parental response–reaction of the child), and (4) Sharing emotions: showing and encouraging parents' affective attunement to the positive and negative emotions of their child.

The themes are ordered in a way that the first two intervention sessions focus on child behaviour only (e.g. by actively 'speaking for the child'; Carter *et al.* 1991). The next two intervention sessions are also directed at parental behaviour, for example by discussing parental behaviour in a 'sensitivity chain'. This specific order is part of the VIPP protocol: addressing parental behaviour is postponed until the parent and the intervener have had more time to build a working relationship. Another advantage is that a primary focus on the child's perspective is already guaranteed in the first sessions.

Additional 'booster' visits (intervention sessions 5 and 6) are used in which all sensitivity themes of the first four intervention sessions are repeated and connected to new video fragments. Giving the parent written information (e.g. brochures) is optional.

VIPP-SD

VIPP-SD is based on an integration of attachment theory (Ainsworth *et al.* 1978; Bowlby 1982) and coercion theory (Patterson 1982). Coercion theory describes how ineffective parental discipline results in increasingly difficult and challenging child behaviour. VIPP-SD can be characterised as an interaction-oriented intervention using video feedback to promote parental sensitivity as well as adequate and sensitive discipline strategies (Mesman *et al.* 2008).

The VIPP-SD programme consists of four specific sensitive discipline themes (see Table 5.1) that are elaborated during the intervention sessions in addition to the sensitivity themes: (1) Inductive discipline and distraction: recommending explanation and distraction as non-coercive responses to difficult child behaviour or potentially conflict-evoking situations, (2) Positive reinforcement: praising the child for positive behaviour and ignoring negative attention-seeking, (3) The use of a 'Sensitive time-out', to sensitively de-escalate temper tantrums, and (4) Empathy for the child: consistent discipline and limit setting should be combined with showing understanding of the intentions and feelings of the child.

For example, in the first intervention session the parent is encouraged to distract the child in occurences of challenging behaviour and direct the child's attention to objects or situations that are allowed, thus creating opportunities for positive behaviours. At the same time, the parent is encouraged to use induction, that is, providing reasons and explanations for a prohibition or parental intervention (Hoffman 2000), thus helping the child to (gradually) understand the consequences of his or her own behaviour and learning to empathise with other people's perspectives.

As with VIPP, in additional 'booster' visits all sensitive discipline themes of the first four intervention sessions are repeated.

Through illustrations and examples we have described how VIPP and VIPP-SD can be used in practice. However, before the implementation of an intervention programme in clinical practice and social work, the evidence-base of the programme should be indisputable. What do we know about the effectiveness of the VIPP programmes?

Evaluating the VIPP programmes

Effectiveness of VIPP

VIPP has been tested in various countries in a number of studies with at-risk parents or children (see Figure 5.1). In all studies, VIPP, or adaptations of the programme, proved to be effective in enhancing sensitive parenting. In most of these studies so-called dummy interventions, for example telephone calls, were given to the control participants to keep in contact with all parents and to prevent attrition (Juffer *et al.* 2008d). In one of the studies both the control group and the intervention group received a cognitive behaviour module to help the parents with their clinical problems. The intervention consisted of a cognitive behaviour module

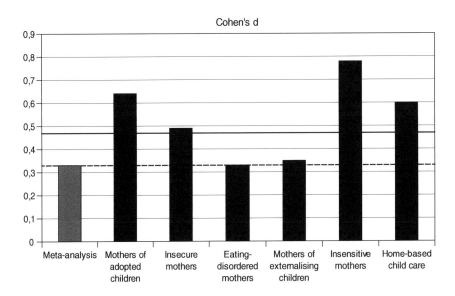

Figure 5.1 Effectiveness of VIPP/VIPP-SD on sensitive parenting in six samples of parents (caregivers) and children (solid line; total *N* = 627), compared to the effectiveness on parental sensitivity in randomised controlled trials in the 2003 meta-analysis of attachment-based interventions (dotted line; *N* = 6,282; Bakermans-Kranenburg *et al.* 2003)

aimed at helping the mother with her eating problem for both groups and an additional adapted VIPP programme aimed at promoting sensitive parenting for the intervention group only (Stein *et al.* 2006).

In a randomised controlled trial with Dutch low-SES mothers classified as insecure with the Adult Attachment Interview (Hesse 2008; Main *et al.* 2003), VIPP implemented in four home visits during the baby's first year of life resulted in a significant increase in maternal sensitivity of the intervention group compared to the control group (Klein Velderman *et al.* 2006a). In a follow-up study of the same sample, it appeared that, compared to the control group, VIPP had significantly protected the children from developing externalising and total behaviour problems in the clinical range at preschool age (Klein Velderman *et al.* 2006b).

Stein and colleagues (2006; Woolley *et al.* 2008) tested a short-term, slightly adapted version of the VIPP in a randomised controlled trial with mothers with eating disorders and their babies in the United Kingdom and found a significant improvement in maternal mealtime interaction with the infant, including mother's appropriate verbal and non-verbal responses to infant cues (components of sensitive parenting behaviour).

In Lithuania, mothers screened on insensitive parenting behaviours significantly gained in sensitivity after receiving VIPP compared to a control group of insensitive mothers in a randomised controlled trial (Kalinauskiene *et al.* 2009). Mothers of adopted children who had received a first version of the VIPP (see before) also outperformed their control counterparts in sensitivity (Juffer *et al.* 2005, 2008a). In another randomised controlled trial, mothers of 1-year-old, 2-year-old, and 3-year-old toddlers screened for high levels of externalising problem behaviour showed significantly more sensitive discipline after the VIPP-SD intervention implemented in six home visits compared to their control counterparts (Mesman *et al.* 2008; Van Zeijl *et al.* 2006).

Further, a randomised controlled trial in home-based child care showed that with some minor modifications the family-based VIPP with six intervention sessions could be successfully applied in a group setting (VIPP-CC: VIPP-Child Care; Groeneveld *et al.* 2011). Global child care quality improved in the intervention group compared to the control group and, after the intervention, caregivers in the intervention group reported more positive attitudes toward sensitive caregiving than caregivers in the control group (Groeneveld *et al.* 2011).

In conclusion, VIPP appeared to be effective with respect to sensitive parenting (see Figure 5.1) and the effect sizes were in the same range or even higher than the combined effect size for parental sensitivity found in the meta-analysis of attachment-based intervention studies (Bakermans-Kranenburg *et al.* 2003). We computed the effectiveness of the VIPP programmes conducted so far with a meta-analysis of the pertinent VIPP intervention studies shown in Figure 5.1 and the combined effect size amounted to a significant medium effect for promoting sensitive parenting, $d = 0.48$, including 627 participants in six studies.

A definite conclusion about the effectiveness of VIPP for enhancing attachment security cannot be drawn yet. Children's attachment security was not reported in the studies on mothers with eating disorders, children with externalising problems, and home-based child care. Mixed outcomes were found in other VIPP studies, with significant, positive outcomes in an adoption sample, and no significant effect in the study on insensitive mothers. Interestingly however, although in the VIPP intervention study of insecure mothers no overall intervention effect on attachment security could be traced, we found that the outcomes varied for children differing in temperamental reactivity: some children gained more from the intervention than others.

VIPP and differential susceptibility

Early-childhood interventions might not always be effective for all families and children (see also Scott & O'Connor 2012), implying that our VIPP intervention might not be equally effective for all children involved. Children may be differentially susceptible to environmental influences and changes (Bakermans-Kranenburg & Van IJzendoorn 2007; Belsky 1997; Belsky *et al.* 2007; Ellis *et al.* 2011; Van IJzendoorn & Bakermans-Kranenburg 2012a).

According to the evolutionary-based differential susceptibility hypothesis, children vary in their susceptibility to parental rearing, for better – when receiving sensitive care, or *improved* sensitive care after a successful intervention – and for worse – when receiving less optimal care. Previous studies have indicated that highly reactive children may be the more susceptible children (e.g. Belsky *et al.* 1998). Against this background, the differential effectiveness of our VIPP intervention was tested in children with high versus average to low negative reactivity.

We found that the mothers of highly reactive infants were more susceptible to the influence of the intervention and gained more in sensitivity, and that highly reactive infants, in turn, were more susceptible to (changes in) their mothers' sensitivity. In the group of highly reactive intervention infants, attachment security and change in pre- to post-test maternal sensitivity were significantly correlated, $r = .64, p < .05$. In the less reactive intervention group the correlation was $r = .11$, ns. The difference in correlations was significant ($p = .03$; Klein Velderman *et al.* 2006a). The experimentally induced *change* in maternal sensitivity appeared to impact more strongly on attachment security in the highly reactive infant group. Thus, the outcomes confirmed the prediction that highly reactive children are more susceptible to experimentally induced environmental change than less reactive infants. Parents of highly reactive infants may therefore be the most rewarding targets of intervention efforts.

Our findings also revealed intervention effects at a neurobiological level: in our sample with 1- to 3-year-old children screened for relatively high levels of externalising behaviour the VIPP-SD programme proved to be effective in decreasing daily cortisol production in children *with* the DRD4 7-repeat allele (a variant of the dopamine receptor gene that is associated with motivational and reward mechanisms and ADHD in children), but not in children *without* the DRD4 7-repeat allele.

These findings indicate that children are differentially susceptible to intervention effects dependent on the presence of the DRD4 7-repeat allele (Bakermans-Kranenburg *et al.* 2008b). Moreover, VIPP-SD proved to be effective in decreasing externalising behaviour in the children with the DRD4 7-repeat allele. Zooming in on parents who showed the largest increase in the use of positive discipline as a result of the intervention, the decrease in externalising behaviour was strongest in children with the DRD4 7-repeat allele, showing that they were indeed the most susceptible to the change in their caregiving environment (Bakermans-Kranenburg *et al.* 2008c).

This first experimental test of (measured) gene by (observed) environment interaction in human development indicates that children might be differentially susceptible to intervention efforts depending on genetic differences.

In summary, we documented the evidence-base of the VIPP programme as an effective intervention for enhancing sensitive parenting and presented promising outcomes regarding children's differential susceptibility to intervention effects based on their temperamental or genetic characteristics.

Against the background of the meta-analytical evidence on attachment-based interventions presented above, the VIPP programmes were developed to include intervention elements that were most effective in the meta-analyses. VIPP and VIPP-SD are brief programmes, confirming the *'Less is More'* feature of effective interventions. VIPP and VIPP-SD both address sensitive parenting, converging with the meta-analytical outcome that effective interventions focus on parental sensitivity.

Before continuing with our conclusions and practical implications, we elaborate on two intervention programmes that also included effective elements from the meta-analyses of attachment-based interventions.

Examples of recent attachment-based interventions

Here we highlight two examples of recent, effective attachment-based interventions tested in randomised controlled trials, and compare their characteristics to the meta-analytic findings described above.

It is not our intention to give a complete overview of all current attachment-based interventions here (other examples of such interventions are the Circle of Security intervention (Hoffman *et al.* 2006), and the Infant–Parent Psychotherapy and Psycho-educational Parenting Intervention (Cicchetti *et al.* 2006, 2011).

ABC Intervention

Mary Dozier and colleagues (Bernard *et al.* 2012; Dozier *et al.* 2006, 2008; Lewis-Morrarty *et al.* 2012) designed an intervention for parents of young children in foster care and for parents identified by child protective services as being at high risk of maltreating their children: the Attachment and Biobehavioural Catch-up (ABC) programme.

ABC was developed to decrease frightening behaviour and encourage sensitive, nurturing care in (foster) parents and to enhance children's relationship formation and their ability to regulate neurobiological aspects of their behaviour (Bernard *et al.* 2012; Dozier *et al.* 2008). ABC appeared to be effective in helping foster infants regulate their neurobiological functioning, as measured after the intervention with cortisol diurnal levels at the post-test (Dozier *et al.* 2008). Also, in a preschool follow-up assessment the intervention foster children outperformed the control foster children in cognitive flexibility and theory of mind skills (Lewis-Morrarty *et al.* 2012).

In their study on parents at high risk of maltreating their offspring, children in the ABC intervention showed significantly lower rates of disorganised attachment (32%) and higher rates of secure attachment (52%) compared to the control children (57% and 33%, respectively) (Bernard *et al.* 2012).

How do the characteristics of this effective intervention compare to the findings from the meta-analyses of attachment-based interventions? As stated by Bernard *et al.* (2012), the home-based ABC intervention was designed to be relatively brief, completed in 10 sessions, converging with the meta-analytical outcome of '*Less is More*' (see above; Bakermans-Kranenburg *et al.* 2003). The ABC intervention was manualised with each session having a specific focus, an important intervention characteristic for promoting treatment adherence (see also Bakermans-Kranenburg *et al.* 2005). Further, the intervention focus of the ABC was on changing sensitive parenting behaviours rather than mental representations of parents, converging with the meta-analytical finding that sensitivity-focused interventions with a focus on interactions appeared to be more effective than other approaches (Bakermans-Kranenburg *et al.* 2003).

Attachment-based intervention for maltreated children

Building on the principles from the VIPP programmes, Ellen Moss and colleagues (Moss *et al.* 2011; Tarabulsy *et al.* 2008) designed an attachment-based home-visiting intervention for maltreating families. The intervention was aimed at enhancing mothers' sensitivity to their child's emotional and behavioural signals, in order to promote the child's attachment security (Moss *et al.* 2011). Outcomes showed that this short-term intervention (8 weeks) was effective in enhancing parental sensitivity, improving children's attachment security and reducing attachment disorganisation (Moss *et al.* 2011).

Like the VIPP and the ABC intervention, this intervention adopted crucial intervention elements identified by the meta-analyses of attachment-based interventions (Bakermans-Kranenburg *et al.* 2003), and it was inspired by the VIPP programme. This intervention for maltreating families was brief, that is, eight home visits, and the main focus of the intervention was on parental sensitivity, for example by encouraging the parent to follow the child's lead. The intervention sessions with video feedback were structured in a fixed order, including a sequence of videotaping interactive behaviour and a sequence of video feedback during which the intervener played back and discussed a video fragment of the parent–child interaction. The interveners followed specific guidelines from a manual. To ensure treatment integrity, interveners were supervised on a weekly basis (Moss *et al.* 2011).

In summary, two recent intervention models incorporated essential elements that distinguished effective from non-effective interventions as found in our meta-analyses on attachment-based interventions. Converging with the VIPP programmes, both interventions confirmed that brief interventions with a focus on sensitive parenting can be successful and effective in changing parenting behaviour and parent–child relationships.

Conclusions and practical implications

Our series of meta-analyses of attachment-based intervention studies (Bakermans-Kranenburg *et al.* 2003) showed that short-term, interaction-oriented interventions that focus on parental sensitivity are most effective. Converging with this meta-analytical evidence, recent effective intervention studies (Bernard *et al.* 2012; Moss *et al.* 2011) made use of brief interventions focusing on sensitive parenting behaviour. Although longer interventions may be needed to address other aspects of parental or family problems (e.g. parent's mental representations or psychiatric disorders, difficulties in multi-risk families), the gold standard for enhancing parental sensitivity and positive parent–child relationships is to use a relatively narrow focus on sensitive behaviour during brief interventions. This rather modest feature of successful and effective attachment-based interventions implies that such an intervention can be quite easily included in more comprehensive and longer treatments of parents and families. It should also be noted that although a brief sensitive parenting intervention may successfully change a parent's behaviour toward the child and the parent–child interaction, it is not a panacea for all parental or family problems. A useful framework is to combine a brief sensitivity intervention with another treatment module. For example, in the study with mothers with eating disorders a brief video-feedback intervention to address parent–child interaction during mealtime was combined with a guided cognitive behaviour self-help module for eating disorders (Stein *et al.* 2006; Woolley *et al.* 2008).

Based on insights from attachment research and the meta-analytical outcome that sensitive parenting is the key to positive parent–child relationships, we developed the Video-feedback Intervention to promote Positive Parenting (VIPP and VIPP-SD: VIPP with an additional focus on Sensitive Discipline). In several studies in various at-risk samples VIPP/VIPP-SD appeared to be an efficient and effective intervention for enhancing sensitive parenting, revealing a significant medium combined effect size in six studies with more than 600 participants.

To date, there are several ongoing studies in which VIPP-SD is being tested in new settings (e.g. centre-based child care) and with other at-risk and clinical samples (e.g. parents of children with autism spectrum disorder; ethnic minority families; parents with intellectual restrictions; children in foster care). The outcomes of these studies will reveal whether VIPP-SD can be successfully applied in these new settings and samples and might also inform us about the possibilities of generalising VIPP-SD to different types of families and child rearing arrangements.

Some questions and issues remain that need reflection and discussion for the future. Interventions such as the ABC intervention and VIPP-SD are usually implemented in home visits. An issue that remains to be resolved is whether centre-based, group interventions (e.g. Hoffman *et al.* 2006; Niccols 2008) are as effective as home-based, individualised programmes. Also, the role of fathers in sensitive parenting interventions needs to be examined. In a first pilot study with five nonclinical fathers and their infant, VIPP was used to improve early father–infant interaction (Lawrence *et al.* 2013). After the intervention, the fathers reported that the intervention helped them to improve the relationship with their baby. Although larger studies are needed to show the effectiveness of VIPP in (clinical) populations of fathers, this promising study demonstrated the feasibility of the VIPP with fathers.

An innovative avenue of intervention research addresses the neurobiological effects of interventions, testing whether attachment-based interventions are not only effective at observed behavioural levels but also at neurobiological levels and, for example, result in altered daily cortisol diurnal levels (e.g. Bakermans-Kranenburg *et al.* 2008b; Dozier *et al.* 2008; Fisher *et al.* 2006).

Also, the role of oxytocin in parental sensitivity and sensitive parenting interventions is an intriguing and still largely unexplored research topic. In human beings oxytocin is associated with delivery and lactation, mood regulation, facial emotion recognition, and trust (Van IJzendoorn & Bakermans-Kranenburg 2012b). An important question is whether oxytocin influences parenting behaviour, not only in mothers but also in fathers. A recent study has shown that oxytocin is indeed associated with differential aspects of parenting style in mothers and fathers: for mothers affectionate physical contact with the child was associated with oxytocin increases, whereas for fathers this was the case after stimulatory contact with the child (Feldman *et al.* 2010). In a first double-blind, placebo-controlled, within-subject experiment with intranasal oxytocin administration in a sample of fathers, Naber, Van IJzendoorn, Deschamps, Van Engeland, and Bakermans-Kranenburg (2010) demonstrated that fathers in the oxytocin condition were more stimulating of their child's exploration and less hostile than fathers in the placebo condition. From this first experiment it can be derived that interventions to promote sensitive parenting might profit from adding intranasal oxytocin administration as an intervention component, and it would be extremely relevant to test the differential and possible cumulative intervention effects on parenting behaviour.

Hopefully, the knowledge from successful and effective attachment-based interventions will be further translated and disseminated and reach practice, policy and clinical work with parents and children. Convincing evidence from theory and research, as well as helpful skills rigorously tested in numerous intervention studies, are now available to offer parents the support they need and promote sensitive parenting and positive family relationships.

References

Ainsworth, M. D. S., Blehar, M. C., Waters, E., & Wall, S. (1978). *Patterns of attachment. A psychological study of the Strange Situation.* Hillsdale, NJ: Lawrence Erlbaum.

Bakermans-Kranenburg, M. J. & Van IJzendoorn, M. H. (2007). Research review: Genetic vulnerability or differential susceptibility in child development: the case of attachment. *Journal of Child Psychology and Psychiatry, 48*, 1160–1173.

Bakermans-Kranenburg, M. J., Van IJzendoorn, M. H., & Juffer, F. (2003). Less is more: Meta-analysis of sensitivity and attachment interventions in early childhood. *Psychological Bulletin, 129*, 195–215.

Bakermans-Kranenburg, M. J., Van IJzendoorn, M. H., & Juffer, F. (2005). Disorganized infant attachment and preventive interventions: A review and meta-analysis. *Infant Mental Health Journal, 26*, 191–216.

Bakermans-Kranenburg, M. J., Van IJzendoorn, M. H., & Juffer, F. (2008a). Less is more: Meta-analytic arguments for the use of sensitivity-focused interventions. In F. Juffer, M. J. Bakermans-Kranenburg, & M. H. van IJzendoorn (eds), *Promoting positive parenting: An attachment-based intervention* (pp. 59–74). New York: Taylor & Francis.

Bakermans-Kranenburg, M. J., Van IJzendoorn, M. H., Mesman, J., Alink, L. R. A., & Juffer, F. (2008b). Effects of an attachment-based intervention on daily cortisol moderated by dopamine receptor D4: A randomized control trial on 1- to 3-year-olds screened for externalizing behavior. *Development and Psychopathology, 20*, 805–820.

Bakermans-Kranenburg, M. J., Van IJzendoorn, M. H., Pijlman, F. T. A., Mesman, J., & Juffer, F. (2008c). Differential susceptibility to intervention: Dopamine D4 Receptor Polymorphism (DRD4 VNTR) moderates effects on toddlers' externalizing behavior in a randomized control trial. *Developmental Psychology, 44*, 293–300.

Beijersbergen, M. D., Juffer, F., Bakermans-Kranenburg, M. J., & Van IJzendoorn, M. H. (2012). Remaining or becoming secure: Parental sensitive support predicts attachment continuity from infancy to adolescence in a longitudinal adoption study. *Developmental Psychology, 48*(5), 1277–1282.

Belsky, J. (1997). Variation in susceptibility to environmental influence: An evolutionary argument. *Psychological Inquiry, 8*, 182–186.

Belsky, J., Bakermans-Kranenburg, M. J., & Van IJzendoorn, M. H. (2007). For better and for worse: Differential susceptibility to environmental influences. *Current Directions in Psychological Science, 16*, 300–304.

Belsky, J., Hsieh, K., & Crnic, K. (1998). Mothering, fathering, and infant negativity as antecedents of boys' externalizing problems and inhibition at age 3: Differential susceptibility to rearing influence? *Development and Psychopathology, 10*, 301–319.

Bernard, K., Dozier, M., Bick, J., Lewis-Morrarty, E., Lindhiem, O., & Carlson, E. (2012). Enhancing attachment organization among maltreated children: Results of a randomized clinical trial. *Child Development, 83*(2), 623–636.

Bowlby, J. (1982). *Attachment and loss* (Vol. 1). *Attachment* (2nd ed.). New York: Basic Books.

Bowlby, J. (1988). *A secure base: Clinical applications of attachment theory.* London: Routledge.

Carter, S. L., Osofsky, J. D., & Hann, D. M. (1991). Speaking for the baby: A therapeutic intervention with adolescent mothers and their infants. *Infant Mental Health Journal, 12*, 291–301.

Chaffin, M., Hanson, R., Saunders, B. E., Nichols, T., Barnett, D., Zeanah, C., *et al.* (2006).

Report of the APSAC Task Force on attachment therapy, reactive attachment disorder, and attachment problems. *Child Maltreatment, 11*, 76–89.

Cicchetti, D., Rogosch, F. A., & Toth, S. L. (2006). Fostering secure attachment in infants in maltreating families through preventive interventions. *Development and Psychopathology, 18*(3), 623–649.

Cicchetti, D., Rogosch, F. A., Toth, S. L., & Sturge-Apple, M. L. (2011). Normalizing the development of cortisol regulation in maltreated infants through preventive interventions. *Development and Psychopathology, 23*(3), 789–800.

De Wolff, M. S. & Van IJzendoorn, M. H. (1997). Sensitivity and attachment: A meta-analysis on parental antecedents of infant attachment. *Child Development, 68*, 571–591.

Dozier, M., Peloso, E., Lewis, E., Laurenceau, J. P., & Levine, S. (2008). Effects of an attachment-based intervention on the cortisol production of infants and toddlers in foster care. *Development and Psychopathology, 20*(3), 845–859.

Dozier, M., Peloso, E., Lindhiem, O., Gordon, M. K., Manni, M., Sepulveda, S., *et al.* (2006). Developing evidence-based interventions for foster children: An example of a randomized clinical trial with infants and toddlers. *Journal of Social Issues, 62*(4), 767–785.

Ellis, B. J., Boyce, W. T., Belsky, J., Bakermans-Kranenburg, M. J., & Van IJzendoorn, M. H. (2011). Differential susceptibility to the environment: An evolutionary-neurodevelopmental theory. *Development and Psychopathology, 23*(1), 7–28.

Fearon, R. P., Bakermans-Kranenburg, M. J., Van IJzendoorn, M. H., Lapsley, A. M., & Roisman, G. I. (2010). The significance of insecure attachment and disorganization in the development of children's externalizing behavior: A meta-analytic study. *Child Development, 81*(2), 435–456.

Feldman, R., Gordon, I., Schneiderman, I., Weisman, O., & Zagoory-Sharon, O. (2010). Natural variations in maternal and paternal care are associated with systematic changes in oxytocin following parent-infant contact. *Psychoneuroendocrinology, 35*(8), 1133–1141.

Fisher, P., Gunnar, M., Dozier, M., Bruce, J., & Pears, K. (2006). Effects of therapeutic interventions for foster children on behavioral problems, caregiver attachment, and stress regulatory neural systems. *Annals of the New York Academy of Sciences, 40*, 1–11.

Groeneveld, M. G., Vermeer, H. J., Van IJzendoorn, M. H., & Linting, M. (2011). Enhancing home-based child care quality through video-feedback intervention: A randomized controlled trial. *Journal of Family Psychology, 25*(1), 86–96.

Groh, A. M., Roisman, G. I., Van IJzendoorn, M. H., Bakermans-Kranenburg, M. J., & Fearon, R. P. (2012). The significance of insecure and disorganized attachment for children's internalizing symptoms: A meta-analytic study. *Child Development, 83*(2), 591–610.

Harlow, H. F. (1958). The nature of love. *American Psychologist, 13*, 673–685.

Hesse, E. (2008). The Adult Attachment Interview: Protocol, method of analysis, and empirical studies. In J. Cassidy & P. R. Shaver (eds), *Handbook of attachment: Theory, research, and clinical applications* (pp. 552–598). New York: The Guilford Press.

Hesse, E. & Main, M. (2006). Frightened, threatening, and dissociative (FR) parental behavior as related to infant D attachment in low-risk samples: Description, discussion, and interpretations. *Development and Psychopathology, 18*, 309–343.

Hoffman, K. T., Marvin, R. S., Cooper, G., & Powell, B. (2006). Changing toddlers' and preschoolers' attachment classifications: The Circle of Security intervention. *Journal of Consulting and Clinical Psychology, 74*, 1017–1026.

Hoffman, M. L. (2000). *Empathy and moral development. Implications for caring and justice.* Cambridge, UK: Cambridge University Press.

Jaffari-Bimmel, N., Juffer, F., Van IJzendoorn, M. H., Bakermans-Kranenburg, M. J., & Mooijaart, A. (2006). Social development from infancy to adolescence: Longitudinal and concurrent factors in an adoption sample. *Developmental Psychology, 42*(6), 1143–1153.

Juffer, F. (1993). *Verbonden door adoptie. Een experimenteel onderzoek naar hechting en competentie in gezinnen met een adoptiebaby.* [Attached through adoption. An experimental study of attachment and competence in families with adopted babies.] Amersfoort, the Netherlands: Academische Uitgeverij.

Juffer, F., Bakermans-Kranenburg, M. J., & Van IJzendoorn, M. H. (2005). The importance of parenting in the development of disorganized attachment: Evidence from a preventive intervention study in adoptive families. *Journal of Child Psychology and Psychiatry, 46,* 263–274.

Juffer, F., Bakermans-Kranenburg, M. J., & Van IJzendoorn, M. H. (2008a). Supporting adoptive families with video-feedback intervention. In F. Juffer, M. J. Bakermans-Kranenburg, & M. H. van IJzendoorn (eds), *Promoting positive parenting: An attachment-based intervention* (pp. 139–153). New York: Taylor & Francis.

Juffer, F., Bakermans-Kranenburg, M. J., & Van IJzendoorn, M. H. (eds) (2008b). *Promoting positive parenting: An attachment-based intervention.* New York: Taylor & Francis.

Juffer, F., Bakermans-Kranenburg, M. J., & Van IJzendoorn, M. H. (2008c). *Manual Video-feedback Intervention to promote Positive Parenting and Sensitive Discipline (VIPP-SD)* (version 2.0). Leiden University: Centre for Child and Family Studies.

Juffer, F., Van IJzendoorn, M. H., & Bakermans-Kranenburg, M. J. (2008d). Attachment-based interventions in early childhood: An overview. In F. Juffer, M. J. Bakermans-Kranenburg, & M. H. van IJzendoorn (eds), *Promoting positive parenting: An attachment-based intervention* (pp. 37–57). New York: Taylor & Francis.

Juffer, F., Bakermans-Kranenburg, M. J., & Van IJzendoorn, M. H. (2009). Attachment-based interventions: Heading for evidenced-based ways to support families. *Association for Child and Adolescent Mental Health, ACAMH Occasional Papers No.29, Attachment: Current Focus and Future Directions,* 47–57.

Kalinauskiene, L., Cekuoliene, D., Van IJzendoorn, M. H., Bakermans-Kranenburg, M. J., Juffer, F., & Kusakovskaja, I. (2009). Supporting insensitive mothers: The Vilnius randomized control trial of video feedback intervention to promote maternal sensitivity and infant attachment. *Child Care, Health & Development, 35,* 613–623.

Klein Velderman, M., Bakermans-Kranenburg, M. J., Juffer, F., & Van IJzendoorn, M. H. (2006a). Effects of attachment-based interventions on maternal sensitivity and infant attachment: Differential susceptibility of highly reactive infants. *Journal of Family Psychology, 20,* 266–274.

Klein Velderman, M., Bakermans-Kranenburg, M. J., Juffer, F., Van IJzendoorn, M. H., Mangelsdorf, S. C., & Zevalkink, J. (2006b). Preventing preschool externalizing behavior problems through video-feedback intervention in infancy. *Infant Mental Health Journal, 27*(5), 466–493.

Lambermon, M. W. E., & Van IJzendoorn, M. H. (1989). Influencing mother–infant interaction through videotaped or written instruction: Evaluation of a parent education program. *Early Childhood Research Quarterly, 4,* 449–458.

Lawrence, P. J., Davies, B., & Ramchandani, P. G. (2013). Using video feedback to improve early father–infant interaction: A pilot study. *Clinical Child Psychology and Psychiatry, 18*(1), 61–71.

Lewis-Morrarty, E., Dozier, M., Bernard, K., Terracciano, S. M., & Moore, S. V. (2012). Cognitive flexibility and theory of mind outcomes among foster children: Preschool follow-up results of a randomized clinical trial. *Journal of Adolescent Health, 51*(2), S17-S22.

Madigan, S., Bakermans-Kranenburg, M. J., Van IJzendoorn, M. H., Moran, G., Pederson, D. R., & Benoit, D. (2006). Unresolved states of mind, anomalous parental behavior, and disorganized attachment: A review and meta-analysis of a transmission gap. *Attachment & Human Development, 8*, 89–111.

Main, M., & Hesse, E. (1990). Parents' unresolved traumatic experiences are related to infant disorganized attachment status: Is frightened and/or frightening parental behavior the linking mechanism? In M. T. Greenberg, D. Cichetti, & E. Cummings (eds), *Attachment in the preschool years: Theory, research, and intervention* (pp. 161–182). Chicago: University of Chicago Press.

Main, M., & Solomon, J. (1990). Procedures for identifying infants as disorganized/disoriented during the Ainsworth Strange Situation. In M. T. Greenberg, D. Cicchetti, & E. M. Cummings (eds), *Attachment in the preschool years. Theory, research, and intervention* (pp. 121–182). Chicago: The University of Chicago Press.

Main, M., Goldwyn, R., & Hesse, E. (2003). *Adult Attachment Scoring and Classification Systems.* Unpublished manuscript, University of California at Berkeley.

Mesman, J., Stolk, M. N., Van Zeijl, J., Alink, L. R. A., Juffer, F., Bakermans-Kranenburg, M. J., *et al.* (2008). Extending the video-feedback intervention to sensitive discipline: The early prevention of antisocial behavior. In F. Juffer, M. J. Bakermans-Kranenburg, & M. H. van IJzendoorn (eds), *Promoting positive parenting: An attachment-based intervention* (pp. 171–191). New York: Taylor & Francis.

Moss, E., Dubois-Comtois, K., Cyr, C., Tarabulsy, G. M., St-Laurent, D., & Bernier, A. (2011). Efficacy of a home-visiting intervention aimed at improving maternal sensitivity, child attachment, and behavioral outcomes for maltreated children: A randomized control trial. *Development and Psychopathology, 23*(1), 195–210.

Naber, F., Van IJzendoorn, M. H., Deschamps, P., Van Engeland, H., & Bakermans-Kranenburg, M. J. (2010). Intranasal oxytocin increases fathers' observed responsiveness during play with their children: A double-blind within-subject experiment. *Psychoneuroendocrinology, 35*(10), 1583–1586.

Niccols, A. (2008). 'Right from the Start': randomized trial comparing an attachment group intervention to supportive home visiting. *Journal of Child Psychology and Psychiatry, 49*, 754–764.

Out, D., Bakermans-Kranenburg, M. J., & Van IJzendoorn, M. H. (2009). The role of disconnected and extremely insensitive parenting in the development of disorganized attachment: Validation of a new measure. *Attachment & Human Development, 11*(5), 419–443.

Patterson, G. R. (1982). *Coercive family process.* Eugene, OR: Castilia.

Pignotti, M., & Mercer, J. (2007). Holding therapy and dyadic developmental psychotherapy are not supported and acceptable social work interventions: A systematic research synthesis revisited. *Research on Social Work Practice, 17*, 513–519.

Schuengel, C., Bakermans-Kranenburg, M. J., & Van IJzendoorn, M. H. (1999). Frightening maternal behavior linking unresolved loss and disorganized infant attachment. *Journal of Consulting and Clinical Psychology, 67*(1), 54–63.

Scott, S., & O'Connor, T. G. (2012). An experimental test of differential susceptibility to parenting among emotionally-dysregulated children in a randomized controlled trial for oppositional behavior. *Journal of Child Psychology and Psychiatry, 53*(11), 1184–1193.

Sroufe, L. A., Egeland, B., Carlson, E. A., & Collins, W. A. (2005). *The development of the person. The Minnesota study of risk and adaptation from birth to adulthood.* New York: Guilford Press.

Stein, A., Woolley, H., Senior, R., Hertzmann, L., Lovel, M., Lee, J., *et al.* (2006). Treating disturbances in the relationship between mothers with bulimic eating disorders and their infants: A randomized, controlled trial of video feedback. *The American Journal of Psychiatry, 163,* 899–906.

Tarabulsy, G. M., Pascuzzo, K., Moss, E., St-Laurent, D., Bernier, A., Cyr, C., & Dubois-Comtois, K. (2008). Attachment-based intervention for maltreating families. *American Journal of Orthopsychiatry, 78*(3), 322–332.

Thompson, R. A. (2008). Early attachment and later development: Familiar questions, new answers. In J. Cassidy & P. R. Shaver (eds), *Handbook of attachment: Theory, research, and clinical applications* (2nd ed.) (pp. 348–365). New York: The Guilford Press.

Van IJzendoorn, M. H., & Bakermans-Kranenburg, M. J. (2012a). Integrating temperament and attachment: The differential susceptibility paradigm. In M. Zentner & R. L. Shiner (eds), *Handbook of temperament* (pp. 403–424). New York: The Guilford Press.

Van IJzendoorn, M. H., & Bakermans-Kranenburg, M. J. (2012b). A sniff of trust: Meta-analysis of the effects of intranasal oxytocin administration on face recognition, trust to in group, and trust to out-group. *Psychoneuroendocrinology, 37*(3), 438–443.

Van IJzendoorn, M. H., Juffer, F., & Duyvesteyn, M. G. C. (1995). Breaking the intergenerational cycle of insecure attachment: A review of the effects of attachment-based interventions on maternal sensitivity and infant security. *Journal of Child Psychology and Psychiatry, 36,* 225–248.

Van IJzendoorn, M. H., Schuengel, C., & Bakermans-Kranenburg, M. J. (1999). Disorganized attachment in early childhood: Meta-analysis of precursors, concomitants, and sequelae. *Development and Psychopathology, 11,* 225–249.

Van Zeijl, J., Mesman, J., Van IJzendoorn, M. H., Bakermans-Kranenburg, M. J., Juffer, F., Stolk, M. N., *et al.* (2006). Attachment-based intervention for enhancing sensitive discipline in mothers of one- to three-year-old children at risk for externalizing behavior problems. *Journal of Consulting and Clinical Psychology, 74*(6), 994–1005.

Waters, E., & Cummings, E. M. (2000). A secure base from which to explore close relationships. *Child Development, 71,* 164–172.

Webster-Stratton, C., Reid, M. J., & Hammond, M. (2004). Treating children with early-onset conduct problems: Intervention outcomes for parent, child, and teacher training. *Journal of Clinical Child and Adolescent Psychology, 33*(1), 105–124.

Webster-Stratton, C., Rinaldi, J., & Reid, J. M. (2011). Long-term outcomes of Incredible Years parenting program: Predictors of adolescent adjustment. *Child and Adolescent Mental Health, 16*(1), 38–46.

Woolley, H., Hertzmann, L., & Stein, A. (2008). Video-feedback intervention with mothers with postnatal eating disorders and their infants. In F. Juffer, M. J. Bakermans-Kranenburg, & M. H. van IJzendoorn (eds), *Promoting positive parenting: An attachment-based intervention* (pp. 111–138). New York: Taylor & Francis.

Chapter 6

Attachment-focused therapeutic interventions

Daniel Hughes

Introduction

This chapter considers therapeutic work for children and teenagers with moderate to severe emotional or behavioural problems as well as work with the adults responsible for their care.

Following the research and theory of A. Sroufe and colleagues (Sroufe *et al.* 2005) we are proposing that the wide range of symptoms reflective of such moderate to severe problems can be understood as reflecting a lack of organisation – or integration – of the child's emotional, cognitive and behavioural functioning. The success or failure of these developing organisational patterns are highly influenced by the child's attachment organisational patterns. To quote Sroufe *et al.*: 'Central aspects of individual organization originate in the organization of early primary relationships' (Sroufe *et al.* 2005: 40). These children and teens are likely to manifest very significant relational disorders, including deficits in emotional regulation and reflective functioning.

A diagnosis of Developmental Trauma Disorder, proposed by a consortium of Child Trauma Centers (Cook *et al.* 2005), may well capture the depth and breadth of these relational problems that are secondary to intra-familial, interpersonal, trauma. However, this diagnosis was not accepted for inclusion in DSM-5. The diagnosis most commonly used is Reactive Attachment Disorder (RAD).

However, given the uncertainty of diagnostic criteria for RAD (see David Shemmings in Holmes & Farnfield 2014) this chapter focuses more on attachment-focused interventions as they apply to a broad range of children and teens with moderate to severe emotional/behavioural/relational problems, irrespective of the particular diagnosis that they have been given.

The organised nature of attachment patterns can be seen as predictive of the integration of one's psychological functioning, including emotional regulation and reflective functioning, from childhood through adulthood. Sroufe *et al.* (2005) say that attachment is the 'dyadic regulation of emotion'. Fonagy *et al.* (2008) indicate that attachment security predicts reflective functioning and the related ability to mentalise, that is being aware of one's own mind and the mind of others (see also Luyten & Fonagy in Holmes & Farnfield 2014).

A central characteristic of the adult classified as being autonomously attached is being able to engage in a coherent discourse about one's narrative with respect to attachment (Hesse 2008). It is suggested here that attachment-focused interventions that facilitate emotional regulation, reflective functioning, and the development of a coherent autobiographical narrative represent great promise for engaging these children and teens successfully in a secure attachment relationship with their therapist and parents or other primary caregivers.

Attachment-focused interventions

Current interventions for children and their caregivers that rely heavily on attachment theory and research for their theoretical foundation are primarily focused on providing interventions to the parents and, less directly, to the child (see Chapter 5 by Juffer and colleagues).

The well-respected Circle of Security Project (Hoffman *et al.* 2006) focuses on the parent in group settings, first by increasing their ability to read the attachment-related cues of their child and to respond in a sensitive manner. This is followed by assisting the parents in exploring their own attachment history, with the goal of assisting the parents in reflecting on their history so that their functioning progresses toward resolved and/or autonomous attachment styles. Parent-Infant Psychotherapies – more recently expanded to include children to the age of 5 – also focus heavily on the parents' own attachment histories so that they may attain attachment resolution and/or autonomous patterns (Lieberman *et al.* 2005). These psychotherapies may also include assisting the parent in becoming engaged with her infant in reciprocal, engaged, attuned activities that emphasise eye contact, infant-directed speech, within contingent, reciprocal interactions.

Video Interaction Guidance (Kennedy *et al.* 2011) uses principles of attachment and infant inter-subjectivity to provide parents with very clear video feedback regarding their interactions with their child. All of these programmes highlight the need to develop a strong relationship between the therapist and parent – with the emphasis on empathy – in order to facilitate the attachment relationship between the child and his parent.

Finally, there is an attachment-focused treatment in which the therapist engages the child in play activities that are similar to those that occur between parent and toddler, and then facilitates such play between the parent and their child of any age. This method of treatment, known as Theraplay (Booth & Jernberg 2010), stresses here-and-now, highly engaging, nonverbal, attuned interactions to facilitate the attachment relationship.

Attachment-focused goals that focus primarily on individual therapy with the child emerged within both a psychodynamic framework and more general play therapy modalities. These therapies have generally not been focused on the treatment of children and teens with moderate to severe relational problems (but see Chapter 2 by Music).

One therapy that became known as 'attachment therapy' was originated in the 1980s by a psychiatrist, Foster Cline (1995), in Evergreen, Colorado. The children being treated by Cline and colleagues were primarily foster or adopted children who had manifested a history of abuse, neglect, and attachment losses including early years in an orphanage. They manifested severe problems with dysregulation, including aggression, impulsivity, and distractibility and were unwilling or unable to rely on their caregivers for comfort, guidance, or support.

These children and teens were extremely oppositional and defiant and most often refused to become engaged in therapy and were not responsive to either nondirective play or dynamic therapy or cognitive-behavioural interventions. The therapist stressed, both in therapy and in the recommendations given to parents, the need for compliance with the directives of the adult as the foundation for any therapeutic change. While the goal was to facilitate attachment security, the interventions were not based on the understanding of how parents facilitate secure attachments in daily life. Rather, 'obedience training', was the guiding principle, not reciprocal attuned interactions. Also in treatment, the child was often provoked toward expressions of rage toward the therapist and parent, in order to facilitate 'rage reduction' during which the child's rigid defences were reduced and the child turned to the parent for comfort and support. This treatment modality was rightfully criticised by many mental health professionals and others and, to my knowledge, has not been taught or recommended openly by therapists since around the year 2000.

The development of Dyadic Developmental Psychotherapy (DDP) and Attachment-Focused Family Therapy (AFFT)

Throughout the 1980s this author had repeatedly failed to provide effective treatment to children and youth who had experienced abuse, neglect, and multiple losses. I had been trained in play therapy, cognitive-behavioural therapy, and family systems therapy and found these traditional interventions to be quite ineffective in assisting these children to both resolve past traumas and to develop new relational patterns. While living in foster and adoptive homes, these children were often not able to enter into relationships with their caregivers that were characterised by attachment security. They often had great difficulty regulating their emotional states while, at the same time, showing little ability to be aware of, or communicate, their inner lives. They tended to be very avoidant and controlling in therapy and had little motivation to become engaged with the therapist whether the approach was nondirective or directive, dynamic or cognitive, within individual or family settings. At the same time they tended to be very resistant to behavioural management approaches based on social learning theory within the home, in spite of motivated and competent foster or adoptive parents. While resisting parental guidance and discipline they also avoided parental efforts to provide them with comfort and support in the face of their developmental challenges and vulnerabilities.

As the 1990s began this author saw these children as manifesting a variety of psychological patterns that were consistent with attachment disorganisation and, to a lesser extent, avoidant or ambivalent attachment patterns. I then began to develop therapeutic interventions that were consistent with attachment theory and research. I went to Colorado to study Dr Cline's programme. I saw the value in taking a more directive stance with children who were so avoidant and controlling, though I did not believe that the provocative and intrusive quality of their interventions was compatible with providing the child with a sense of psychological safety. I saw the value in actively involving the foster and adoptive parents, not to confront the child, but rather to convey safety, commitment, and support for the child when he was asked to explore his trauma, terror, and shame. I saw the value in providing touch and nurturing holding for the child, but not the mandated and provocative holding practised by Dr Cline and colleagues. Initially I would hold the child when he was in distress, as this seemed to be easier for him than being held by his caregiver.

I then realised that this was not as productive as taking a slower pace and facilitating the child's readiness to initiate or be receptive to the comfort and closeness of parental hugs and support. In going slower, I focused more on developing the overall relational patterns between parent and child, rather than taking a more narrow attachment perspective of providing safety. By 1998, touch – by parent or therapist – to encourage a sense of safety, became a secondary intervention, with the central therapeutic activity and goal being to facilitate and maintain a therapeutic dialogue that was based on attuned, reciprocal, moment-to-moment, nonverbal and verbal interactions. I was greatly guided by the theory and research of Colwyn Trevarthen (2001) and Daniel Stern (1985).

Over the past 15 years, a consistent therapeutic model has emerged for children with serious psychological problems secondary to trauma and attachment problems. This became known as Dyadic Developmental Psychotherapy (DDP) (Hughes 2004, 2006). As this treatment model became applied to general populations it was called Attachment-Focused Family Therapy (Hughes 2007, 2009, 2011). This chapter focuses only on DDP – the application of this treatment to children and teens with moderate to severe emotional and behavioural problems and those adults responsible for their care.

Characteristics of DDP

DDP involves developing and maintaining a reciprocal, dyadic, relationship where both safety and exploration are valued, with safety preceding exploration and being continuously re-established whenever exploration generates fear or shame. The relational quality of safety and exploration are emphasised, with dysregulating emotions being co-regulated by the therapist (or the therapist and parent when a child is in distress) and the experience of past and present events being co-created into a coherent narrative. Thus, DDP adheres to 'the wider view of attachment' which focuses on 'psychological security' and includes both 'security of attachment and security of exploration' (Grossman et al. 2008: 873).

Attachment theory has expanded from the understanding of the infant and his inherent need for safety to the understanding of development over the entire life span and the human being's inherent need for a coherent autobiographical narrative. In a similar manner, DDP focuses on the entire autobiographical narrative where all experiences are valued, understood, explored, and accepted.

The therapeutic relationship develops within the context of the child's entire narrative, with the therapist and foster carer or adoptive parent adding their inter-subjective presence to the child's efforts to make sense of all of the events of his life. From this 'wide-angle' focus, the child is likely to experience sufficient safety to remain fully engaged in the immediate relationships while focusing more narrowly on specific traumatic events. The therapist and caregiver's inter-subjective presence enables the child to co-regulate the stressful emotions associated with these events, while co-creating new meanings of the events. The therapist and caregiver attend to the event and experience it with their reflective functioning, enabling the child to also be reflective while experiencing the event again, and so increase his mentalising abilities while integrating his experience of the event into his narrative.

Inter-subjectivity

Inter-subjectivity refers to a primary source of learning about self, other, events and objects of the world (Trevarthen 2001). The infant develops his 'inner working model' of self, other, and the larger world, primarily through joining his attachment figures in their experience of him and the world. As the attachment figures experience and express nonverbally – in their eyes, face, voice, and bodily gestures as they interact with him – their joy, delight, interest, and love, the infant experiences himself as being joyful, delightful, interesting, and lovable. If the attachment figure conveys safety in the presence of an object – a dog or a stranger – or an event – a loud noise or sudden movement – then the child is likely to experience safety. As the attachment figure begins to explore the meaning of that object or event, the child explores it with him. For infants these inter-subjective communications are nonverbal. Their nonverbal component remains central in such communications within a safe relationship throughout life. When we inhibit the nonverbal expression of the experience, the other is much less likely to experience our experience and so the inter-subjective component is reduced and/or distorted.

Inter-subjectivity in therapy

Similarly, in therapy, as the therapist and caregiver convey safety – inter-subjectively – while exploring a past traumatic event of the child, the child is likely to be able to remain safe while attending to that event. Then as the therapist and caregiver convey their experiential meanings of that event – inter-subjectively – the child is likely to attend to that event, experiencing it again within the light of the therapist and caregiver's experience of it. It is the therapist and caregiver's nonverbal expressions – contingent with the child's present experiences or his memories of past events – that convey their inter-subjective experience of that event within the child's narrative. The therapist becomes an attachment figure alongside the caregiver.

When the therapist remains in an ambiguous, or neutral stance, the child is less able to be influenced by the therapist's inter-subjective experience of both himself and the events of his life. When children have had a lack of positive inter-subjective experiences with attachment figures associated with safety, then it seems reasonable for the therapist to clearly express the positive impact that the child is having on him in order to broaden his self-identity to include the capacity to have a positive influence on a caring person (Gelso 2011). The therapist's inter-subjective experience of the child's past traumatic events will enable the child to integrate these events into his narrative with new meanings, without the associated states of emotional terror and shameful meanings that had been embedded into those events by the perpetrator of the abuse. The therapist's inter-subjective meaning of the past event serves as a balance to the meaning given by the perpetrator and enables the child to safely experience it anew.

This open and engaged therapeutic relational stance is the same stance characteristic of secure attachment interactions as well as the most influential inter-subjective experiences of exploration and learning. It involves the ongoing activation of the ventral vagal neurological circuit that has been explored in such detail by Stephen Porges (2011).

According to Porges' polyvagal theory and associated research findings, the ventral vagal circuit is activated when the infant or child is feeling safe. It enables the social engagement system in the brain to become active and to optimise the young child's social and emotional learning. Under threat, the ventral vagal system becomes inactive and the dorsal vagal circuit is activated. The dorsal vagal system is the defensive system that focuses on the protection of the self, not on learning about the environment. Thus, the activation of the ventral vagal circuit and social engagement system requires the sense of safety and enables safety to be maintained (through the open and engaged stance of the attachment figure), while the child explores and learns about the world (either the world of the present or the world represented in memories of the past), while integrating the inter-subjective experiences of the attachment figure.

In DDP this open and engaged inter-subjective therapeutic stance is facilitated through the therapist maintaining an attitude that is characterised by playfulness, acceptance, curiosity, and empathy (PACE). These relational features are evident in the attuned interactions between parent and infant and so might be seen as highly suitable for facilitating attachment security for neglected and abused children who had insufficient quality and quantity of such experiences during their infancy.

Playfulness conveys a light optimism and confidence in the dialogue and general nonverbal interactions. It indicates an enjoyment and acceptance of the other and his past and present experiences. Playfulness does not refer to telling jokes or distracting someone from painful experiences or memories. Rather, it represents a light emotional closeness that shows acceptance, not evaluation, of the other person.

Acceptance is a central means of activating the ventral vagal circuit and generating a sense of safety and closeness. The inner life of the other – any thoughts, feelings, intentions, wishes, memories, perceptions, values, beliefs – is met with acceptance, though certain behaviours will be evaluated and may elicit consequences. Acceptance creates the sense of safety that is necessary to give expression to one's inner life and to explore it openly and so understand it and integrate it into the autobiographical narrative. For example, if a teenager who had been sexually abused, behaves sexually toward a child, the behaviour is evaluated as not being 'acceptable' and restrictions and supervision follows to make such behaviour very difficult or impossible to engage in. However, if the teenager is to be able to openly explore it in therapy, he needs to feel safe in knowing that the thoughts, feelings, wishes, and intentions that were associated with that behaviour, are themselves accepted. The therapist will be helping the teenager to focus on those features of his inner life in order to make sense of them without judgement, understand their probable connection to his own history, and develop new meanings of the behaviour. These new meanings greatly increase the likelihood that those behaviours will be less likely to have a purpose in the child's life.

Curiosity involves an open stance of not-knowing about the inner life of the other. It also conveys a fascination with, a desire to understand, without judgement, whatever is in the mind and heart of the other person. Such open, non-judgemental curiosity from the therapist conveys a sense of safety for the child necessary for him to begin to explore and share his inner life. This is not a passive stance where the therapist waits for the child to give expression to his inner life. Rather, the therapist takes an active, inter-subjective stance, openly wondering about possible thoughts, feelings, wishes, memories, perceptions, intentions, all the while not judging anything that is being explored. Over time, the child may well increase his sense of curiosity toward himself, increasing his tolerance for ambiguity and enabling the development of his reflective functioning and mentalisation.

Children who have been abused and neglected have little curiosity about their mind and often do not have the words necessary to think about or communicate their experiences about the events of their past as well as their current experiences (Cicchetti *et al.* 1995). Communicating with these children often elicits the response of 'I don't know'. Very often this response is truthful. For that reason, engaging in dialogue with these children about their experiences tends to be difficult, if not impossible, unless the therapist is willing and able to take the lead in assisting the child in 'finding the words' that describe his experiences. These treatment interventions will be discussed shortly.

Empathy conveys a sense to the child that the therapist will be with him when he addresses and explores painful, frightening, or shameful events from the past. Empathy functions to facilitate attachment security, encouraging the child to rely on his attachment figures to face the difficult moments of his life. With empathy, the therapist is able to co-regulate intense negative emotions that may be associated with past traumas. As these emotions remain regulated the child is then able to explore the events, and co-create new meanings, joining with the experiences of the attachment figures. The message of empathy is much like the message of attachment figures who generate security: 'I will not abandon you when you need me the most.'

Affective-Reflective (A-R) Dialogue

Therapeutic conversation, known as Affective-Reflective (A-R) Dialogue is characterised by nonverbal affective expressions involving modulated, rhythmic, voice prosody, clear facial expressions, gestures, movement, posture, rather than the monotone of a lecture or rational discussion. Within this 'story-telling' conversational stance, the therapist openly reflects with the child on his autobiographical narrative, facilitating its increasing depth and coherence.

The therapist is responsible for maintaining the flow and momentum and coherence of the A-R Dialogue, uncovering, developing, co-creating the experience of events. The therapist follows the child and parent's lead in the evolution of the dialogue and narrative, while leading the child or parent into areas that are being avoided, and then following the client's response to those leads. This reciprocal nature is characteristic of all intimate relationships. It is neither a directive stance nor a nondirective stance. Any initiative of the therapist has only one step. The next step in the dialogue is the child's and the child's response which determines the therapist's following step. This communicates to the child that his response has an impact on the therapist. It is a true reciprocal dialogue where the two individuals are having an influence on each other. It is not a one-directional lecture.

DDP: a two-phased treatment

Phase One

The treatment of the child with moderate to severe emotional/behavioural problems secondary to intra-familial trauma and attachment disruptions and disorganisation begins with the therapist meeting with the parents without the child. This first phase is necessary for a number of reasons:

- The parent needs to experience safety within her relationship with the therapist if she is to provide safety for her child during the treatment session. The parent needs to experience the therapist's unconditional acceptance of her, if she is going to remain open and engaged with the therapist who is addressing the parent's behaviours that the therapist thinks might be hurting the child's ability to form a secure attachment with the parent.
- The therapist needs to explore the parent's attachment history to determine if the parent's attachment pattern is resolved and autonomous since these

classifications are related to the parent's ability to facilitate attachment security. If the parent manifests an unresolved pattern then it might be necessary for the parent to engage in his own psychological treatment before beginning joint sessions with his child.

- The therapist needs to explore the parent's parenting history with this particular child in order to determine the nature of the past and present parent–child relationship, including the nature of conflict resolution and repair, communication, comfort and support, discipline, and shared activities.
- The therapist needs to determine the strength of the parent's commitment to the child in order to ensure that it is sufficient to manage the stress of the treatment over a period of time that is necessary to effect change.
- The therapist needs to make the parent aware of the nature of the treatment in order to ensure that the parent is open to the basic treatment premises and interventions. In particular, the parent needs to understand the necessity of co-regulating the child's emotional states and co-creating the past and present meanings of his symptoms.
- If the therapist is not successful in facilitating the parent's psychological safety in the session and believes that the child will not be safe in joint sessions with the parent, the therapist may recommend that the parent pursues treatment for themselves prior to and/or during the course of the joint sessions with the child. A second therapist is likely to be necessary to provide such treatment if it is of any duration.

When the therapist meets with the parent without the child, the therapeutic relationship contains the same features that will be present during the joint sessions. A-R Dialogue, with inter-subjective sharing and PACE, generates psychological safety for the parent and prepares them for maintaining a similar way of engagement when their child is present.

Phase Two

Once the alliance with the parent is established and the parent and therapist agree on the course of the treatment, they are ready to begin the joint sessions with the child. Throughout the treatment, the therapist and parent continuously monitor and ensure that the child is experiencing psychological safety as she explores aspects of her past and present, including those that might generate negative emotions such as anxiety and shame. This is done by communicating PACE (in this instance, acceptance, curiosity, and empathy but not likely playfulness) whenever the child may experience any distress of the discourse.

Empathy is the primary communication, helping the child to experience that the parent is experiencing the child's distress with him, accepting the events that may precipitate the distress, and then exploring the factors that are eliciting the distress. The therapist's nonjudgemental curiosity helps the child to know that understanding and expressing whatever thoughts and feelings are emerging is safe. The child

– and his inner life – are never judged. Therapy is about understanding the child's experience and making sense of it and its origins, not judging the child, fixing him, nor giving him a lecture and consequence. Through such nonjudgemental understanding, the child is much more able to face his experience, understand it in a way that reduces his sense of shame, and develop a sense of safety that his parents, too, understand his experience and continue to love him and be committed to him.

The process of attachment-focused treatment attends continuously to assisting the child in regulating any emotions that are emerging in the discourse. This facilitates both the ability to explore and integrate traumatic and shame-inducing events but also in learning to be more able to regulate intense emotional states. Co-regulation of emotion is central – and must precede – the developing ability to auto-regulate emotional states.

The therapist and parent do so through remaining regulated themselves if the child begins to dysregulate. Their regulation enables the child to feel safe and confident in his and their ability to manage any emerging emotional states. They also co-regulate the child's emotional state by matching the child's affective, nonverbal expression of his emotional state without feeling the emotion themselves. Dan Stern (1985) defines this as 'attunement' and it is a central means by which parents facilitate the development of their child's ability to regulate their emerging emotional states. Within attuned states, the therapist and parent match the rhythm and intensity (as well as beat, duration, contour, and shape according to Stern) of the child's bodily expressions (voice, facial expressions, gestures and movements) of his underlying emotion, showing that the emotions are understood (with empathy) and are able to be managed.

It cannot simply be assumed that the therapist and caregiver will remain regulated when the child experiences distress over the memory of traumatic events. The therapist is continuously aware of the caregiver's psychological state to ensure that he or she is able to be emotionally strong for the child. Any doubt requires that the therapist meet with the caregiver alone and address any areas of distress that she or he is experiencing. The same holds true for the therapist. The therapist must have ongoing supervision to ensure that the therapist is able to remain fully engaged and regulated when the child is exploring past traumatic events.

The process of DDP also greatly assists the child in making sense of the overwhelming traumatic and shame-inducing events of his life. The therapist's nonjudgemental curiosity enables the child to begin to safely explore these events, while being open to their underlying meanings. The therapist's – and parent's – reflective functioning enables the child to reflect on these events as well. The child begins to develop a sense of what he thinks about them, what they mean in light of his history and symptoms, and what implications they have regarding his future. The child experiences the therapist and parent's experience of those events and through this inter-subjective experience is able to develop – with their active minds interwoven with his – new meanings of those events. The therapist and parent's inter-subjective experience serves as a balance to the perpetrator's experience of those events and so frees the child to begin to experience them anew, rather than assuming that the perpetrator's experience represents objective reality. As this happens again and again in treatment, the child is learning how to reflect himself and so develop his mentalising abilities which are so important for his developing mental health.

As was mentioned earlier, the therapist needs to facilitate the child's ability to develop the words to describe and communicate his inner life. To ask the child to use his words or giving him time to tell his story often ends in failure because the child does not have the ability to associate words with the traumatic, confusing, or shame-inducing interpersonal events of his past. His inner life was not often seen, recognised or valued by his attachment figures and he was not given an adult's mind to use to develop his own mind. In therapy the therapist can greatly facilitate this process by – with the attitude of PACE – speaking for the child to the parent or therapist or speaking about the child to the parent or another person (or even a stuffed animal or puppet).

When the therapist speaks for the child he does so with the child's permission and with the acknowledgement that he is only guessing what a child might be thinking or feeling and so the child is encouraged to correct the therapist whenever the guess is seen as being 'wrong' by the child. The therapist never disagrees with the child. The therapist also takes the child's nonverbal response to his guesses as valid, so that if the child demonstrates confusion nonverbally over the therapist's guess, the therapist then suggests that his guess might be wrong, while asking for clarity regarding the child's response. This process resembles 'doubling', a technique used in psychodrama (see Holmes 1992).

When speaking for the child, the therapist begins tentatively:

> I wonder if you sometimes think: 'I really don't like having to think about this stuff.'

or

> I really have a hard time thinking about what my dad did. I sometimes think that I'm being selfish when I get mad about it.

Or the therapist guesses what the child might want to say to the parent:

> I wonder if you sometimes want to say to your mom: 'Mom, sometimes when you say "no" to me, I think that you say it because you really don't care what I want. That what I want is not important to you. And then I get really mad at you. It even seems that you don't like me! And then I don't like you!'

When the therapist speaks about the child to the parent, the child – relieved from the need to respond or even to listen – will often listen in a more open and engaged way to what the therapist is saying. The child hears the therapist's words with less defensiveness and more open curiosity about what the therapist thinks. Often, the child remembers what the therapist says much more fully and deeply, allowing the therapist's thoughts to influence the development of his own. For example, the therapist might say to the parent, in the child's presence, rather than to the child:

> When your son has a hard time when you are correcting him or when we dis-
> cuss some of his challenges in therapy, I really can understand why. He starts
> to have doubts, wondering if you really care for him, wondering if you are
> so angry with what he did that you might give up on him, wondering if there
> is any hope that the problem can work itself out. Your son really cares about
> these things, even when he might just show his anger or says that it's not
> important to him. He tries, I know he does, even if it seems that he isn't trying.
> He has had a hard life and looking at these things is very hard. We need to be
> patient, and understand why he might give us a hard time sometimes.

Such words, when expressed with the open and engaged voice prosody characteristic of PACE – are often heard, felt, and integrated by the child in a way that
would not occur if the therapist spoke directly to the child.

In summary, the attachment-focused interventions proposed represent both
the process and content of treatment. DDP establishes a therapeutic relationship
between the therapist and both the parent and child where both are able to remain
open and engaged in their relationship with each other and the therapist in order
to broaden and deepen their relationship. At the same time, they explore their conflicts and stress as well as the child's shame and traumas in a manner that leads to
their co-regulation of associated emotions and co-creation of new meanings. The
therapist is an attachment figure to both parent and child, while at the same time
being a midwife to facilitate the child's attachment to his parents.

References

Booth, P. & Jernberg, A. (2010). *Theraplay: Helping parents and children build better relationships through attachment-focused play*. San Francisco: John Wiley.

Cicchetti, D., Toth, S., & Lynch, M. (1995). Bowlby's dream comes full circle: The application of attachment theory to risk and psychopathology. *Advances in Clinical Child Psychology*, 17, 1–75.

Cline, F. (1995). *Conscienceless acts, societal mayhem: Uncontrollable, unreachable youth in today's desensitized world*. Golden, CO: Love & Logic Press.

Cook, A., Spinazzola, J., Ford, J., Lanktree, C., Blaustein, M., Cloitre, M., *et al.* (2005). Complex trauma in children and adolescents. *Psychiatric Annals*, 35(5), 390–398.

Fonagy, P., Gergely, G., & Target, M. (2008). Psychoanalytic constructs and attachment theory and research. In J. Cassidy & P.R. Shaver (eds) *Handbook of attachment (2nd ed.)*. New York: Guilford Press, pp. 783–810.

Gelso, C.J. (2011). *The real relationship in psychotherapy: The hidden foundation of change*. Washington, DC: American Psychological Association.

Grossmann, K., Grossmann, K.E., Kindler, H., & Zimmermann, P. (2008). A wider view of attachment and exploration: The influence of mothers and fathers on the development of psychological security from infancy to young adulthood. In J. Cassidy & P.R. Shaver (eds) *Handbook of attachment (2nd ed.)*. New York: Guilford Press, pp. 857–879.

Hesse, E. (2008). The adult attachment interview: Protocol, method of analysis, and empirical studies. In J. Cassidy & P.R. Shaver (eds) *Handbook of attachment (2nd ed.)*. New York: Guilford Press, pp. 552–598.

Hoffman, K.T., Marvin, R.S., Cooper, G., & Powell, B. (2006). Changing toddlers' and preschoolers'attachment classifications: The Circle of Security intervention. *Journal of Consulting and Clinical Psychology*, 74, 1017–1026.

Holmes, P. (1992) *The inner world outside: Object relations theory and psychodrama*. London and New York: Tavistock/Routledge.

Holmes, P. & Farnfield, S. (eds) (2014). *The Routledge handbook of attachment: Theory*. London and New York: Routledge.

Hughes, D. (2004). An attachment-based treatment of maltreated children and young people. *Attachment & Human Development*, 6, 263–278.

Hughes, D. (2006). *Building the bonds of attachment (2nd ed.)* Northvale, NJ: Jason Aronson.

Hughes, D. (2007). *Attachment-focused family therapy*. New York: W. W. Norton.

Hughes, D. (2009). *Attachment-focused parenting*. New York: W. W. Norton.

Hughes, D. (2011). *Attachment-focused family therapy workbook*. New York: W. W. Norton.

Kennedy, H., Landor, M., & Todd, L. (2011). *Video Interaction Guidance: A relationship based intervention to promote attunement, empathy, and well-being*. London: Jessica Kingsley.

Lieberman, A.F., Van Horn, P., & Ippen, C.G. (2005). Toward evidence-based treatment: Child–Parent Psychotherapy with preschoolers exposed to marital violence. *Journal of the American Academy of Child and Adolescent Psychiatry*, 44, 1241–1248.

Porges, S.W. (2011). *The polyvagal theory: Neurophysiological foundations of emotions, attachment, communication, self-regulation*. New York: W. W. Norton.

Siegel, D.J. (2012). *The developing mind: How relationships and the brain interact to shape who we are (2nd ed.)*. New York: Guilford Press.

Sroufe, L.A., Egeland, B., Carlson, E., & Collins, W.A. (2005). *The development of the person*. New York: Guilford Press.

Stern, D. (1985). *The interpersonal world of the infant*. New York: Basic Books.

Trevarthen, C. (2001). Intrinsic motives for companionship in understanding: Their origin, development, and significance for infant mental health. *Infant Mental Health Journal*, 22, 95–131.

Chapter 7

Clinical implications of attachment in immigrant communities

Elaine Arnold

An understanding of the nature and dynamics of attachment *informs* rather than *defines* intervention and clinical thinking.

(Slade 1999: 577)

Introduction

This chapter focuses on the clinical implications for treatment in individuals who have experienced disruptions of their attachments in childhood or have suffered other traumas and losses. Such problems are not uncommon in communities where families have travelled abroad either as economic migrants or because of war and strife in their home countries (see Avigad & Pooley 2002).

Jafar Kareem, the founder of Nafsiyat the Inter-Cultural Therapy Centre in London, expressed the view that 'the concept of loss of a very early love object and subsequent maneuvers to cope with such loss constitute, according to some, the basis for many later emotional traumas' (Kareem 1992/2000: 34). Attachment theory has always considered the processes of loss and trauma in individuals and in communities. Indeed John Bowlby was commissioned by the World Health Organization in 1949 to study and report on the needs of children left homeless at the end of the Second World War in 1945. This gave him the opportunity to research in the United Kingdom and in France, the Netherlands, Sweden, Switzerland and the United States of America. He studied the literature and interviewed professionals who worked in child care and child guidance. Bowlby observed that in these various cultural groups there was a high degree of agreement regarding the principles underlying the mental health of the children and the practices that safeguarded this.

His report for the World Health Organization 'Maternal Care and Mental Health' (1952) was abridged and entitled *Child Care and the Growth of Love* (1953) and made available to the general public. The book became a best seller and was translated into ten different languages. According to Jeremy Holmes (1993: 38) the change of title of the book was a significant shift since, rather than confining itself to the mental health of the child, it gave a universal message about mothers and children. Bowlby stated that 'what is essential for mental health, the infant and young child should experience a warm, intimate and continuous relationship with his mother (or permanent mother-substitute) in which both find satisfaction and enjoyment' (Bowlby 1952: 11). It should be noted that although Bowlby held strong views of the importance of the mother caring for the young child he did not rule out the possibility of someone other than mother caring for the child.

This chapter describes clinical work in which those involved have, for different reasons, experienced a disruption or a failure of these ideal experiences for an infant. Such experiences are of course all too common not only during national crises such as occur in war, but also at other times, and so to this extent they are not dependent on cultures. However, such experiences occur more frequently in some communities than in others.

Issues of race and culture were considered in research into attachment when Mary Ainsworth, one of John Bowlby's most senior collaborators, undertook some of her original studies on the Ganda tribe in Uganda (Ainsworth 1963). Race and culture have been considered further in many other studies (see, for example, reviews by Van IJzendoorn and Kroonenburg 1988 and Reebye *et al.* 1999).

On Ainsworth's return to the United States of America, building on her observations in Uganda, she observed children aged 12 months to 20 months with their mothers at home and subsequently in a university laboratory play room in Baltimore. She stated: 'The laboratory procedure was designed to capture the balance of attachment and exploratory behaviour under conditions of increasing, though moderate stress' and then to observe the child's behaviour on reunion (Ainsworth *et al.* 1978). She called this procedure 'the Strange Situation' (SSP) and it remains one of the standard assessments of attachment (discussed in Farnfield and Holmes 2014), and is considered as 'the cornerstone' of the current understanding of infant–mother attachment behaviours. Ainsworth observed that the attachment relationships between mothers and children from the two different backgrounds of race and culture were similar, and she recognised difference in some patterns of *attachment behaviour*. For example, in the Ganda sample, when there was a secure attachment between mothers and children before the separation, upon reunion the children clapped their hands while the American children hugged and kissed their mothers (Reebye *et al.* 1999).

Attachment, separation, and loss

These are the main titles of Bowlby's three linked books on the subject of attachment (Bowlby 1969, 1973, 1980).

Attachment

In *Attachment and Loss Volume 1: Attachment*, Bowlby described the emergence of attachment behaviour in early childhood and stressed that if the principal figure is absent, another in the hierarchy of the attachment relationships can be a substitute (Bowlby 1969/1982: 321). While this process occurs in all cultures, the smooth progress to the development of secure attachments may be more disrupted in some communities than in others. He also asserted that

> children tend unwittingly to identify with parents and therefore adopt when they become parents, the same patterns of behaviour that they themselves have experienced during their own childhood. Patterns of interaction are transmitted more or less faithfully from one generation to the next.
>
> (Bowlby 1969/1982: 323)

Separation

In *Attachment and Loss Volume 2: Separation, Anxiety and Anger* (1973) he proposed the idea that children who are confident of the consistent availability of the attachment figure will be less prone to chronic fear, and the converse for children who are not confident that the attachment figure will be available. This confidence is acquired slowly through childhood and adolescence so that the expectations regarding the responsiveness of attachment figures are reflections of the actual experiences the child has with their parents and tend to persist at the level of the unconscious throughout life (Bowlby 1973: 235). These seem to be universal features in human development.

Loss

In his third volume of the trilogy, *Attachment and Loss Volume 3: Sadness and Depression* (1980), Bowlby stated that he believed that the cause of unhappiness, psychiatric illnesses and delinquency could be attributed to loss and that in working clinically with individuals, this was often missed. He expressed the view that 'the loss of a loved person is one of the most intensely painful experiences any human can suffer' (Bowlby 1980: 7), and advocated that the individual needs help to mourn the loss.

Too often this is unrecognised when individuals, whether of the indigenous population or migrants, asylum seekers or refugees, who have been traumatised, are assessed by therapists. An individual may be labelled as uncooperative when he/she is unable to respond to the interviewer but, because of fear, they might be more accurately described as 'frozen'. The behaviour of such individuals might be classified in a fourth category of insecure attachment, disorganized/disoriented (Main and Solomon 1986), consequent upon his/her early experiences of having been subjected to abuse – physical, emotional, sexual – or when the mother or primary carer themselves showed frightened or fearful behaviour when the child signalled the desire for nurture and comfort. According to George, Kaplan and Main (1985/1996) if an Adult Attachment Interview (AAI) is conducted with these carers, they often recall separation, loss or traumatic violence in their child-hood which has remained with them and is still unprocessed so it continues to have an impact on their lives and on their capacity to parent.

Pressures on the care of children in urban communities

In most cultures the care and protection of the young is undertaken by the mother or mother-substitute, with or without the support of fathers, and with other mem-bers of the extended family, or friends of the family; but specific practices dif-fer among peoples with different cultural norms. Regardless of the practices the aim is to protect and safeguard the health and survival of members of the family. Strong and supportive families within communities where individuals feel a sense of belonging are conducive to good mental health.

In some urban areas in England, up to 80 per cent of the population come from communities in which previous generations have suffered displacement from their familiar environments to which they had been attached. This is particularly true of migrants who came to Britain and who settled in the areas where employ-ment was to be found. According to Marris: 'the calculations of economic devel-opment seldom take account of the psychological cost of this vast displacement. And these costs will come to haunt us as alienation, rage, humiliation, violence – all the ways that frustrated attachment seeks compensation and revenge' (Mar-ris 2008: 30).

The counsellor/therapist working in Greater London, which contains only one eighth of the British population but of which nearly half are from minority groups (Owen 2002–3), will find a population with very diverse cultures, some members of which will have suffered personal and social upheaval.

Marci Green (2008) observes that most research on attachment is on the individ-ual's experiences of attachment separation and loss and admonishes us to widen our vision to the public domain. She argues that 'attachment experiences matter for both the health of individuals and the quality of the human community within and across generations' (Green 2008: xv).

I will now describe some of my clinical work structured around Bowlby's three book titles: Attachment, Separation, and Loss.

Attachment

An inner London mothers' group

One neighbourhood community centre in a London Borough, committed to pro-viding excellent service for families, engaged in outreach work, and encouraged young mothers to use the facilities provided at the centre and organised various courses for them. It is in this context that I was invited to work with a group of six mothers.

There were five mothers, four from ethnic minority groups – Jamaica, Ghana, India, Greece – and one English. They were in the age group 25–30 and of lower socioeconomic backgrounds. Their children were aged from one year to just over two.

I introduced them to attachment theory as part of a course on Parents' and Young Children's Relationships. The trainees viewed video tapes of the Strange Situation procedure compiled by Bowlby's son, Richard Bowlby, and listened to the explanations of the classifications of the attachment patterns. We then discussed the children's reactions to being left. The mothers were unanimous in their disagreement with the classification of the SSP rated as secure. Their views were that the child's crying and trying to follow mother (protest) and not settling with the stranger indicated that the child was 'too tied' to mother. They argued that since most mothers needed to go out to work and to leave their children with carers, either at home or in the nursery, children needed to learn to be independent. The children who did not protest when mothers left were considered to be more accepting even though they appeared 'sad'.

It seemed that the trainees thought that children of that age were capable of assessing their mothers' needs and were on good behaviour in order to please them.

We discussed the concept of mother being 'a secure base' to which the child could return when stressed and the trainees were asked to observe the reunions more closely. They acknowledged that the children's behaviour in seeking comfort from the mother or not acknowledging mother on reunion, and mother responding to the child's discomfort, gave them some insight about how mother and child reacted to each other before they were separated. If the child was used to being comforted by mother when in distress, she went to her and mother was able to calm her, while the child who was uncertain of mother's reaction did not seek comfort from a mother who did not attempt to give any. This had been missed on the first viewing of the procedure.

The trainees expressed the view that the mother of the child who did not cry or try to follow her when she left the room, and who sat looking dejected, and whose pattern of attachment was classified as 'insecure', needed to be more 'active' in engaging the child who seemed unsure of whether to seek comfort and was unable to resume her play. The mothers recalled how they felt when they left their children in the nursery, and how their children responded to being left and appreciated that the nursery allowed them to stay with the children until they were settled and engaged in play.

At the end of the course, the mothers had gained an understanding of the concepts of attachment and of the Strange Situation and were more accepting of the classifications in the video. This allowed them to reflect on their own early experiences and conclude that they realised how early childhood experiences remained in one's mind into adulthood, and how present feelings and behaviour were influenced by these experiences.

Some of those who had experienced their primary carers as 'matter of fact' (that is, 'dismissive'), and not demonstrative with hugs and kisses, described this pattern of behaviour as common within families of their countries of origin so that it could be considered as cultural. Others attributed this to the fact that mothers who worked were tired and did not have much time to devote to 'cuddling', but their behaviour could not always be interpreted in terms that their children were not loved. Those from the Caribbean recalled that mothers and others in the extended family paid great attention to grooming children, especially with plaiting and braiding the hair and massaging the skin with oil and telling the children how pretty they looked. Nevertheless, it was considered necessary that the children learnt from an early age to be independent of others. They were not encouraged to show their emotions if hurt or sad by crying. This was particularly stressed with boys.

This discussion prompted the mothers to reflect on the attachment behaviour patterns of their mothers and their own behaviour towards their children, and they realised that they were repeating the pattern set by their mothers/carers and began to understand what was meant by intergenerational transmission of attachment patterns.

The mothers felt themselves enabled to respond to the emotional needs of their children more effectively and, after learning the developmental stages of the child, said they would be able to observe these in their child/children as they matured and would be able to respond to them appropriately. The concept of mother as a secure base for the young child was accepted and the mothers agreed that they were helped in beginning to understand how important it was to communicate with their children, to tell them goodbye when they left and reassure them that they would return, and so begin to meet the emotional needs of their children more effectively.

The staff commented that the mothers seemed calmer and spoke to the children more than previously, and the children settled to play more quickly when they arrived at the centre.

Five of the women in the above group had been left by their parents as young children in their countries of origin and were from different cultural backgrounds. They had been cared for by grandmothers from whom they did not want to be separated to come to Britain to join parents who had preceded them. The reunions with mothers were painful, and sometimes they met siblings whom they thought were loved and preferred by their mothers/parents. These life events had markedly impacted on their attachment styles and thus on the care of their children.

Separation

The impact of early separation is not a new phenomenon but may have been more marked in Britain as during the last few decades it has become more multiracial and multicultural. Following the destruction of the country and the loss of many people during the Second World War (1939–45) there was an influx of migrants from the Caribbean, at the invitation of the government, to assist in rebuilding 'the mother country'. Others came from the Asian and African continents and former British colonies, often following political upheaval or civil wars in those countries. More recently, with the establishment of the European Union which allows free movement of people from the various European member states, there has been an increase of migrants, who have added to the demographic change in British society, with families of three and four generations.

Some of the original migrants, including many from the Caribbean, settled for longer than they had planned, mainly due to a lack of economic success in this country. They then sent for their children whom they had left with extended families in their countries of origin. However, they often became parents to children born in this country. This had implications for attachments within the families. The reunited children had not been helped to grieve and mourn the loss of their carers and country left behind and felt marginal to their new families after having been at the centre of the extended family now so far away and with no hope of seeing them again. Their perceptions of the close relationship between their mothers and the younger children who had not been separated for long periods of time, were that they were preferred and loved and they were not. The children born in England who had not been prepared for the newcomer felt that their territory had been invaded by a stranger. When the younger children had been prepared for their older siblings' arrival they were more able to accept the reunited children (Robertson 1977, now Arnold).

It is not uncommon for those children, who felt no sense of belonging in their new families when they became adults, to be unable to express their anger and the distress experienced in their early childhood. Frequently their emotional distress manifests itself in physical symptoms. Attachment theory provides a theoretical basis for understanding their difficulties and argues for its inclusion in the training of all professionals involved in the helping professions.

Some parents who left young children in the care of extended family members for long periods of time before being reunited with them, have had disappointing reunions as they were virtual strangers and unable to communicate with each other. Mothers were surprised to find that the children had become attached to their carers in their country of origin, the loss of whom they mourned silently. The birth parents and their children were unable to establish relationships with each other. The reunited children suffered the discontinuities of all that was familiar to them and while some have adapted to living in the new environment, there is little doubt that history has left its own psychological impact on individuals and the communities which have developed within the host country (Arnold 2012).

Many of the younger members of the migrant groups who were born in Britain and reared by parents to whom they are attached have adapted to the cultural norms of the host country. Even when parents and grandparents maintain links with their homelands some of these children consider that they would feel like strangers if they visited their homeland and consider themselves British (conversations with young people, 2012) but do not have a sense of belonging, especially when they suffer racial discrimination from the various sections of British society, school, church, employers, the police, the justice system. Nevertheless, some of these individuals have put down roots and formed stable relations, families and work patterns.

The following case study demonstrates the long-lasting nature of the traumatic effects of broken attachments through separation.

Tina – separated from and then deserted by her mother

Tina, a 45-year-old woman of Afro-Caribbean origin was referred for counselling. Her doctor described her as being depressed, but she was unwilling to take anti-depressants for fear of becoming dependent on them. She spoke of being over worked and tired; she was a single parent and the father of her 15-year-old son, Ben, was inconsistent with any financial help and had stopped visiting.

Ben had expressed anger towards her for his father's absence and she was very hurt by his accusations. Tina described herself as being a strict parent as she did not want him to 'go astray'. Ben's relationship with his father was a close one and she realised that the loss of him was painful for Ben.

When Tina was six years old, the youngest of eight children of various ages, her mother, two aunts and a friend of the family had migrated and left their children to be cared for by her grandmother. Tina recalled that she always felt left out and said of her grandmother, 'She tried to care for us but there was not enough love to go around.' When she joined her mother in England they were strangers to each other and did not develop a relationship. When her mother returned to the Caribbean they had no opportunity to talk about the past. Tina had hoped that she would have been married and experienced a loving family and was very disappointed that this did not happen and was very anxious for the future.

Tina's history, although not unique to her African-Caribbean culture, was one shared by many of her peers. A secure therapeutic environment enabled Tina to disclose her long repressed feelings and accept a recommendation that Ben too needed to discuss his painful feelings of loss and his anger and that he be seen by the child psychotherapist. In this instance, the counsellor's knowledge of Tina's background and an understanding of the effects of broken attachments, separation and loss assisted in the development of the therapeutic work.

There are a number of families of all cultures who are experiencing difficulties in parenting and may come to the attention of helping professionals, who think that it would be beneficial for mothers to be assessed in order to appraise their parenting skills and their attachment to their children or that their children are struggling with issues of attachment. Working inter-culturally does not only mean that the professional and the client come from different races, but also that for the client 'any kind of difference in culture is reflected in their attitudes and concepts of life, in their manifestations of distress and in their personal ideas about what might be done or can be done' (Kareem 1992/2000: 34).

Loss

There are some young people who live on the margins of society, unloved and unable to love and are often angry. They may have experienced insensitive parenting for a number of reasons such as acute poverty, poor housing, neglect because of their mother's physical or mental ill health or substance abuse and lack of paternal support in the family: 'after all when you are going through problems of adjusting to a society which in many ways and forms is rejecting you, it doesn't really help if your father for whatever reason, decides to leave the family' (Phillips 2006: 147). They may also have histories of emotional, physical, sexual abuse, and several changes of care arrangements, with inconsistent careers in their early lives, or have spent long periods in children's homes or various institutions managed by the state or voluntary agencies. Many will have suffered significant losses in their lives. They have not developed a secure attachment to their primary carers and they are detached and unable to build relationships.

At some time in their lives they may be referred for psychotherapeutic help, through contact with other agencies. Since these young people have not had their basic needs met it is important that the therapist is fully aware of their attachment history and, according to Pearce (2009), that they are given reassurance by understanding their needs without the therapist trying to be too emotionally close or too distant. Maintaining consistency in the range of affect expressed and behaviour reassures the young person and gives a sense of attunement which has been missing in their early lives.

There are also numbers of asylum seekers and refugees who were forced to flee from war-torn countries and who have suffered persecution, abuse and threats of death. They have experienced broken attachments, separation from and loss of family and friends and have been traumatised by the events that caused them to leave the security of their own homes, and have been disappointed at not finding Britain to be the safe haven that they had imagined it to be. They might not be aware of whether parents or relatives have survived in the countries from which they fled. Depending on their early experiences and their level of resilience, some have been able to adapt to the new environment and cope reasonably well. Some have come from countries where therapy is not practised and the concept of telling their problems to a stranger is not acceptable to them. However, there are instances when doctors or other professionals recommend therapeutic help with the services of a counsellor or therapist of the client's own ethnic and cultural background, who speaks the language and who possesses knowledge of attachment theory. Where this is not possible, carefully and well-trained interpreters need to be employed.

The acceptance of grief and the need for mourning loss are not only applicable when there is the death of a loved one; there are others among this population who will have suffered the discontinuities of their minority cultures. There will be issues of dislocation and trauma often resulting from unwanted separation and living among strange people and strange environments. There are also those who deal with ambiguous loss where the person who is 'lost' is not dead and is thought of and being grieved for. This may occur with children in foster care or who have been adopted, and those whose parents are divorced, or in prison or in long-term hospital care.

Older children who are adopted and who experience difficulty in settling may be having difficulty in resolving ambiguous loss and their adoptive parents need to be helped to appreciate the grief which the children suffer. The need to be encouraged to summon up 'the willingness to connect with children about their adoption, instead of denying the difference of entering a family through adoption rather than through birth, is an essential part of helping them grieve this important loss and make sense of their circumstances' (Hall and Steinberg 2000/2013: 179). These authors state that sometimes adoptive parents are reluctant to address their children's questions, usually because of their fear of pain, anger, blame and their own loss. Working therapeutically with adoptive parents' knowledge of attachment, loss, separation, anger and anxiety is invaluable in order to help them to process their feelings and enable them to empathise with their children.

There are also situations where the 'lost' person may be physically present but psychologically absent (Boss 2006), for example where a couple share the same house but maintain no relationship.

Somatised distress: a case study

Julia was a 21-year-old woman of African origin who was referred for an assessment when her GP was unable to find anything wrong. She had complained of frequent stomach pains and had been given leave from attending college as she found it impossible to sit up in the class. Julia was very anxious about missing time from college as she was eager to do well, urged on by her parents who set great store on education. Julia spoke softly and said she hoped that she could be helped in order to return to college as soon as possible.

This was her first year at college and she had not yet made any friends and found the lecturers intimidating and she was not able to concentrate as much as she would like. On returning home she helped with preparation of meals; the younger siblings, a sister aged 12 and brother 14, did not help. She volunteered that they were born in this country and their upbringing was different from hers. Julia was asked to tell her story. She had been reared in an African country by her grandmother whom she loved and regarded as mother. Her father left home first for the UK followed by her mother soon after. Her childhood was a happy one with other children in the extended family. She did well at school and when her parents decided that she should join the family here, she was very reluctant to leave home and all of her family and friends. What was arresting in her narrative was Julia's description of her reaction to her mother's presence. 'When she enters the room, I freeze. I am so afraid of her.'

Julia's emotional pain was focused on her physical symptoms. According to Wallin (2007: 130) 'the impacts of acute trauma as well as disorganized attachment are frequently somatic'. This implies that it is observed in individuals in any culture. A knowledge of her attachment issues allowed her therapy to focus on her insecurity and fear of authority figures on whom she seemed to project the feelings she held towards her frightening mother, with whom there was an insecure disorganised attachment.

Attachment theory and issues of race and culture

Slade (1999) issues a warning that although attachment theory can assist clinicians in understanding the dynamics of the therapeutic relationship, changing their views and responses to their clients, all aspects of human experience are not defined by understanding attachment organisation. It is particularly important to bear this in mind when assessing migrants, asylum seekers, refugees and all those persons who have been displaced and who are of different ethnic groups. How safe is the environment in which they live, and how unsettling are some of the policies to which they are expected to conform?

Jeremy Holmes (1994), in his discussion of attachment theory and its theoretical base for counselling, states that the therapeutic process could be considered as being based on the movement of the client from insecure to secure attachment. Attachment theory should not be seen as yet one more form of psychotherapy, but rather as defining features that are relevant to therapy generally. Certain key elements shared by all therapies include a relationship with the client, which provides a secure base from which to explore the problem. The task of the therapist is both to encourage appropriate emotional responses to past trauma, and to encourage discussion and ventilation about losses.

These aspects of the therapeutic process are not culturally based. The pain and the anguish need to be experienced if the client is to feel safe enough to form new attachments. According to Holmes the central context emerging from attachment theory is that of narrative, and the individual's core state is a condensed form of his/her primary relationship which gives the individual 'a sense of ownership of their past and their life' (Holmes 1993: 150).

However, there are also the social and historic factors that impinge upon the individual which need to be taken into account. There are some professionals who, when working with clients from black and other minority groups, are anxious about being called 'racist' if they probe into their clients' cultural beliefs and practices. These anxieties can hamper workers in making accurate assessments of the needs of their clients. Training in intercultural therapy would assist workers to maintain a balance between, on the one hand, awareness of shared and universal human characteristics and, on the other, not neglecting cultural variability by treating everyone 'the same' or attributing the client's problems to a cultural peculiarity.

Jafar Kareem founded the intercultural therapy centre in north London, where therapeutic help was offered to adults and families, mainly from black and minority groups. Some of them needed to be spoken to in their own language and by a therapist of a similar background with whom they felt secure and able to build a relationship. Kareem was explicit in stating that:

> for intercultural therapy it is necessary to understand how patients first experience and perceive their illness or problem, in effect to allow them authenticity as a person. It is therefore useful to involve patients themselves from the outset to let them explain and define how they see their own problem whether in terms of bodily disease or emotional distress.
>
> (Kareem 1992/2000: 34)

Many of the clients were immigrants or children of immigrants and their experiences of broken attachments and the issues stemming from this were explicitly recognised.

Within any one community there are usually different interpretations of the culture and, therefore, it is always important to discover the individual family's cultural pattern of behaviour. Sharpe (1997: 266), commenting on the mental health and socialisation in the Caribbean, expressed the view that the mental health issues attributed to attachment, separation and loss, 'are central to much of the psychopathology that may be associated with the specifics of Caribbean family socialization'. Fletchman Smith (2000: 79), working with clients of Caribbean origins in London, stated that, generally, children seem to suffer particularly badly when problems occur in families from 'an extended network background, described as headed by women, and in which women take sole charge of caring for the children, sometimes including the children of several generations'. In these instances there undoubtedly will be issues of attachment for the children and for the women who are parenting them and they could benefit from therapeutic help if their needs are recognised by professionals with the knowledge of attachment disorders.

Conclusions

The understanding and knowledge of attachment theory and sensitivity to the client's verbal and nonverbal communication, as in all forms of counselling or therapy, helps to build trust in establishing a working relationship. It is also necessary to consider how the client's ethnic background and the attachment behaviour patterns of parents from that background have influenced his or her behaviour.

Some of the elements of the task of the therapists as suggested by Bowlby (1988) are:

- the provision of a secure base from which the client would be able to explore past painful experiences;
- helping the client to consider how she engaged in relationships with significant attachment figures and what the client's expectations and behaviours were;
- encouragement of the client to examine the relationship with the therapist/social worker and the way that she is thought of as an attachment figure;
- helping the client to think about childhood and adolescent experiences, particularly in relation to parents' influence on the present. This task is often painful and it may be hard to express feelings or ideas about parents which previously seemed unthinkable;
- helping the client to understand that images of self and of others which might have been derived from life experiences or from parents might not be appropriate for the present nor the future.

The nonverbal communication of the client is extremely important in working with those who are sometimes so overwhelmed by their experiences they are unable to find the adequate words, and also when the language is not their mother tongue. The quality of the nonverbal communications will, in time, influence the attachment relationship and help the development of trust and security which will help the client to recognise difficult feelings and to begin to process them. Within every individual there is the potential for change and this can be possible when positive and meaningful interventions are made by those in the helping professions who are sensitive, empathic and patient.

References

Ainsworth, M. D. S. (1963) 'The development of infant–mother interaction among the Ganda', in B. M. Foss (ed.) *Determinants of Infant Behaviour*, Vol. II, pp. 67–112, London: Methuen.

Ainsworth, M. D. S., Blehar, M. C., Waters, E. and Wall, S. (1978) *Patterns of Attachment: A psychological study of the Strange Situation*, Hillsdale, NJ: Laurence Erlbaum Associates.

Arnold, E. (2012) *Working with Families of African Caribbean Origins: Understanding issues around immigration and attachment*, London and New York: Jessica Kingsley Publishers.

Avigad, J. and Pooley, J. (2002) 'Strangers in foreign lands', in B. Mason and A. Sawyer (eds) *Exploring the Unsaid Creativity, Risks, and Dilemmas in Working Cross-Culturally*, London: Karnac Books.

Boss, P. (1999) *Ambiguous Loss: Learning to live with unresolved grief*, Cambridge, MA: Harvard University Press.

Boss, P. (2006) *Loss, Trauma, and Resilience: Therapeutic work with ambiguous loss*, New York: W.W. Norton and Company.

Bowlby, J. (1952) *Maternal Care and Mental Health*, Geneva: World Health Organization.

Bowlby, J. (1953) *Child Care and the Growth of Love*, London: Penguin.

Bowlby, J. (1969/1982) *Attachment and Loss*; Vol. 1 *Attachment*, London: Hogarth Press.

Bowlby, J. (1973) *Attachment and Loss*; Vol. 2 *Separation: Anxiety and Anger*, London: Hogarth Press.

Bowlby, J. (1980) *Attachment and Loss*; Vol. 3 *Loss: Sadness and Depression*, London: Hogarth Press/Penguin.

Bowlby, J. (1988) *A Secure Base: Clinical applications of attachment theory*, London: Routledge Kegan Paul.

Farnfield, S. and Holmes, P. (eds) (2014) *The Routledge Handbook of Attachment: Assessment*, London and New York: Routledge.

Fletchman Smith, B. (2000) *Mental Slavery: Psychoanalytical studies of Caribbean people*, London: Rebus Press.

Green, M. (2008) *Risking Human Security: Attachment and public life*, London: Karnac Books.

George, C., Kaplan, N. and Main, M. (1985/1996) *Adult Attachment Interview*, unpublished manuscript, University of California at Berkeley.

Hall, B. and Steinberg, G. (2000/2013) *Inside Transracial Adoption*, London and Philadelphia: Jessica Kingsley Publishers.

Holmes, J. (1993) *John Bowlby and Attachment Theory*, London: Routledge.

Holmes, J. (1994) 'Attachment Theory: A secure theoretical base for counselling', *Psychodynamic Counselling*, 1(1): 65–78.

Holmes, J. (2000) 'Narrative in psychiatry and psychotherapy: The evidence', *Medical Humanities*, 26: 92–96.

Kareem, J. (1992/2000) 'The Nafsiyat Intercultural Therapy Centre', in J. Kareem and R. Littlewood (eds) *Intercultural Therapy*, Oxford: Blackwell Scientific Publications.

Main, M. and Solomon, J. (1986) 'Discovery of a new insecure-disorganized/disoriented attachment pattern', in M. Yogman and T. B. Brazelton (eds), *Affective Development in Infancy*, pp. 95–124, Norwood, NJ: Ablex.

Main, M., Kaplan, N. and Cassidy, J. (1985) 'Security in childhood and adulthood: A move to the level of representation', in I. Bretherton and E. Waters (eds) *Growing Points of Attachment Theory, Monographs of the Society for Researching Child Development* 50 (1–2), Serial No. 209.

Marris, P. (2008) 'Attachment and loss of community', in M. Green (ed.) *Risking Human Security: Attachment and public life*, London: Karnac Books.

Owen, D. (2002–3) 'Profile of Black and Minority ethnic groups in the UK', The University of Warwick.

Pearce, C. (2009) *A Short Introduction to Attachment and Attachment Disorder*, London and Philadelphia: Jessica Kingsley Publishers.

Phillips, M. (2006) *The Name You Once Gave Me*, London: HarperCollins Publishers.

Reebye, P. N., Ross, S. E., Jamieson, K. and Clark, J. M. (1999) Research report: A literature review of child–parent/caregiver attachment theory and cross-cultural practices influencing attachment. Available online at www.attachmentacrosscultures. org/research/.

Robertson, E. (1977) 'Out of sight, not out of mind', in British Association of Social Workers (ed.), *Studies in Intercultural Social Work* (pp. 26–35), Birmingham: British Association of Social Workers Publications.

Sharpe, J. (1997) 'Mental health issues and family socialization in the Caribbean', in J. L. Roopnarine and J. Brown (eds), *Caribbean Families: Diversity among ethnic groups*, Norwood, CT: Ablex Publishing and London: Jai Press.

Slade, A. (1999) 'Attachment theory and research: Implications for the theory and practice of individual psychotherapy with adults' in J. Cassidy and P. R. Shaver (eds) *Handbook of Attachment Theory, Research, and Clinical Applications*, pp. 575–594, New York and London: The Guilford Press.

Van IJzendoorn, M. H. and Kroonenburg, P. M. (1988) 'Cross cultural patterns of attachment: A meta-analysis of the Strange Situation', *Child Development*, 59: 147–156.

Wallin, D. J. (2007) *Attachment in Psychotherapy*, New York and London: The Guilford Press.

Chapter 8

Attachment

A British lawyer's perspective

Mary Ann Harris

Introduction

This perspective, from a British child care lawyer's point of view, is written at a time of immense change taking place in a bid by the government to reform the family justice system through reducing delay, and consequently cost, in care proceedings.

The courts have traditionally used senior professionals to act as expert witnesses to assist them in understanding often complex issues in a case in the family courts. In the current climate of change, the use and appointment of experts will be affected, in that any expert put forward in public law (care) or private law (contact and residence) proceedings, will be closely scrutinised by the court and subject to a test of 'necessity' for the purpose of concluding the proceedings. In the past the test was whether the expert was 'reasonably required' to assist the court in concluding the proceedings. In the revised Public Law Outline (PLO) – the government's guidance for case management of child care proceedings, the emphasis is on local authorities formulating a detailed case plan prior to issue of proceedings.

In reality this is nothing new, except that more is now expected of them. They will have to produce more succinct and relevant paperwork by way of social workers' statements and any appropriate assessments. From the outset of proceedings, they should be in a position to set out their case for the court, saying what case work, therapy or assessments they have done with the family and detailing what still needs to be done to make final decisions for any relevant children.

It is also envisaged that the court proceedings will conclude within 26 weeks. In effect, local authority teams will need to have carried out some of the work that in the past has been done by senior independent experts. These changes have been a long time coming and are, in reality, the latest in various waves of reforms since *The Children Act 1989* first became law. They are government led, and are supported by the President of the Family Division, Sir James Munby (the senior family judge in England and Wales).

The view from the President's chambers

In Sir James' first two statements published in 2013 about reform, entitled 'View from the President's Chambers', he outlines the needs for change and the steps to be taken.

Sir James's first view

He states: 'The family justice system is undergoing the most radical reforms in a lifetime'. Sir James outlines three strands of reform:

1   a new single Family Court (to incorporate all levels of the court possibly sitting under the same roof and subject to a unified system of administration);
2   the implementation of the Children and Families Bill 2013–2014;
3   the goal of improving transparency in the family courts.

He states, 'I do not accept that either of those reforms will prejudice the quality of justice or the interests of those who appear before us'.

There are those who express concern about the implications of such reforms and, indeed, to what extent they are achievable. A joint parliamentary briefing in May 2013 by the College of Social Work and the Family Rights Group regarding the 26-week deadline for the conclusion of care proceedings from their implementation warn that '[t]here is a genuine risk that the proposed 26 weeks could result in too much focus on procedure and not enough on the welfare of the child'. They suggest there should be an amendment to the Children and Families Bill to provide for an extension of the 26-week time limit where, in the judgement of the professionals involved, the case calls for it.

That begs the question who are the professionals making these decisions?

Sir James' second view

In his second view, Sir James states that he hopes the revisions in both law and procedure effect a change in the status of social workers 'as trusted professionals playing the central role in care proceedings which too often of late has been overshadowed by our unnecessary use of and reliance upon other experts'.

In a statement published in Local Government Lawyer on 9 May 2013, by the Children and Family Court Advisory and Support Service (Cafcass), set up to safeguard and promote welfare of children in family court proceedings, they note there has been a 70 per cent increase in new care applications since the tragically notable case of 'Baby P' in London in 2008/2009. The Baby P case concerned the death of a baby aged 17 months at the time. The case shocked the community when the details were released at the conclusion of the criminal trial as Baby P was found to have suffered more than 50 injuries during an eight-month period, during which time social services and other agencies had been involved with the family.

Tragically this was not the first case where a child suffered harm or death while social services were monitoring the family.

In a time of increasing number of care proceedings coupled with a climate of reforming policies to reduce cost and delay, it is difficult to predict with any precision how these changes will affect the use of experts, in particular, assessments of attachment (which in the past have usually been undertaken by such senior professionals) and the outcomes for children in court proceedings.

The appointment of expert witnesses

The change in the test regarding appointment of experts (the standard having been altered from 'reasonably required' to 'necessary') will make it more difficult for lawyers to seek the appointment of professionals with specific specialist expertise to assist them in preparing cases for court.

The view of many solicitors is that it is an exceptional case (i.e. one which is very straightforward) which can and should conclude within 26 weeks. Even in those cases that are fairly clear cut as to harm caused to the child, finding the answers as to what is in the child's best interests in the future can still be a challenging and lengthy process.

The process of assessment

There are various stages of the court process in public law children proceedings which can be summarised as the pre-proceedings, fact-finding and welfare stages.

Pre-proceedings

In the pre-proceedings stage (unless there are emergency proceedings necessary to protect a child) the local authority will carry out a core assessment and other assessments required to decide whether court proceedings are necessary to protect the child. This sometimes includes assessments by medical or other professionals, however usually these pre-proceedings assessments are undertaken by social workers.

Such preliminary input is extremely important and, as stated by Sir James:

> Work done by local authority in the period pre-proceedings – front loading – is vital for two quite different reasons. Often it can divert a case along a route which avoids the needs for proceedings. When that is not possible, and proceedings have to be commenced, work done beforehand will pay rich dividends later on.

I would agree wholeheartedly with this point. However, it will be essential for there to be transparency in the work/assessments carried out by the local authority, and for the relevant parents/family members to be fully involved with their own legal support and advice. If much of the assessment of the family has been completed before court proceedings are initiated, challenging those early assessments will be difficult, particularly with the changes regarding the appointment of independent experts.

It might, in the future, become incumbent on local authorities to seek expert assistance at the pre-proceedings stage to strengthen their case. These changes in the legal process will also demand much better training and supervision of social workers to support them in meeting the tasks ahead. There is no doubt that social workers already carry a heavy burden, are often over-worked and expected to manage very difficult complex situations. Increasingly, in this country, many social workers are relatively young and inexperienced and, in my experience, there are enormous variations in the quality of social work practice, from excellent to very poor, which impacts directly on outcomes for children.

The children ignored and a lawyer's question – a case example

One of my cases in the last five years involved a young mother who had been assessed by an adult psychologist prior to the proceedings as having significant learning disability. The assessment was excellent, setting out recommendations to professionals working with this mother about how to talk to her and explain issues. This lady's child who was under the age of ten at the time, was removed from her care early on in the case. It was alleged she failed to protect her from harm, and she failed to take seriously the local authority's concerns.

I spent many an hour with her trying to explain to her what 'emotional abuse' meant, and why social services were taking court action, in the hope of improving her ability to work with them. Somewhat shockingly to me, it was many months into the case when I fully realised she just could not understand the basic concepts. It also became clear that social services did not follow the psychologist's recommendations about working with the mother. I recall the moment when the mother asked me what an 'emotion' was. The combination of poor social work practice and the mother's inability to work with social services resulted in the child remaining in foster care.

There was an independent assessment by a specialist learning disability team, which focused on the mother's shortcomings, in my view, rather than the child's needs. There was little focus on long-term contact issues, although a contact order was made with a full care order, but there had been no independent assessment of the child's needs and her attachment with the mother.

Three years after the conclusion of the court proceedings, the child had moved through three different foster placements, her behaviour deteriorated, and she was receiving therapy. Her mother remained involved through regular supervised contact, and tried her best to understand what was expected of her. The case lasted two years in court and, on the face of it, this should have been a straightforward case, but the complexities were not in assessing the 'harm' caused, but rather in deciding what would be in this child's best interests in the future. I have little doubt the mother is still involved in this child's life, doing her inadequate best for her.

Could the outcome have been better?

In my opinion this family was not well served by the system. There was little doubt the child suffered significant harm while living with the mother, but the harm was as a result of the mother's ignorance, and she herself had little support. Could there have been a better outcome for the child if more work was done with the family, looking at the dynamics including the mother's and child's attachment styles? Maybe, but if this case were to occur today, I do not think the outcome would be different, as it would be even more unlikely that a court would agree an expert assessment on attachment would be necessary to conclude the case. The question really is whether that serves the child's best interests or the short-term interests of saving time and costs.

The lawyers become involved

It is during the pre-proceedings process that a lawyer first becomes involved, having been consulted by a parent or family member about social services' involvement in their family. It is at this stage when the parent either receives a 'pre-proceedings letter' from social services stating their intention to issue court proceedings, or they are considering the issues as to whether there are genuine child protection concerns. At this stage the local authority is largely in control.

If the family receives a pre-proceedings letter, the parent together with a lawyer are invited to a meeting to try to agree a way forward without the need for court intervention. If agreement is reached, and the parents acknowledge the concerns and comply with the agreement, court proceedings can be avoided. Social services would have produced a list of concerns and expectations for the parents to work with. In my view this process, which was only introduced in the last few years, can be very helpful as it crystallises what needs to be done to avoid court proceedings being issued. The issue of attachment is not usually a point of discussion at this stage, as social services are focused on whether they can work with the family and, if necessary, whether there is sufficient evidence to intervene and instigate court proceedings.

In my experience social services' assessments rarely question the parents' capacity to meet the needs for a secure base, an essential step to protect the children's emotional development (see Holmes and Farnfield 2014).

Lawyer and client – is this an attachment-based relationship?

The lawyer's task at this early stage is not only to analyse the information and advise the parent, but also to develop a trusting relationship with the parent so that the lawyer can explain what social services are saying, and the consequences of the parent's response. This process can be understood as the development of an attachment-based relationship in which, to a degree, the lawyer becomes a 'secure base' for their client at the time of their possibly great distress and emotional need. It may be easier for lawyers to develop such relationships with parents as their responsibility is to their client alone and not to the child, local authority or the state.

In a similar vein, it is important for the lawyer to work with social services in a constructive although often challenging way.

However, if a relationship of trust cannot be forged with the parent, and the parent remains argumentative and unaccepting of social services' concerns, it is almost impossible to run the parents' case successfully (unless of course social services' assessment of the risk of harm is flawed).

Although many lawyers manage this process intuitively, this is an area in which lawyers might benefit from a better understanding of the attachment process and its relevance to their relationships with their clients. In the typical neglect or abuse case, it is crucial for the parent to trust the lawyer's analysis and advice, and believe that if they cooperate with social services they might get their child back.

The fact-finding and welfare stages – the battle for the appointment of expert witnesses

I have dealt with many cases which have resolved at the pre-proceedings stage. However, much also depends on the willingness of social services to share information regarding the family, and their willingness to work with the parents. If the pre-proceedings, negotiation, route is not successful then the dynamics of the situation change and court proceedings will be issued.

Under the new revised Care Proceedings Protocol, with a 26-week deadline to conclude cases from the start, it is anticipated that lawyers will be kept in the loop as to what evidence social services have and local authorities will have to state their care plan for the child and suggestions for expert assessment clearly and early on. Lawyers for parents will have to be quick off the mark to give careful thought as to how they will challenge the local authority case, and what experts they wish to put forward.

In the past, lawyers have argued the need of an expert witness to assist the court with complex psychiatric and psychological issues. However, increasingly, the issues required to be dealt with by expert assessment will have to be more clearly defined. Lawyers will need more assistance in their efforts to persuade a judge that the appointment of an expert is 'necessary' for the welfare of the children to be adequately protected. As a consequence lawyers will need to be well informed about issues such as attachment, both from a theoretical but also a practical assessment perspective. It will be helpful for individual experts to set out general statements of their expertise and usefulness or relevance to different issues in care proceedings.

Mothers and babies

It is common knowledge that if the child is a newborn baby and the local authority want to separate the mother and baby, a court will be loathe to allow separation except as a last resort. In some cases, social services will argue they have enough information about the parent, but in many cases the court will consider whether there should be a further assessment, often in a residential unit, which allows the case to progress without separating parent and baby.

A residential assessment might only inform the court about the parent's basic abilities to parent. However, some residential units are multi-disciplinary, including a psychologist or psychiatrist to assess dynamics in the family. Ideally any such assessment should use evidence-based tools to look at the parent's attachment and the dynamics of their relationship (see Farnfield and Holmes 2014).

If the parent successfully completes the residential assessment and the local authority has not brought the case back to court to remove the child, then the plan is likely to be gradual rehabilitation of the child and parent in the community. The main issue at the end of the proceedings will be under what type of court order should social services need to share parental responsibility with the parent. If, on the other hand, the residential assessment throws up more concern, it is likely the local authority will bring the matter back to court with a view to separation of the child and parent.

At this point the issue of separation and its impact not only on the child but also on the parent's ability to fight the case is important. Although, as the law stands, if a child is removed at an interim stage, that fact is not supposed to prejudice the parent's case to seek the child's return, the reality is that, in practical terms, it is far more difficult to get a child back from foster care than if the child were never separated from the parent.

How can an assessment of attachment assist?

An assessment of attachment could be very useful at this interim stage, to inform the court about the parent's ability to become a 'secure base for the child'. In light of the move towards reducing the length of care cases, it is likely lawyers representing parents or children will need to be considering the instruction of an expert to assess attachment at a very early stage in the proceedings. Such assessments should include an Adult Attachment Interview (AAI) with the parent and a mother–infant assessment, such as the CARE-Index with mother and baby. Issues of attachment should also be considered in wider terms of a child's extended family. The issues of assessment and the protocols that can be used are considered in *The Routledge Handbook of Attachment: Assessment* (Farnfield and Holmes 2014).

There is no doubt professionals and parents will have to not only think of expert assessments, but also give early consideration to other family members who might be able to care for the children to avoid their being removed from their family home. In my view it is important for any assessments of extended family members to be looked at inclusively, rather than exclusively, in other words, to look at the family holistically and systemically rather than from a 'them and us' scenario (see Dallos, in Farnfield and Holmes 2014).

Court proceedings

In relation to the process of court proceedings, it is fair to say they are considered in two stages: the first stage is fact-finding and agreeing the issues regarding the threshold criteria (has the child suffered, or are they at risk of suffering, significant harm), and the second stage, or welfare stage, considers what final orders should be made and decides where the child should live and with whom he should have contact. In many cases, these two stages evolve together, although before the case can proceed at all, a court must be satisfied that the grounds for intervention in family life are met, i.e. the interim threshold is met.

The legal test for threshold is set out in ss 31 and 38 of *The Children Act 1989*, the interim test being based on reasonable grounds that the child is at risk of significant harm caused by the parent, whereas the test for a final care order must show that the child has suffered significant harm, or will in the future if not removed. These tests are far more complicated and take up much of the court's time. In my experience there are not many cases where threshold is not met, and the court then goes on to decide what is in the child's best interests in the future.

Interestingly, and perhaps uniquely in this country, much of the time spent at court revolves around discussions outside of court, where lawyers thrash out the issues and agree the way forward in a case. It is only the issues on which the parties cannot agree that are argued and determined by the court. There are differing views about the benefit of lengthy discussions outside of court. There is no doubt it saves court time, and can avoid unnecessary conflict, but it can sometimes result in the parents of the child being left out of the loop – as the discussions are usually conducted by lawyers only.

The use and abuse of expert witnesses

Judith Mason, Professor of Socio-legal Studies, School of Law, Bristol University, in an article entitled 'The use of experts in child care proceedings in England and Wales: benefits, costs and controls' (2010), analysed data from two studies in particularly looking at why there were so many experts instructed in care proceedings. She argues that the focus of care proceedings is more on what will happen in the future rather than what has happened. In other words, whether threshold is met is not the main focus of care proceedings, but what is the best outcome for this child.

She also points out that, based on her research, many of the issues in care proceedings, including issues of assessment, 'were largely negotiated by the parties' lawyers, not determined by the court'. I would agree with her analysis that, in many cases, the negotiations outside of court will often result in an 'agreed' list of directions to be presented to the court for its approval. Of course, there are the hearings where issues cannot be agreed or negotiated, and have to be scheduled for a contested hearing before the court, whether that issue is the appointment of an expert, or other issue.

However, a full and adequate assessment process requires both time and expertise. In this jurisdiction, a court has to be persuaded that the instruction of an expert is 'necessary' rather than 'reasonably required', and recent court decisions show that the bar for 'necessary' is set very high.

Further, in recent years the Ministry of Justice, which at the end of the day pays a proportion of an expert's fee, has set prescribed rates of pay at increasingly low levels. Some experts will work at these rates, however there is concern that many professionals will not, resulting in a loss of the necessary expertise required to ensure that the needs of children in care proceedings are best met.

The lawyer's dilemmas and confusions in public law

Lawyers will need to think carefully about the particular expert to be instructed, but also about the questions to be addressed. Generally speaking, it is common practice for such letters of instruction to be agreed by the parties outside of court, and there are precedents for standard letters and questions for each type of expert which are well known and used in care proceedings.

If the lawyer is acting for a parent, it can be more difficult to frame the questions, and it is important to ask about support and therapy for the parent. If, on the other hand, the lawyer is acting for the child, one's goal is always to have in mind what is best for the child, and therefore usually the more information/expert assessment, the better.

In many cases, where I have represented children, the Children's Guardian (the social worker appointed by the court to represent the children's welfare in the court proceedings) may raise attachment or behavioural issues and will express the view that an expert on attachment is necessary. Such an opinion might be based on behavioural issues the Guardian has observed or read about in social services documentation, and which the Guardian considers an expert is necessary to assess.

It is probable that such an assessment would provide the court with a more detailed and sophisticated opinion than can currently be provided by most social workers; one which should assist in analysing and identifying the needs of the child in the immediate and long term. This assessment would also assist in considering what type of therapy would be helpful for the child and, possibly, the parent.

I think attachment assessments are particularly helpful in allowing for a deeper understanding of the members of the family and thus looking at the bigger picture. This allows the identification of the types of support from which parent and child might benefit, whether the child is to remain at home, or, if the child is to remain in care, looking at continuing contact, and whether a particular therapy will help the child overcome or address any insecurity in his or her attachment style.

As I understand it the early attachment style of the child will continue throughout adulthood, unless altered by loss, trauma or abuse, and if it is an insecure attachment, that will continue throughout adulthood, having an impact on personality, behaviour and relationship patterns. But the issues and processes are complex.

A case example

Why did David continue to wish to see his abusive father?

About 10 years ago I represented a teenage boy who was separated from his family at the age of 15 years – he had been sexually abused by his father from a very young age, but had not told anyone. The mother had left the home when the child was very young, so the father was the main care giver. The child went to the police to report the abuse at the age of 15, and social services became involved. The father was arrested, convicted of sexual offences against the child, and sent to prison for several years. The issues in the care proceedings were narrow. The father admitted the abuse and was ruled out as a carer. The mother was assessed after it was decided she did not know of the abuse, and the child eventually went to live with his mother. What I thought was interesting, was that the child insisted he wanted to visit his father in prison and stay in contact with him. This was against social services' and the Children's Guardian's advice.

What does that say about this child's attachment with each of his parents, a mother who effectively abandoned him as a young child, and a father who sexually abused him from a young age? The child's contact with the father would undoubtedly be supervised, but what would happen when he became an adult? Was the child's attachment with his mother irretrievably broken down, or could that be improved? I do not know, but in my mind it poses interesting questions about an assessment of each individual's attachment and how that might have assisted in understanding this child's relationship with his parents. Could it have provided a better understanding of this child's long-term needs? Might it have suggested how the attachment to the mother could have been improved, or helped to resolve in some way the issues with the father?

Such apparently paradoxical behaviour in children is not uncommon. I have been involved in many cases over the years where a child has been abused or neglected and who is then separated from their family and placed in foster care, and as they get older, the child seeks out advice to be reunited with their family. These long-term issues for children in care, and their relationships, if any, with their families are not well served in care proceedings, perhaps necessarily, and can be sadly minimised by social services in the planning for the child on leaving care.

The short- and long-term views of remaining in care – the role of attachment assessments

In my view, assessments in care proceedings tend to focus on short-term issues, even when considering what is in the child's best interests long term.

There can be a lack of consideration given to outcomes in the longer term in court cases, although perhaps it depends on what is meant by long term. When I first became involved as a lawyer in care proceedings, there seemed to have been more argument about balance of harm issues, balancing the harm suffered at the hands of the parent with the harm likely to be suffered in care. Of course, the court's monitoring role is extremely limited in time, and once the care plan has been approved by the court, and the case finished, neither the court nor the Children's Guardian are involved in that child's life, unless someone brings the matter back to court. I have seen so many children and young people in long-term foster care who desperately seek out being reunited with their families, knowing the abuse or harm suffered but still choosing their families as soon as they are old enough to realise they can do this.

These older children in care have fewer options and are heavily reliant on good social work practice and being listened to. There are so few avenues for these young people to change their lives, so many run away, only to be found and returned to the foster placement. Some will seek legal advice, often in desperation having failed to make the social worker listen and getting nowhere with their Independent Reviewing Officer (IRO) who has been allocated to them by social services. Such cases, in my view, are desperately sad, as these are children who have already suffered abuse or neglect, have been separated from their families, and who then suffer poor care or treatment in the care system, and whose voice is not listened to. In one such case I dealt with, it took four months to even get confirmation from the local authority that the child was in their care (which triggered my ability to obtain legal aid to represent the child) and it then took another few months to get specific responses to questions about the child's living arrangements in care and ascertain the local authority's views on contact with the parents.

You might think the solution would have been simply to make an application to the court to discharge the care order. The reality is that information gathering to assess the merit of the case, and then obtaining legal aid, are the hoops through which one has to jump before making such an application. Social services would have to assess the family fully, including their attachment patterns, before simply releasing the young person back home and this all takes time. This may be an area where expert guidance as to attachment would be helpful, particularly to inform any work that might need to be done within the family, including support and therapy.

Julie aged 13

In one case where I acted for a 13-year-old girl who was subject to a care order and placed in long-term care (along with her siblings), the court refused the parents' application to discharge the care order as it determined that the parents' situation had not significantly changed since the original care proceedings. The child desperately wanted to return to her parents' care. She was represented by me through a Children's Guardian. At the final hearing, the Guardian did not support the child returning to her parents' care, and the court decided the child was not competent to represent herself (i.e. without a Guardian). Although the court took into account the child's wishes and feelings it decided there was no merit in the parents' application. The child, therefore, remained in the foster placement. Subsequently, the child ran away, on several occasions, each time to be returned to the foster placement. Eventually, what changed was a change of position by social services. Through negotiations with the leaving care team it was agreed the child could return to her parents' care with a support package, and while remaining under a care order.

This was an unusual outcome, but the other option was that this young person would probably have continued to run away, exposing herself to harm and possibly leading to the local authority applying for a secure accommodation order.

The point I wish to make in this regard is that the practicalities or reality of whether or not a care plan will work in the long term are extremely important, and the monitoring of children in long-term care, although subject to precise procedures and regular review, would benefit in my view from the inclusion of a truly independent monitoring system. The role of the IRO needs to be redefined so that they are independent of social services' pressures as to how well they perform their functions.

Lawyer's dilemmas in private law

In public law proceedings, the court's focus is on child protection and determining what is in a child's best interests. In contrast, in private law proceedings the emphasis is on conciliation, mediation and trying to achieve a compromise in the child's best interests. Thus in private law, child protection issues, although relevant, are not the forefront consideration. These cases are about competing parents who disagree about some issue or issues regarding their child's upbringing.

When I first started practising in this area of law, I recall a robust judge who would take the opportunity at the first conciliation hearing to shout at all parties in the courtroom, including the parents, appearing quite threatening and unpleasant, telling them that if they did not sort out their differences about their children, they would have to accept him making the decision for them. In many cases this worked, at least temporarily, and the parents would walk away from court having reached some sort of compromise. I am not suggesting this is the solution to most cases, but I think it highlights the essential difference in public law and private law cases.

Of course, if there are child protection issues in a private law case, for example domestic violence or other abuse, and where there has been social services involvement with the family, the court will ask social services to carry out an assessment and consider if there is a need for them to intervene by way of public law proceedings.

Cafcass (the Children and Family Court Advisory and Support Service which looks after the interests of children in family proceedings) would also be involved at the onset of proceedings. It is not usual to have psychiatric or psychological assessments of children in private law proceedings as a general rule. However, if the issues are complex and demand the need for an expert, particularly if the child is made a party and is separately represented, this will be considered by the court. I think it likely in the current climate of change, in private law proceedings, the use of experts will become more scarce and the use of compromise more prevalent.

There are also further restrictions on obtaining legal aid, public funding, for a parent to be represented in private law cases, and it is anticipated this will result in more litigants in person. If there are child protection concerns, or domestic violence, legal aid will be available, and the case will follow a different process, with a fact-finding hearing before consideration of the issues in dispute. There is no doubt some private law cases can be as complex as their public law counterparts, and that the use of attachment assessments in particular could play an important role in examining the nature of the child's attachment to each parent, and the long-term consequences for that child.

A lawyer's confusion

In my experience there can be considerable confusion about the importance, and implications of, attachment assessments as different psychologists and psychiatrists seem to analyse the issues differently. Indeed they may even be using the term 'attachment' differently and might not be in agreement that the processes they are observing and describing are indeed attachment at all. This can lead to considerable confusion in the minds of lawyers and judges. These issues are discussed in *The Routledge Handbook of Attachment: Theory* (Holmes and Farnfield 2014). It is important that assessors use terminology that is consistent and clear.

The way ahead

It is a daunting task to endeavour to ensure that all children who are subject to court proceedings are not only protected from harm, but also that their basic human rights including the right to family life are protected. Social work practice needs to be on top form to ensure good cooperative working practice with families, and in those cases where court intervention is necessary, appropriate expert evidence will continue to be available to assist the courts in making long-term decisions in children's best interests.

Reflecting on the difficulties that lie ahead, with reforms designed to reduce delay and cost, it would be helpful to put in place safeguards to ensure a more transparent process pre-proceedings, where the costs of the expert professionals involved are borne by the local authority. This would necessitate a shift in attitude of all professionals involved to include training of those professionals (the former 'experts') working with local authority teams and more extensive supervision and training of social workers, and for all those involved to actually work together, otherwise pre-proceedings assessments will continue to be challenged subsequently in the court proceedings.

Some local authorities do better than others in regard to their attitude and practices towards working with families. I have come across differing approaches working with a number of different local authorities. As a lawyer, I suspect I do not fully understand the implications of attachment and separation issues, however, I have seen such assessments significantly assist the court in making the right decisions for children.

These are such difficult and complex issues which will continue to benefit from the input of an expert focused on the child's needs and, in particular, his or her attachment needs.

References

Farnfield, S. and Holmes, P. (eds) (2014) *The Routledge Handbook of Attachment: Assessment*, London and New York: Routledge.

Holmes, P. and Farnfield, S. (eds) (2014) *The Routledge Handbook of Attachment: Theory*, London and New York: Routledge.

Mason, J. (2010) The use of experts in child care proceedings in England and Wales: benefits, costs and controls, Annual Legal Research Network Conference 2010.

Munby, J. (2013) View from the President's chamber: the process of reform, *Family Law*, May 2013.

Chapter 9

The applications of attachment theory in the field of adoption and fostering

Jeanne Kaniuk

Introduction

Attachment theory has a special place in adoption and fostering as it provides a conceptual framework for the practitioner who is grappling with major decisions about the future of vulnerable children. It offers a scaffolding for thinking about the children's experiences, the impact of these experiences on the children's internal expectations of parental figures and information as to how best to support both the children and the substitute parents who are charged with their care.

The significance of an infant's attachment to her primary caretaker (usually mother) was first recognised by John Bowlby, who understood that attachment was a basic biological drive, as significant for the infant's survival as nourishment, and that separation from the mother was potentially catastrophic, especially if there was not a substitute carer available (preferably one already familiar to the infant) who could provide responsive care, accepting the infant's distress (Bowlby 1988).

Later work by Mary Ainsworth enabled the development of a system for classifying the types of attachment of infants to their mothers based on the care she provided, particularly her responsiveness to their communications, both positive and negative (Ainsworth *et al.* 1978). When these attachments to the primary caregiver are disrupted, particularly if there are repeated disruptions accompanied by the absence of an available and sensitive substitute caregiver, there may be far reaching consequences for the infant's later emotional, psychological, cognitive and social development. Alternatively, if the infant's primary caregiver is neglectful or abusive rather than a reliable source of protection, the parent who should be the source of protection and security is experienced as threatening and the infant will have no strategy for keeping safe (Main & Solomon 1986).

The consequences of attachment trauma are far reaching for the children who are fostered or adopted. Many of these children have huge difficulties trusting the adults with whom they are placed and, rather than expecting them to be essentially nurturing and attentive, anticipate hostility and neglect. Children who have been abused will have these experiences 'hard wired' into their nervous system, as it is essential for survival to learn from dangerous situations and to be alert to avoid them in future. Thus these children are often slow to develop trusting attachments to their new parents even, or particularly, when they offer benign caregiving that runs counter to their previous experience (Steele *et al.* 2007).

The child's negative expectations require enormous reserves of hopefulness and perseverance on the part of the adopters or other long-term carers, as well as the professionals who are charged with the responsibility for planning for the children's future care. It is an understandably complex task, which is open to mis-interpretation and requires careful assessment to ensure that communications from the children to their new parents are understood, and that the parents who might be struggling to care for children are not misjudged when they express frustration and possibly despair. There is often a tendency to seek someone to blame when plans for vulnerable children prove difficult to realise, and the adopters might be the ones who are seen to be failing when their attempts to nurture the children placed with them are rejected. In turn, the adopters might be tempted to give up and reject the children.

The context for contemporary adoption and fostering

Children in foster care need stable placements where they can experience attach-ments to carers who are attuned to their difficulties. Some of these children are in short-term care and may return home, or be placed with members of their extended family or be adopted. Others are in long-term care. Of 67,050 children in England who were looked after on 31 March 2012, 50,260 were in foster placements. This is a fluctuating population, with very different leaving care pathways. In 2011–12, 27,350 children left care but 28,220 started to be looked after. Of those who left care 10,160 returned home, 2,620 became subject to Residence or Special Guard-ianship Orders, 3,720 moved to independent living and 3,450 were adopted (DfE 2012).

There are no figures relating to the number of children in long-term foster care whether designated as such or by default, but they might be in excess of 20,000. These are children for whom adoption is not an option for a variety of reasons such as: the child's age (age at placement is the most significant factor with regard to whether children are likely to be placed for adoption); the nature of the child's psycho-social difficulties; the child's status as an asylum seeker. In the last case the child might be emotionally attached to parents and others in the home country, who are prevented from offering care because of social strife in that country.

This represents a major challenge for local authorities charged with their care, and for the social work staff to find appropriate placements for these children, who will have suffered similar trauma as the general population of children who need adoption, but might be older or more emotionally damaged.

By definition, adoption practitioners are concerned with children who have suffered separation and whose attachments to their birth parents are insecure or disorganised. It is sadly not uncommon for them to experience changes in placement leading to further disruptions of attachment while in care.

If a child comes into care at birth and is made the subject of care proceedings, ideally she should be in a stable foster placement where the foster carer will temporarily become the child's primary attachment figure until her future is decided by the courts. Inevitably this means that the child will suffer a broken attachment and will have to make a new attachment with her adoptive parents or re-establish a primary attachment with her parent/s. Some children suffer several changes of foster carer and thus broken attachments before being permanently placed, which makes the process of building an attachment even more difficult for the child.

The population of children who require adoption in the UK generally come from backgrounds of multiple disadvantage with parents who might be substance abusers, have mental health problems, suffer from domestic violence, and/or where the children might be abused or neglected or both. These children have often experienced adversity pre-birth (26 of 41 infants studied by Ward *et al.* (2006) were born with neonatal abstinence syndrome). In addition they may have genetic vulnerabilities.

Within the care system there is a risk of multiple placements or of repeated and unsuccessful attempts to return the child home, and many children experience protracted delays during the court proceedings to determine whether they are to return to the care of parents or extended family members or to be adopted. All these factors compound the likelihood of damage to the infant or growing child's capacity to build attachments.

In the UK the number of children who are relinquished by their parent/s for adoption and adopted at less than 12 months has dropped dramatically. In 2011/12, there were just 70 adoptions of children under 12 months of age out of a total of 3,450 adoptions. The average age was 3 years 8 months. Thus the vast majority of adoptions in the UK involve children who are older at placement and may have experienced considerable early trauma. The current UK government has introduced an Adoption Reform Programme which aims to reduce the length of court proceedings in care cases to 26 weeks and to ensure that children who cannot return home are adopted at younger ages to maximise their opportunity for developing secure attachments (Children and Families Act 2014: section 14).

In the USA there is also a tradition of placing children from the care system, who have experienced deprivation and trauma, into adoptive families. The mandatory imposition of an adoption plan in the USA has resulted in over 50,000 adoptions a year but over 100,000 children wait for an adoptive home. Many of these children are over the age of five, including a significant number of adolescents.

A different model of adoption involves inter-country adoptions where some of the issues are similar, but where there are also significant differences with regard to greater uncertainty about the child's background, why she needs to be adopted and her birth parents' circumstances. There is usually a less full and reliable medical history. Step-parent adoption is also possible. This chapter does not address either step-parent or inter-country adoption.

The task of professionals involved in placement planning

The theoretical framework provided by attachment theory can provide scaffolding for the social worker engaged in the following tasks:

- understanding the needs of children: how the child's experience of care and of broken attachments and placement moves has influenced her expectations of parental figures which informs the search for adopters or a foster family;
- providing a supportive relationship to the child which is marked by the reliable and ongoing involvement of a familiar adult who takes responsibility for talking to the child in an age-appropriate way about the plans for the child, preparing the child for any moves, and ensuring that the child has a record of the significant people and events in her life (life story work);
- assessing potential adopters or foster parents;
- matching the strengths of adopters with the needs of children;
- foster placements may be made in an emergency, and there may be little choice of family, but insofar as possible, matching the foster family's strengths with the child's needs, and providing support to the foster family;
- supporting both children and new parents as well as the foster family through the period of introductions; i.e. the move from a temporary placement to the permanent placement – whether foster care or adoption;
- supporting families post placement, including advising the new parents/ carers on behaviour management likely to reduce the child's defensive behaviour, and to allow attachments to develop;
- therapeutic interventions or referral for more specialist support, for example from child and adolescent mental health services.

This chapter cannot consider all these tasks and will concentrate on:

- assessing attachment in children;
- understanding the child's needs;
- supporting the child;
- assessing adopters and foster carers;
- supporting adopters, carers and children.

Assessing attachment in children

Professionals working with children needing substitute family care can be greatly assisted by a formal assessment of the child's attachment status. There are a number of such valid and reliable assessment tools. These are discussed in the *Routledge Handbook of Attachment: Assessment* (Farnfield & Holmes 2014). This chapter discusses those tools on which work familiar to the author is based.

The Strange Situation procedure (Ainsworth *et al.* 1978) is not used very often in adoption and so has been omitted.

Story stems

Older children's attachments have been assessed using narrative story stems, and Jill Hodges, a consultant child and adolescent child psychotherapist has developed a set of story stems for use with children who have suffered abuse and neglect. Narrative stems are a useful tool for exploring children's internalised expectations of parental figures as opposed to other assessments which measure external aspects of the child's functioning. This approach can be used with children who are verbal – approximately aged three or four to nine years. The story stems draw on children's unconscious expectations of parental figures – their Internal Working Models (IWMs) – by inviting the children to supply the ending to 13 story stems which all pose a dilemma of some sort in terms of the outcome. However, they do not ask direct questions about the child's own experience and are therefore less threatening. The child's responses are not taken literally as a concrete representation of the child's actual experience, but as indicating the quality of that experience. The worker illustrates the story with toy figures representing a family or toy animals, depending on the story, and the child's completions are videoed, so that the assessment of the story stems can use both verbal and non-verbal cues. For example, there is a story about a child (boy or girl depending on the sex of the child being assessed), who knocks over a glass of juice at the tea table. The children's story completions may range from mother mopping up the juice and simply saying to be a bit more careful next time, to bizarre events and extreme punishments. Some children who feel anxious about the scenarios, which do all pose a dilemma, are unable to complete a story and disengage (refuse to complete the story).

Story stems have been used in a longitudinal research study exploring the way attachments develop between older children (aged 4–8 years at placement) and their adopters. All of the children had come from backgrounds of adversity and were assessed soon after placement, after one year and again after two years (Hodges et al. 2003). The research demonstrated that all the children developed significantly more secure themes within their narratives over time; for example, an increase in parents helping children and being aware of the children's needs. However, all the children also retained a significant level of insecure themes; for example, representing parents as rejecting and aggressive. These findings suggest that past experiences are not simply wiped out by later, good experiences of attuned care. The adopters' task is one of actively disconfirming children's negative IWMs of attachment by provision of attentive care, and the daily lived experience with adults who are attentive and responsive builds up a competing set of expectations (IWMs) in the child's mind which, over time, it is hoped will become increasingly strong and gradually outweigh the negative expectations. Nevertheless these children will remain vulnerable, especially at times of change and transition, and their parents will need to remain vigilant and supportive.

Some clinicians within children's mental health teams use story stems as a diagnostic tool which can also be used to provide detailed, focused advice on parenting strategies to a parent. This is discussed below.

Understanding children's needs

Children who are in the care system depend on a team of adults working together who will mediate the external world and ensure that the child is protected from danger. It is the foster carer's responsibility to provide day-to-day care, physical nurture and also responsive, sensitive care. However, carers might be eager to help a child catch up and meet their milestones and encourage the child to learn and to become independent rather than attending to the deficits and gaps in their early experience to give them a firmer emotional foundation on which to build.

The child's social worker holds responsibility for ensuring that plans are made for his permanent care, whether at home, with members of the extended family, or via adoption. The social worker needs to work closely with the foster carer and the child's parents to ensure that plans are made and implemented thoughtfully and without undue delay, and that all parties are supported through the process. The social worker also has the responsibility of working with the child to ensure that she understands the plans and has an opportunity to express her own views and to be heard. This does not mean giving the child responsibility for adult decisions, but treating children with respect and ensuring that they are not left in limbo. This can only be achieved by a worker who takes time to get to know the child and develop a relationship of trust.

Kenrick (2000) has written an account of psychotherapy with children who have been subjected to repeated separations. She comments: 'some of our most vulnerable children already with unprocessed trauma, are subjected to further trauma from repeated separations while in the care system. This often reactivates early trauma and too often ensures the failure of the next placement.' She goes on to say that children who lack a benign internal representation of a parental figure to support them, as well as lacking a reliable caregiver in the external world, 'may . . . develop defences of not thinking or of flight to action against experiences that it would be hard for anyone to comprehend'. Children who are unable to think, or who take refuge in unthinking action are challenging to care for and can be frightening to the adults, who need to be reminded that they are children and that they are likely to be frightened themselves. It is often these children who suffer repeated moves between foster families and breakdowns in adoption placements.

The move to an adoptive family

It is important to recognise that when children in foster care have to move to an adoptive placement, this will be experienced as another disruption, and is likely to evoke resonances of earlier moves and a sense of insecurity. This will be true even for a child who has had a relatively stable period of foster care, where he came to feel safe. Such a child may be able, in the course of time, to use his experience of a relationship with an attentive caregiver as the basis for taking the risk of building a new attachment, but the scars of repeated moves and broken attachments are likely to have an ongoing impact. Adopters should be prepared to anticipate that the child they hear about in the foster home is likely to behave differently for a period, and will need support and reassurance to help them to settle and feel safer. Alternatively there are children who have been in foster families where the adults have made few demands on them, and in turn the children have responded by 'blending in' without making demands as a strategy for remaining 'safe' in an uncertain world. These children are often described as not presenting any management issues in their foster home.

Given the traumatic backgrounds from which children who are removed from their families via the courts generally come, it is unlikely that they are so well adjusted that the fact that they do not present overt problems is an indication of their positive mental health. It is more likely that many of these children are presenting a 'false self' which will not be possible to maintain in an adoptive family where the dynamics are very different, and the new parents are keen to build a caring relationship. Children in such a situation are expected to relate to their new parents in a way that demands skills in building relationships which they might never have had the opportunity to develop. Children who have been abused will frequently associate the intensity of intimate family relationships with danger, and may respond in the unthinking 'flight to action' described by Kenrick. It is important to recognise what is happening, and not to assume that it is the lack of commitment or warmth on the part of new parents that is responsible for the child's reaction. It is more likely to be that the child is re-experiencing fears and trauma associated with the past, and will need the adults to remain calm, not to over-react and panic, to convey that they can think about the child's feelings and anxiety, and that the child is safe in his new home.

The need for a coherent life story

Children who have suffered separations and moves often lack a coherent narrative of the significant events of their life and reasons why they needed to be adopted (or fostered). In order to process the feelings associated with the separations and the events which preceded their removal from home, the child will need an explanation that is factual and age appropriate. Loxtercamp (2009) has worked extensively with adopted children and writes about his experiences of working with angry adopted children who display intense hostility towards their adopters. He suggests that often social workers have attempted to protect the children from knowing that their birth parents abused or neglected them, providing bland reassuring accounts of the reason for their adoption. These reassurances do not chime with the child's non-verbal memories of intense fear and distress which remain unprocessed because they have not been understood and acknowledged. Since the child has no understanding that the experiences that have left them dealing with this distress are located in past relationships, they project their despair and rage on the adopters, holding them responsible for their unhappiness. Loxtercamp makes a strong plea for children to have an honest account of the reasons for their removal from their birth family in order to allow them to process the residue of feelings and inchoate memories.

Based on her experience as a post adoption worker, Joy Rees (2009) has developed an approach to Life Story Books (LSBs) which encourages the child's attachment to her adoptive parents, while giving an age-appropriate and truthful account of the significant events of the past that can be developed and elaborated as the child grows and is able to comprehend the complexity of past events. Rees suggests that adopted children's LSBs should not start with the child's birth and an account of her family of origin as has been traditional, but rather with her present (adoptive) family, confirming that she belongs there and is loved. The story then moves on to acknowledge that this has not always been her family, and gives an account geared to her age and understanding which is nevertheless honest. Choosing the words to convey a difficult story which is clear and developmentally within the child's understanding and which the adopters feel comfortable in sharing and discussing is important.

Rees stresses that it is not appropriate to give lengthy descriptions of the birth parents' own difficulties, which might leave the child feeling burdened with concern. The process of unpicking the difficulties experienced by the previous generation is a task for a later developmental stage.

Supporting children

Children in adoptive or long-term foster placements are, by definition, in an environment which it is hoped will provide 24/7 reparative experience. This is the most radical treatment option available. However, many of these children will also require professional intervention at times. It is important to ensure that children experience continuity of their social worker throughout the period of moving and settling into their new family as she acts as a bridge between past and present and supports them in processing the losses involved as well as the task of settling into their new family.

Story stems can be used in a therapeutic way either before the child is placed or once the child is in placement. A careful analysis of the themes that emerge allow an individualised map of the issues which are particularly sensitive for that child to be constructed, enabling the worker to assist the new parents to devise strategies to disconfirm that child's negative expectations and to augment the positives. For example, a child might have no expectation of parents who notice when he is hurt. Such parents might be advised to maximise any opportunity to show the child that they are indeed aware when the child has a fall or scrapes his knee for example, and provide overt comfort. Another child might have experienced criticism and mockery of his efforts, and might prefer to destroy any achievements such as drawings rather than risk ridicule. Such children might need particular parenting strategies in order to approach below the child's 'radar' for detecting and rejecting praise, and accustoming them to accepting that they can be appreciated, thus gradually building their self-confidence. For example, by ensuring that any small achievement is noticed and celebrated – not waiting for major achievements, but thanking the child for coming to the table, or for shutting the door when asked.

A number of child and adolescent mental health services (in the UK CAMHS) employ clinicians who are trained to administer and evaluate story stems. If local authorities are commissioning services from their local CAMHS for looked-after and adopted children, they could specify such assessments as an important method of understanding the challenges posed by some children, and of supporting their parents.

Assessing adoptive parents

The training of child care social workers in the 1960s took cognisance of Bowlby's teaching, which emphasised the importance of attachment and the impact of separation on babies. In the 1970s the specialist training of child care, mental health and welfare social workers was abandoned in favour of a generic model of training and service provision, at the same time as attachment theory and a psychodynamic model of practice were overtaken by an empowerment/rights-based approach. Nevertheless the assessment of adopters and foster carers retained a focus on what parents bring to their role from their own experience of having been parented, along with an understanding that healthy psychological adjustment requires that past losses (including the experience of infertility) have to be processed if they are not to remain as 'ghosts in the nursery' affecting the ability to build new attachments on a healthy emotional basis (Fraiberg et al. 1975; Steele et al. 2008).

The Adult Attachment Interview

The development of the Adult Attachment Interview (AAI) by Mary Main, enabling the classification of the attachment status of adults, provided a theoretical validation of what had been developed and retained as practice wisdom.

The AAI is a semi-structured interview in which the interviewer asks a series of questions about the subject's experience with his mother and father as a child, five adjectives to describe the relationship with each of his parents (plus an example to illustrate the adjective); to whom he would turn if upset or hurt; any experiences of loss or separation, and also of abuse. Any later experiences of supportive relationships are also explored. The respondent is also asked what he makes of those experiences in retrospect, and whether/how they have shaped the person he is today.

The assessment of the adult's attachment is made on the basis of the quality of the narrative, rather than on whether the history of childhood reflects a secure attachment, or experiences of loss and trauma; i.e. it is not what happened but how the subject thinks about it now, in the present, that is important; the respondent's ability to assume the perspective of their parent and understand why they acted as they did, and their ability to reflect on the past in sufficient detail to convey a sense of something real rather than bland generalisations. The qualities upon which the classifications are made include accounts which are either lacking in any detail to confirm generalised statements, or alternatively, overly long, involved and delivered with a sense that the issues are still live and unresolved for the respondent.

Adults who are rated as 'Autonomous' give an account of their childhood which is clear and balanced, reflecting both positive and painful experiences, and not idealising their parents, but acknowledging their weaknesses as well as their strengths. The respondent is able to evidence his descriptions of his parents and experiences by giving examples that are vivid and convey something real. Their stories convey a sense that the subject is 'psychologically minded' – i.e. they can see other people's points of view, and in retrospect make allowances for their parents' shortcomings. They are truthful, and the detail provided is relevant to the point being made. Adults whose interviews are classified as 'autonomous' might have experienced a good quality of care from their parents so they would have been assessed as 'securely attached' as children. Alternatively they might have experienced considerable adversity which they have subsequently processed and have consequently developed resilience so their interviews are classified as having 'earned' autonomous status. Resilience is the capacity to deal with adversity and to persevere in the face of the difficulties and challenges that life might present. It is based on having had good enough experiences of being cared for, having learned to deal with and process loss and other difficult experiences. It can also be the result of later experiences of therapy or of a relationship within which the person could confide about their past and have support in thinking about it and making sense of it such that the person no longer feels responsible and is able to make sense of why things happened as they did.

Adults who are rated as Insecure/Dismissing (minimising) have narratives that tend to minimise the importance of relationships and the impact of separations or losses. They might show difficulty in remembering relationships and may also idealise their parents, despite some evidence of emotional difficulties in their childhood which are glossed over. They have difficulty in giving specific examples to verify their account of their childhood, and minimise the impact of their childhood on their current functioning.

Adults who are classified as Insecure/Preoccupied (ambivalent) have narratives that are long and confused. They give examples to illustrate their story, but they tend to lack focus and to be lengthy and rambling. They might display high levels of anger with their parents regarding incidents in the past. They might not convey a clear impression of their childhood. There are references to childhood difficulties which still preoccupy them.

Adults who are rated as Disorganised or with Unresolved patterns of response to past trauma or loss have narratives which refer to the past losses or traumas in a way which conveys ongoing bereavement, guilt or irrational thinking about these events. They may be similar to the dismissive adults described above, but with this additional overlay. Adults who are in other ways rated as secure may display this pattern in relation to recent bereavements or losses which are still being mourned.

Steele and Steele (2005) followed up the transmission of patterns of attachment from parents to their children in a study that measured AAIs of both parents during pregnancy and followed up their children to middle childhood. There was a significant correlation in attachment status, especially between mothers and their children measured between the ages of 5–6 years and 11–12 years. A significant correlation was also found between fathers' AAI scores during pregnancy and their children's ability to make friends and manage conflict with peers at age 10 years, perhaps indicating that in general the fathers' influence is more marked in respect of relationships with the outer world.

Steele and Steele (2005) comment that

> the AAI is a uniquely valid measure of competence in the parenting role, i.e. pointing to the adult who will or will not be likely to meet the child's needs for care and love in the first year, and manage effectively most if not all later parenting tasks appropriate to each developmental stage in the child's life.

Kaniuk and colleagues studied the attachment profiles of adoptive parents and the children they had adopted (Kaniuk et al. 2004). The majority of the children showed significant increases in their secure attachment construct over the two years. Those who did not were children who had adoptive mothers who had unresolved losses. In addition as long as children have one adoptive parent who has autonomous attachment status, that child will make progress in developing more positive expectations of parental figures, more secure attachments and managing better in the family and at school (Kaniuk et al. 2004). Having two parents with autonomous status leads to better outcomes, but as long as one parent is able to hold the child in mind and reflect on their experience, rather than being preoccupied with their own issues, the child is able to benefit.

Other researchers have developed different tools to assess adults' attachment status. Patricia Crittenden developed the Dynamic-Maturational Model of patterns of attachment in adulthood. The Crittenden model has some significant differences from Main's AAI. These are discussed in Farnfield and Holmes (2014).

The AAI as a tool for assessing prospective adopters

Administering and scoring the AAI requires intensive training and there are a limited number of trained professionals in the UK. A few adoption agencies have brought the AAI in as either a standard aspect of their assessment, or to use in cases where the standard assessment highlights concerns and a more in-depth assessment is judged necessary. As far as is known, there is currently no study of the outcomes of using the AAI in this way, nor of the costs of introducing this as a standard aspect of assessments. There is also some evidence of a few agencies who have attempted to use the AAI without having appropriately qualified personnel to undertake this work. This is plainly inappropriate. Nevertheless the insights from the AAI and the longitudinal research referred to above do indicate that the conceptual framework provided by the AAI has an important contribution to make to the field. The thinking behind the AAI has been significant in confirming the importance of taking an account of the applicant's childhood and relationships with their parents (which is already a standard aspect of the assessment of adopters). It also alerts the social worker to pay attention to losses suffered by the applicant and to look for evidence that they have been resolved. The importance of identifying applicants who can discuss both the positives and the negatives in their childhood, and who give a balanced account of their lives which addresses both the positives and the more challenging or painful experiences they have had; people who demonstrate the capacity for reflecting on relationships – the ability to see other people's perspective and be empathetic – these are all important qualities needed by a child who has suffered adversity, and who is likely to come with expectations of parental figures which are at odds with what is offered by the prospective adopters. It is important to identify adopters with the capacity to be reflective rather than responding in a reactive and possibly angry way when the child is rejecting or challenging.

It is important that social workers receive supervision where these qualities of the prospective adopter can be considered. Building up experience of working with adopters and using the framework provided by attachment theory and the AAI, enables social workers to make better assessments, but will not replicate the level of accuracy obtained from the AAI. Having said that, the longitudinal research study where the adopters all completed an AAI before their child was placed revealed that of the sample of 48 adoptive mothers, 70 per cent were rated as having Autonomous attachment status, as opposed to 50 per cent in a community sample (i.e. people in a general population group) (Kaniuk *et al.* 2004). Thus the assessment process had identified a significantly higher proportion of these mothers as secure than would be in the general population. Only one of the children had a placement which disrupted (broke down) over the first two years of placement, although there was also a small group of children whose story stems did not reflect an increase in secure constructs over that period.

Given the very disadvantaged group of children and the severe levels of adversity they had experienced prior to placement, this represents a huge improvement in their emotional functioning and their life chances. As Rustin comments (Rustin 1999: 60): 'Something new is always a possibility. Without this element of optimism adoption could never have been invented as a solution to something that has not worked. But the complexity of the task never fails to fill me with wonder.' It is suggested that part of the 'magic ingredient' which does enable the child to have such a reparative experience lies in the transformative power of parental devotion when it is freed from preoccupations arising from losses and unresolved conflicts and the adults are able to concentrate their energies on the child in a way which values the individual child and respects his past as well as his present and his future.

Recent theoretical developments have suggested that Reflective Function (RF) is the key factor which provides the mechanism whereby parents who have autonomous status (secure) influence the attachment trajectory of their children. Arietta Slade defines RF thus: 'Reflective functioning refers to the capacity not only to recognise mental states, but to link mental states to behaviour in meaningful and accurate ways' (Slade 2005). This concept clearly links to the ideas of 'psychological mindedness' and the way adults describe previous losses, reflecting whether these have been processed and understood, or whether they are still in some way 'live' and interfering with the individual's ability to manage current relationships.

Attachment Style Interview

The Attachment Style Interview (ASI) (Bifulco *et al.* 2008; Bifulco 2014) aims to assess the strength of people's current relationships and support network. It was originally developed for research with depressed mothers. Training to use the ASI is available in the UK, and a number of adoption agencies use it as part of their assessment of prospective adopters. It does not attempt to 'surprise the unconscious' in the way the AAI does, revealing the quality of people's early relationships in a way that they might not be consciously aware of themselves, but does provide a framework for assessing current relationships in a consistent manner.

Assessing foster carers

Many of the same considerations apply to the assessment of foster carers as described in the section regarding adopters, particularly where long-term fostering is concerned. Carers need help to understand the children's vulnerability and to interpret behaviour that may be challenging or which might appear, on the surface, to indicate that they do not require much individual attention. As described above, the carers need to have the capacity to stand back and reflect in order to understand the child's communications, and will need to disconfirm the child's expectations which are likely to be of harsh or neglectful care. The carer will need support from a worker who understands these complexities. This is at odds with the advice foster carers are sometimes given, to remain emotionally distant in order not to encourage the development of an attachment which might make it more painful for the child to move. It is true that a child who is attached is likely to have more difficulty separating from the carer, and moving to his new home; however, it is more damaging to a child for the foster home to confirm his expectation that adults do not hold him in mind and are not available to establish a relationship within which the child can feel supported.

Both Dozier (2003) and Steele *et al.* (2008) have demonstrated that if children are placed with carers who have secure attachments, they can recover from insecure and disorganised attachments and develop more positive IWMs of parental figures' representations than if placed with carers who are themselves insecure or suffering from unresolved loss.

Dozier (2003) has demonstrated that infants who have been neglected may be unresponsive to attempts by their foster carers to provide nurture and care, and might appear independent. The temptation of the carer is to respond to the child's cues that he does not need attention, by assuming that the child is, indeed, self-sufficient, and to reduce the level of interaction and nurture offered. However, if the foster carers are trained to over-ride the child's signals of self-sufficiency and to reach out to the child, providing sensitive care and reassurance, the children respond to this and within a matter of two or three months their behaviour becomes responsive to the level of care they receive. In other words, their expectations or IWMs of parental/caregiving figures has been transformed.

Wakelyn (2011) describes the observation of a baby in foster care from birth to 12 months when he was placed with adopters, having been relinquished by his young parents at birth. The foster carer was repeatedly advised by the social workers that the baby would move as soon as adopters had been identified, which resulted in a sense of uncertainty and impermanence permeating the foster mother, who was not able to make plans, for example to take the baby to visit her own mother who lived at a distance.

It is evident in the account of the observation that the uncertainty affects the carer deeply as she struggles to provide care while also worrying about the baby's future. The carer's own sense of uncertainty also seems to impact on the baby's development. Even at such a young age, and within a stable foster placement the anxieties that are an inevitable part of the experience of separated children and their carers have an impact on the baby.

Dozier notes that repeated experiences of having to move children on to a new placement having formed a bond with the child depletes the carers' emotional resources. She suggests that the more children a carer has moved on to a new placement, the less sensitive to the needs of the next child the carer becomes (Dozier 2003). If we want to enable carers to retain their capacity to relate to distressed children and to reach out to them, it is important that the carers' own needs are recognised and they are not treated as a commodity on a conveyor belt. Carers need support at the time a child moves, and to have their own feelings acknowledged. They need a space in which to process the loss and to recover before the next child is placed – even a week or two would offer them some respite. They should continue to be paid a fostering retainer during this time. Failure to give carers this kind of support is likely to result in 'burn out' with the result that either they will resign after a certain number of placements, or they will become hardened and less responsive to the needs of the individual child.

If a carer develops a bond with a particular child who needs to be adopted, and offers to adopt that child, her offer should be carefully considered. In such a case the carer's motivation to adopt the child, in the knowledge of that child's difficulties, provides a foundation for a positive outcome particularly if the child is also attached and wants to remain in the placement, as the adopter will have chosen the child on the basis of real knowledge about the issues that child presents, which is usually not possible in adoptions by strangers. If we are truly child centred in our decision making, the needs of that individual child to a secure family placement will outweigh the organisation's need to ensure a good supply of foster carers available to care for children when needed.

Supporting adoptive parents and carers

Many children do respond to the daily lived experience of sensitive caregiving by their new parents, and many do not require specialist professional input. However, if children are not able to respond to the care of their new parents after a period of months, a referral to CAMHS may be considered. Generally speaking it is important for children and parents to have an opportunity to get to know each other and for the parents to establish themselves in their new role before a referral is made. Parents need to be treated with respect; professionals should appreciate that the parents know the child and their concerns should be treated seriously. They should be offered an opportunity to speak to the professional team without the children present in the first instance – both so that they feel free to speak openly about their concerns which they may be reluctant to voice in front of the children, but also because as the parents, they need to feel some confidence in the professionals before their children are involved. In some cases consultation to the parents is the most helpful intervention. Other helpful approaches include story stem assessments which can provide insights into the nature of the child's internalised beliefs about parental figures. Where there is a child psychotherapist on the team, many of these children will benefit from the opportunity to process some of their early, pre-verbal experiences and to have somewhere other than their adoptive family to deposit some of the rage and upset they have endured. Parenting skills courses or support groups for adopters/foster carers may provide a forum for shared learning and support for these parents.

Adopters report that the response they receive at clinics is not universally well informed. Adopters are sometimes made to feel responsible for their children's difficulties, which makes it very difficult for the adopter to develop a positive working relationship with the therapist. It is important that professionals who offer a service to families who care for children who have been looked after, understand the powerful long-term sequelae of such early experiences, and manage to convey to the adopters respect for what they manage. Adopters are often distressed and conscious of their 'failure' as parents at the point of seeking help. It is, therefore, important that the professionals convey awareness that the children's difficulties pre-dated their placement, even if their responses are sometimes unhelpful to the child. It is difficult for parents to maintain a positive stance in the face of consistent rejection which some children who have been abused and neglected in the past may present as their default position.

Parenting skills training groups which are tailored to the needs of adoptive or foster parents provide them with insight into the reasons for their children's difficult behaviour within a supportive peer group which facilitates sharing and learning. Some programmes also provide a 'toolkit' of strategies to use to improve their relationship with the child and enable them to manage the child's challenging behaviour without being drawn into a negative spiral.

There are a range of such groups available in the UK. Adoption UK which is a self-help organisation for adoptive parents offers a course entitled 'A Piece of Cake', which spends time exploring the reasons why children from backgrounds where they have experienced trauma have behaviour difficulties before discussing strategies to support them. The voluntary adoption agency After Adoption has developed a package called 'Safebase' which also offers adopters a programme of groups designed to support the development of more positive strategies and interactions.

Dr Stephen Scott and his team at the Maudsley Hospital have developed a programme for a support group for foster carers entitled 'Fostering Changes', which draws on 'The Incredible Years' developed by Carolyn Webster Stratton in the USA, initially for children with conduct disorders (not foster or adopted children). Researchers from the Anna Freud Centre and Coram conducted a study over three series of the Webster Stratton groups (Henderson & Sargent 2005), from which they identified additional themes relevant to adopters, and the package has since been modified in the light of this study. The package is highly rated by the participants, and an evaluation carried out established that the parents had an increase in their confidence and ability to manage as parents to their children (Henderson & Sargent 2005).

All the parenting skills groups mentioned above provide the adopters or foster carers with the opportunity to share their experiences with a group of peers where they feel understood and able to speak frankly about the difficulties they encounter. However, the parenting skills groups provide only one aspect of the support needed by these families. Many of the children will require individual therapy, and the parents might need access to consultation and advice from time to time. Access to a multi-disciplinary team is valuable as these children often have a multiplicity of needs and may require assessments by educational psychologists, speech therapists, occupational therapists, child psychotherapists, neurologists, and/or psychiatrists.

Conclusion

Adoption and foster care social workers are responsible for providing services to some of the most vulnerable children in our society as well as supporting the adults who make themselves and their homes available on a full-time, and in the case of adopters, a permanent basis. The care these parents offer is the most potent source of therapeutic experience available for these children. However, their role makes huge demands on people who are not mental health professionals, but ordinary folk who are child centred and motivated to help a child as well as wanting the satisfactions of parenthood. They need to be persevering, patient and to have an optimistic outlook, even though they will at times experience despondency and despair. Indeed, one of the most significant qualities of adopters is that they should withstand attacks (psychological but sometimes physical) and survive as parental figures. Children who have been catastrophically let down by adults will test them to destruction, and need to know that they can survive. Remarkably, a very high proportion of these placements do endure (reliable statistics are not available, although a research study by Julie Selwyn has been commissioned by the Department of Education). However a report produced for the Prime Minister in 2000 (Prime Minister's Review 2000) set the disruption rate at 20 per cent, which many in the field believe is considerably higher than the true figure. Nevertheless, even if 20 per cent disrupt, that means that 80 per cent endure, and a study by David Howe (1996) gives cause to hope that some of the troubled children who leave their adoptive families in distress during adolescence, will have benefitted from living in their adoptive family and will re-establish a cordial relationship in their twenties.

This high rate of positive outcomes is a testament to the powerful drive of children to make an attachment when the opportunity presents, and when they are able to be persuaded that their new parents are indeed benign and able to care for them. It is also testament to the level of devotion which enables the parents to keep going even when things might appear hopeless, thereby finally convincing children who have learned to expect rejection and discontinuity, that relationships can be different. It is important not to impose arbitrary cut off points in evaluating the success of adoptions. Adoption is a lifelong process, not an event, and as people grow up, mature and age, they are capable of seeing things in a fresh light and making different choices. Although much about the attachments people make relates to the trajectory they set out on early in life, individuals do remain capable of change in response to changes in their circumstances and the other relationships they forge as they mature.

Applying attachment theory to this complex field is not a straightforward process, but the insights it provides gives the context within which professionals and parents can make sense of the complex and contradictory messages they receive from children, and indeed from the adults who care for them, who are themselves inevitably affected by the children's projections and sometimes extreme behaviour. The message is one of optimism, hope and respect for the human spirit.

References

Ainsworth, M. D. S., Blehar, M., Waters, E., & Wall, S. (1978). *Patterns of Attachment*, Hillsdale, NJ: Erlbaum.

Bifulco, A. (2014). 'The Attachment Style Interview', in S. Farnfield & P. Holmes (eds) *The Routledge Handbook of Attachment: Assessment*, London and New York: Routledge.

Bifulco, A., Jacobs, C., Bunn, A., Thomas, G., & Irving, K. (2008). 'The Attachment Style Interview (ASI): A support-based adult assessment tool for adoption and fostering practice', *Adoption and Fostering* 32, 3, 33–45.

Bowlby, J. (1988). *A Secure Base: Parent–child attachment and healthy human development*, New York: Basic Books, p. 146.

DfE (2012). 'Children looked after by local authorities in England, including adoption'. Statistical first release. Available online at www.education.gov.uk/rsgateway/DB/SFR/s001084/index.shtml

Dozier, M. (2003). 'Attachment-based treatment for vulnerable children', *Attachment & Human Development* 5, 3, 253–257.

Farnfield, S. & Holmes, P. (eds) (2014) *The Routledge Handbook of Attachment: Assessment*, London and New York: Routledge.

Fraiberg, S., Adelson, E., & Shapiro, V. (1975). 'Ghosts in the nursery: A psychoanalytical approach to the problems of impaired infant-mother relationships', *Journal of the American Academy of Child Psychiatry* 14, 387–421.

Henderson, K. & Sargent, N. (2005). 'Developing the *Incredible Years* Webster–Stratton parenting skills training programme for use with adoptive families', *Adoption & Fostering* 29, 4, 34–44.

Hodges, J., Steele, M., Hillman, S., Henderson, K., & Kaniuk, J. (2003). 'Changes in attachment representations over the first year of adoptive placement: Narratives of maltreated children', *Clinical Child Psychology and Psychiatry* 8, 3, 347–363.

Howe, D. (1996). 'Adopters' relationships with their adopted children form adolescence to early adulthood', *Adoption & Fostering* 20, 3, 35–43.

Kaniuk, J., Steele, M., & Hodges, J. (2004). 'Report on a longitudinal research project: Exploring the development of attachments between older, harder to place children and their adopters over the first two years of placement', *Adoption & Fostering* 28, 2, 61–67.

Kenrick, J. (2000). '"Be a kid": The traumatic impact of separations on children who are fostered and adopted', *Journal of Child Psychotherapy* 26, 3, 393–412.

Loxtercamp, L. (2009). 'Contact and truth: The unfolding predicament in adoption and fostering', *CCPP* 14, 3, 423–435.

Main, M. & Solomon, J. (1986). 'Discovery of a new, insecure-disorganised/disorientated attachment pattern', in M. Yogerman & T. Braxelton (eds) *Affective Development in Infancy*, Norwood, NJ: Ablex, pp. 95–124.

Prime Minister's Review of Adoption, Permanence and Innovation Unit (2000) The Cabinet Office, London.

Rees, J. (2009). *Life Story Books: A family friendly approach*, London: Jessica Kingsley.

Rustin, M. (1999). 'Multiple families in mind', *Clinical Child Psychology and Psychiatry*, 4, 51–62.

Slade, A. (2005). 'Parental reflective functioning: An introduction', *Attachment & Human Development* 7, 3, 269–281.

Steele, H. & Steele, M. (2005). 'Understanding and resolving emotional conflict: Findings from the London Parent–Child Project', in K. E. Grossman, K. Grossman & Waters, E. (eds) *Attachment from Infancy to Adulthood: The major longitudinal studies*, New York: Guilford Press, pp. 137–164.

Steele, M., Hodges, J., Kaniuk, J., D'Agostino, D., Blom, I., Hillman, S., & Henderson, K. (2007). 'Intervening with maltreated children and their adoptive families: Identifying attachment-facilitative behaviours', in D. Oppenheim & D. F. Goldsmith (eds) *Attachment Theory in Clinical Work with Children: Bridging the gap between research and practice*, New York: The Guilford Press, pp. 58–85.

Steele, M., Hodges, J., Steele, H., Hillman, S., & Asquith, K. (2008). 'Forecasting outcomes in previously maltreated children: The use of the AAI in a longitudinal adoption study', in H. Steele & M. Steele (eds) *Clinical Applications of the Adult Attachment Interview*, New York: Guilford Press, pp. 427–451.

Wakelyn, J. (2011). 'Therapeutic observation of an infant in foster care', *Journal of Child Psychotherapy* 26, 3, 393–412.

Ward, H., Munro, E., Gearden, C., & Nicholson, D. (2006). *Outcomes for Looked After Children: Life pathways and decision making for very young children in care or accommodation*, London: Jessica Kingsley.

Chapter 10

Attachment and social work

David Howe

Introduction

Social workers get involved with people of all ages, from the young and vulnerable to the old and dependent. They work with children and families, individuals with mental health problems, and the disabled. They work with the troubled and troublesome, the endangered and dangerous. Their work might involve duties of care or control. And the more ambitious might grow excited by the possibilities of treatment and cure as they seek to ape the evidence-based success of other people-based professions including medicine and clinical psychology.

They are *social* workers in the sense that their concerns are with people who either have problems with society or with whom society has problems. This being the case, social workers find much of their work determined by welfare legislation and social policy. Although concise definitions are difficult, Wilson and colleagues characterise social work as:

> a professional activity which takes place at the boundary of many different spheres of society: private and public, the civil and judicial spheres, and the personal and political arenas. However, it is above all about relationships. We see at the heart of social work the provision of relationships to help people (children, young people and adults) negotiate complex and painful transitions and decisions in their lives . . . Our book, then, is based on the belief relationships are at the heart of effective social work and that the essential and distinctive characteristic of social work is its focus on the individual *and* the social setting and context.
>
> (Wilson *et al.* 2011: xiv, original emphasis)

So, although such broad definitions mean that practitioners are required to know something of social policy and the law, the many schools of psychology and their applications, sociology, systems theory, philosophy and the political sciences, a perennial interest has remained in social relationships and human development. And to the extent that this has remained true, attachment and its theories have retained a significant fan-base among many of the profession's practitioners. Nevertheless, because much of the content, manner and purpose of social work is governed by the state and its agencies, practitioners tend to have a complex, often constrained relationship with social science's theories and their evidence-based practices.

Origins of social work's interest in attachment

James Robertson, a social worker, practised with John Bowlby during their time together at the Tavistock Clinic. His close observations of young children's highly distressed reactions when they were separated from their parents, for example when they went into hospital or foster care, offered early empirical support for Bowlby's immanent ideas on attachment (for example, Robertson 1953). In particular, Robertson's recognition of the several stages of loss through which young children progress upon separation from their parents (protest, despair and detachment) not only provided an important contribution to early ideas about attachment but also began to influence people's thinking on how best to mitigate the more distressing effects of loss and separation when children were admitted to hospital or went into foster care. Indeed, attachment's earliest and most significant impact on social work practice was in the placement of children in short- and long-term foster care (also see Kaniuk, Chapter 9, this volume).

And for a couple of decades, until the early 1980s, that was almost the extent of social work's interest in attachment. Social work in the 1970s and 1980s was under assault from two ideologically opposed groups. The group interested in empirically robust and evidence-based approaches to social work wanted the profession to be more treatment-oriented which, at the time, meant practices based on behaviour modification. Those supporting this approach were particularly dismissive of any social work practice that had even a whiff of psychodynamic thinking about it, including attachment theory.

The second band of would-be reformers were inspired by a range of radical political theories including 1970s' Marxism, feminism and early post-structuralism. For them, attachment theory at best merely offered a plaster on the deep wounds of inequality and injustice caused by the iniquities of capitalism, and at worse offered a theory that subjugated women as well as blamed them for many of society's man-made ills. Social workers with attachment sympathies, therefore, tended to lie low or simply tread water for a while, confining their interests mainly to children moving in and out of foster care.

Nevertheless, in spite of the ideological buffeting that social work suffered during these times, most practitioners continued to value the theories and practices associated with loss, grief and mourning, often unaware of attachment's contribution to our understanding of these shared experiences.

However, gradually, throughout the 1980s, attachment-based thinking began to find its way back into the profession's practices. Again, it was foster care and adoption work that acted as the stimulus. In particular, the shift in adoption practice from placing babies to placing older children forced workers to think about how early life experiences affected children's psychosocial development and behaviour. This coincided with significant developments in attachment theory and research. Ainsworth's work on caregiving, attachment patterns and personality was particularly influential (Ainsworth *et al.* 1978). And the recognition that child abuse, neglect and trauma could have profound consequences for the developmental pathways taken by some children had major implications for adoption policy and practice.

The early work of researchers such as Main and Solomon (1986), and Crittenden and Ainsworth (1989), also began to transform social workers' thinking about the causes and consequences of child abuse and neglect. In particular, ideas about the quality of caregiving, the making and breaking of affectional bonds, and attachment in situations of abuse and neglect began to offer social workers much more sophisticated understandings of the nature of dangerous and neglectful parenting and their effect on children, their behaviour and development. As well as the intuitive appeal of these ideas, their strong research underpinnings gave attachment-informed practices increasing credibility in the world of child protection social work.

Thus, by the mid-1990s, attachment was firmly back on social work's agenda, especially in the fields of child protection, adoption and foster care.

We now follow the child protection story in more detail. This gives a particularly good idea of how social workers, along with many other professional groups, have understood (and sometimes misunderstood) and used (and sometimes misused) some of attachment's key concepts and categories.

Social work and child protection

In child protection and welfare work, the key concerns of social workers are children's developmental wellbeing and safety. In order to assess and make judgements on these concerns, they have to assess the quality of parents' caregiving, the developmental prospects and condition of their children, whether or not the children are safe, and whether or not the children should be removed, either permanently or temporarily. As attachment has many interesting things to say on all these matters, by the mid-1990s the theory began to play an increasingly important role in the way social workers assessed, judged, supported and worked with parents and their children.

One of the first consequences of this interest was to determine whether a particular child in a particular family was securely attached or not. This was, and continues to be assessed most typically by observing parent–child interactions both in the home and, in cases where children are separated from their parents, during contact visits.

Although very few social workers are trained to use any of the fully validated instruments now available, such as the Strange Situation procedure or the CARE-Index, they might make up for their lack of methodological rigour by undertaking repeated observations, over time, in the home setting, under different conditions.

However, in order to assess and interpret the quality and character of these parent–child interactions, social workers do need a full and proper understanding of attachment and what it is. In particular, the part that parents play in acting as safe havens and secure bases at times of need and distress is an especially helpful idea. When attachment is not properly understood, it is possible that some secure children happily playing on their own in an independent fashion, having no particular need of their attachment figure at that time, might be mis-classified as insecurely attached.

Perhaps more critically, some children who might be classified as 'ambivalent' in their attachment organisation using a reliable, validated measuring instrument, who, when observed in the home setting, seem to be constantly engaged with the parent, might wrongly be judged 'secure' inasmuch as they seem to show no fear of their parent, indeed seem particularly anxious to remain close and energetically engaged with their caregiver at all times. Here, proximity seeking in and of itself is mistakenly perceived as an indication of security.

Furthermore, the rather low-grade value that secure versus insecure gives in terms of making key decisions in a child's life is not always appreciated. 'Secure good, insecure bad' is too crude a division on which to base life-changing judgements. Given that between 30 and 40 per cent of children in any normal population might be classified insecure, we learn a little, but not a lot from the distinction.

The past as a guide to understanding the present

Of more value has been the research evidence that has looked at the relationship histories of abusive, rejecting and neglectful parents and how these relate to their caregiving. Social workers have had a long-standing interest in people's social histories. This, coupled with opportunities to collect detailed observational information on parent–child, parent–partner and parent–professional interactions in the home and other community settings, affords rich material on which to base sound assessments on parenting capacities and children's safety. Good assessments lead to good problem formulations. Good problem formulations guide decision making and intervention strategies.

Attachment theory has proved particularly useful in terms of helping social workers make sense of complex, long-standing, often turbulent cases. It is all too easy on a home visit to feel overwhelmed or intimidated by the behaviour of highly dysfunctional parents and their families. Practitioner anxiety, of course, does not lead to sound or safe practice. Attachment theory's ability to see pattern and logic in what otherwise might seem like random chaos helps reduce professional stress. Low anxiety increases emotional availability and helps sharpen the worker's intellectual bearings. If the social worker knows where she is and where she's going, it also helps clients feel less stressed and more confident.

Attachment theory and research has recognised a variety of caregiving patterns and styles, each one of which has its origins in the parents' own attachment and relationship history (George & Solomon 2008). The more information social workers can collect on parents' past and present relationship experiences, the more they can make sense of current caregiving environments.

The presence of unresolved states of mind in parents with respect to their own attachment experiences of abuse, rejection and neglect provide powerful clues about the way they are likely to respond to current stresses and strains, particularly those associated with parenting their own children. When current stressors evoke unresolved and painful memories of their own childhood experiences of abandonment and abuse, parents employ the defensive and adaptive strategies that helped them survive their own traumatic childhoods. Thus it is that when their own children are in a state of need and distress that parents' own attachment systems become activated. This triggers attachment behaviours with all their attendant demands and feelings of threat and danger. The challenge and stress of their children's arousal and attachment behaviours then evokes unresolved and distressed states of mind in parents who, at the very moment their children need them to be emotionally available, attuned, regulating and responsive, actually shift into one of their own threatened states of mind and the defensive strategies that go with it. Crudely, these might be characterised as ones of fight, flight or freeze. These, in turn, might be loosely associated with various forms of avoidant or ambivalent attachment behaviours including one or more of their many refinements, including the use of compulsive and coercive strategies following Crittenden's Dynamic-Maturational Model (DMM) (Crittenden 2008 – also see Farnfield & Stokowy 2014), and controlling and punitive behaviours as explored in the ABC + D model (Main & Cassidy 1988; also see Van Rosmalen et al. 2014; Shah & Strathearn 2014). In either case, the parent's ability to perceive, process and respond to the needs of their children is disturbed.

In Fonagy's (2006) pithy phrase, parental mentalisation at these key moments 'goes off-line'. The parents' defensive responses in fact become ones of abuse (fight), neglect (flight), or abandonment (freeze) as they attempt to deal with their own distressed and threatened state. Each one of these responses represents a danger to the child whose attachment behaviour triggered the feeling of threat and distress in the first place. The child is then obliged to find his or her own adaptive and defensive survival strategy with its own distortions and disturbances which, unless recognised and treated, is likely to result in development following a sub-optimal pathway.

In the ABC + D model (see Chapter 1 and various chapters in Holmes & Farnfield 2014) abused and neglected children experience their parents' behaviour as either frightened or frightening (Main & Hesse 1990; Lyons-Ruth et al. 1999). Under these caregiving conditions, young children may find it difficult to find any behavioural strategy that helps reduce their feelings of arousal, fear and distress. In the presence of an attachment figure who frightens them, children appear to experience the simultaneous activation of two incompatible behavioural responses – fear (triggering an escape response) and attachment (recover proximity with your attachment figure). However, as the attachment figure is both the source of danger and is the ostensible provider of safety, children find themselves in a behavioural dilemma. Their attachment systems remain highly activated and their levels of arousal and distress quickly escalate. They suffer 'fear with escape' and 'fright without solution'. Unable to find a behavioural strategy that helps terminate their highly activated attachment system, their attachment behaviours are classified as disorganised or disoriented. However, under less stressful conditions, their attachment behaviours often possess more organisation. They might, therefore, also be classified as either avoidant, ambivalent or even secure (also see Farnfield & Holmes 2014 for a DMM's alternative interpretation of these behaviours).

Understandings and misunderstandings of attachment classifications

The proper recognition and correct classification of an attachment as disorganised, or indeed the recognition of any other attachment pattern, requires the use of the correct measurements and codings along with the reliability training that goes with them. Very few social workers are trained, or indeed likely to be trained in the use of these measuring instruments. Care should therefore be taken before any classificatory or diagnostic label is attached to a child or a parent. However, labels such as 'disorganised' and 'disordered' do have an evocative ring to them and there is a temptation to use them whenever a child, parent or family seem to be leading lives that are chaotic, turbulent or violent. This is wrong and should be avoided. It is particularly worrying when attachment labels and jargon are used by the untrained to support radical decisions such as the removal of a child or condemnation of a parent's caregiving.

Here is Crittenden in similar vein:

> Far too often, clinical opinion regarding attachment is relied upon, even in court cases, where custody and placement in care are issues . . . Most of the 'experts' rendering the opinion have no formal training in attachment
>
> (Crittenden 2008: 276)

> When life-changing decisions will be based in part on the outcomes of the assessment of attachment, fully qualified and authorized professionals should code, classify and write up the results of the assessment, it being certain that they are not the same individuals who carried out any of the assessments.
>
> (Crittenden 2008: 284)

Even more hesitation is required when it is acknowledged that there are relatively weak or unproven correlations between many of attachment's major measures. It can be the case that a child or parent might even be classified as avoidant on one measure and ambivalent on another. This lack of measurement consensus must surely mean that professionals and courts alike should view attachment diagnostics with some considerable caution.

The companion volume to this book, *The Routledge Handbook of Attachment: Assessment* (Farnfield & Holmes 2014), considers these issues and describes the various formal, evidence-based tools currently available to assess attachment.

Even if the classification of a particular child's attachment did have validity, social workers cannot, in the Humean sense, simply argue from an *is* to an *ought*. That is, recognising that a child has a disorganised attachment say, or is using a compulsively compliant or coercive strategy, does not, in and of itself, determine statutorily what should be done. Decisions about removal and custody involve social, legal and moral issues as well as scientific facts and opinion. In Stevenson's (1974) immortal words, social workers are inevitably brokers in shades of grey. So although knowledge about attachment styles and types can be extremely useful, they should never be the sole determinants of a decision, a recommendation or a course of action.

Social workers, therefore, should be cautious, even queasy about their use of too much attachment jargon, particularly the more evocative terminologies such as 'disorganised' and 'disordered'. It is lazy, immoral and dangerous to be over-reliant on the use of single, contestable labels to make life-changing recommendations.

The profession's strengths lie in knowing clients over time, in different settings, and under different conditions. This knowledge provides powerful information. A good understanding of attachment certainly helps social workers perceive, recognise, collect, organise and make sense of complex information about troubled lives but on its own it cannot be the whole story.

Attachment and relationship-based social work

However, it is possible, maybe even preferable, to think about attachment's value to social workers in a different way. There is a strong argument that social work remains an essentially relationship-based practice (Wilson *et al.* 2011; Baim & Morrison 2011). Yet, in most countries the profession has a large number of statutory duties, some mandatory, some discretionary. It is required to deliver a wide range of services. But most of these work best when the social worker establishes a good working relationship with the client. 'Good relationships, it seems, are a universal therapeutic good', argues Bentall (2009: 260), 'and yet may turn out to be the single most important ingredient of effective psychiatric care'. The good-enough relationship is the medium in which most therapeutic change takes place.

Attachment theory provides social workers with a sophisticated, subtle and nuanced understanding of human behaviour and social relationships, particularly in situations where people find themselves feeling under stress. When clients feel anxious, threatened and uncertain, their attachment systems become activated. It is then that their internal working models and dispositional representations (Crittenden 2008) guide their perceptions of, understandings of, and responses to the people with whom they are in relationship. These people might include partners, children and professionals, including social workers themselves. Clients will employ in the present those established and familiar behavioural strategies that have kept them safe and helped them survive in the past. There are longer discussions on these topics in *The Routledge Handbook of Attachment: Theory* (Holmes & Farnfield 2014).

Attachment theory, therefore, with its interest in people's relationship histories, adaptive strategies, defence mechanisms, and personality traits can be extremely useful in helping workers make sense of why clients are doing what they do, and saying what they say. Such understandings can help social workers make sense and so keep their bearings in difficult cases. And the more the worker can make some kind of sense of what is going on and why, the less anxious she is likely to be. In short, like all good caregivers, she can provide a relationship in which she is experienced as both 'stronger and wiser' (Bowlby 1997).

In the lives of many social work clients, it is relatively unusual to find yourself in relationship with someone who remains emotionally available for you under conditions of stress, who is willing to try to understand you and where you are coming from, and who is willing and able to communicate and connect with you. To the extent that the social worker is able to create such a relationship, she is acting as a *transitional attachment figure* (Crittenden 2008: 292; also see Winnicott 1965). And one of the key things that sensitive, responsive attachment figures do is keep the other in mind.

The minds of babies form, both neurologically and psychologically, as they relate with others who view and interact with them as 'mental state' beings, as having a mind. Parents' capacity to keep their children in mind facilitates children's general understanding of minds – their own and other people's. Thus, we learn to think of others in psychological terms because we were thought of in psychological terms (Fonagy *et al.* 2002). Our ability to improve the skill of keeping others in mind by feeling psychologically understood ourselves continues across the lifespan. Workers who understand, acknowledge and communicate their clients' thoughts and feelings help clients take on board and reflect on their own and other people's mental states and the behaviours to which they give rise.

Social workers who are able to stay with and process the strong feelings of clients offer *containment*. Worker–client relationships based on collaboration, cooperation and containment help clients to self-regulate. Practitioners who are not emotionally available leave clients with feelings that go unrecognised and unprocessed (Bion 1962). Bower suggests that:

> Bion's theory of containment is immensely valuable in providing not only a model of the development of the capacity to manage emotional states, but a way of understanding how a thoughtful and emotionally receptive stance to clients can have therapeutic value without anything fancy being done.
>
> (Bower 2005: 11)

Mind-mindedness and mentalisation

Recent developments, many fashioned by developmental psychologists, have produced a variety of concepts similar to containment. Parents whose children are observed to be secure in their attachments typically relate with their babies in a way that Meins terms *mind-minded* and Fonagy and colleagues call *mentalisation* (Fonagy *et al.* 2002; Bateman & Fonagy 2006; see also Fonagy *et al.* in Holmes & Farnfield 2014).

In a series of studies, Meins (1997, 1999) found that caregivers who are interested in what their children are thinking and feeling, and seek to share and enjoy this understanding with their children, possess what she calls 'mind-mindedness'. Mind-minded parents are good at translating psychological experiences into an active, coherent dialogue with their children. They help children attend to their inner thoughts and feelings and how these affect mind and body. Such mind-minded interactions facilitate emotional understanding, regulation and secure attachments. Parents who focus on their children's subjective experiences help them understand their own and other people's psychological states, and how these are linked to actions and behaviour.

Many of the clients of social workers, particularly parents who maltreat their children, suffered deprived and difficult childhoods. Their own parents lacked sensitivity and interest in their children's growing minds, their thoughts and feelings. They lacked mind-mindedness and, as a result, did their children a profound developmental disservice increasing the risk of them growing up with impaired social cognition, poor affect regulation, low empathy, limited emotional intelligence, insecure attachments, behavioural problems and poor mental health (Howe 2005). Any one or more of these impairments is likely to increase the chance of an individual becoming a social work client.

The concepts of 'mentalisation' and 'reflective function' are similar to mind-mindedness but take matters of psychological awareness a step further (Fonagy *et al.* 2002). Mentalisation is the capacity to understand how one's own and other people's mental states affect behaviour. It also involves an appreciation of how 'my behaviour affects your thoughts and feelings, and how your behaviour affects my thoughts and feelings'. The process includes the idea that 'I also recognise that as I am "mentalising" our interaction and modifying my behaviour accordingly, you are probably doing exactly the same'.

In order to develop the capacity to mentalise, an individual must have been in a relationship, particularly a parent–child relationship, in which the other was mentalising. In other words, to understand, one must have been understood. People who are able to recognise and reflect on themselves and others as meaningful and understandable become more competent social beings. Mentalisation correlates with secure attachments, a coherent sense of self, resilience, good mental health, and the ability to self-regulate.

Many clients of social workers, whether in mental health, child and family work, or youth offending, have problems mentalising, making sense of, and reflecting on their own and other people's psychological states. This results in miscued responses, feelings of confusion and distress, emotional arousal, and *problematic behaviour* in most significant relationships – with partners, children, professionals and officials. Never having been fully engaged as an independent, complex psychological being themselves, they have problems relating to others as complex, reflective, psychological beings.

In the case of working with parents of maltreated children, Slade (2008: 220) writes that 'it is more often the case that mothers and fathers find it very difficult to enter their child's experience as a means of understanding them'. Their children's needs and behaviour are therefore difficult to read. This is stressful and can precipitate strong feelings of fear, anxiety and anger leading to abuse, neglect or both.

The inability to mentalise not only makes relationships inherently more puzzling and stressful, it can also trigger the defensive responses of fight, flight and freeze which, if experienced in the parent–child relationship, can lead to feelings of helplessness and hostility resulting in abuse or neglect. Similarly, if the parent's relationship with the worker is experienced as officious and impersonal, stress and the defences associated with it are likely to increase.

To help clients, including abusive and neglectful parents, feel less confusion and stress as they interact with significant others, clients might be helped by being in relationship with social workers who are able to hold their clients' thoughts and feelings in mind. In the case of working with abusive and neglectful parents, it also helps if the worker can also hold children in mind for parents. In this way, other people's mental states and their links to behaviour, including the mental states of children of maltreating parents, are re-presented back to clients. This is how Slade describes her psychotherapeutic work with parents:

> [W]hen I work with a parent, I am trying to create a context in which he or she can slowly shift from a physical to a reflective or mentalizing stance. That is, *I hold the child in mind for the parent as a mentalizing being*, as a person whose feelings and behaviors are inextricably intertwined with theirs as a parent. Most important, I see the child's behaviour as *meaningful*. Hopefully the parent will come to internalize this view of the child, which will in turn allow them to hold this in mind for the child.
>
> (Slade 2008: 220, original emphasis)

> Creating an environment in which the parent can begin to hold the child in mind depends upon our capacity to first – and perhaps for a very long time – hold the parent in mind.
>
> (Slade 2008: 222)

In relationship-based social work, practitioners relate with clients in the same way that they want clients to relate with their children, partners, parents, professionals, and other authority figures, that is, develop a reflective, mentalising stance.

From a practice point of view, social workers first have to establish a working or therapeutic alliance – a secure base from which clients can begin to explore difficult thoughts and feelings, hopes and fears. Exploring from the secure base allows feelings and mental states to be linked to behaviour, whether the behaviour is that of the other or the client. Being held in mind by practitioners is a powerful way of containing clients' anxieties, fears, anger and sadness.

Practice, therefore, needs to re-focus. Rather than simply concentrate on what has gone wrong, much more attention needs to be paid to the psychological processes that get clients into distress and difficulty. In the case of parents who abuse and neglect their children, it is necessary to tune into their world:

> In order to understand parents' intent, we will need to get 'inside' [their] adaptive strategies. That is, understanding how they develop over childhood (patterns, strategies, dispositional representations, distortions of cognition and affect), we will need to think and feel like someone using their strategy if we are to understand parents who harm their children. Once we can do that, we may be able to join parents meaningfully and guide them safely to a less dangerous reality. Without understanding them as they understand themselves, we may not be able to help.
>
> (Crittenden 2008: 120)

The social workers aim is behavioural reorganisation and not symptom reduction. There is a need to be empathic, to see and understand how the world looks and feels from the client's point of view, and *accurately convey that understanding* (Gross & Capuzzi 2007).

Assessments, supports and interventions

Attachment-based thinking is also useful in helping social workers understand why and how they might be being perceived, interpreted and responded to by clients when they meet and communicate.

For example, a client with a history of rejection and abuse might approach the relationship warily and without trust, keeping themselves and their feelings at a distance. Their attachment style is essentially avoidant and dismissing of attachment-related cues. A hostile, intimidating attitude is the default mode for all new relationships, especially those with professionals. If they are to remain emotionally available, cognitively interested, and not react counter-aggressively or with trepidation, social workers needs to know and understand these things. In order to establish a secure base, social workers need to be consistent, contingent, congruent, predictable, sensitive and open. Maintaining this degree of responsivity and attunement means that social workers must be in regular receipt of good quality, critically reflective supervision.

It might also be the case that knowing that avoidant clients, for defensive reasons, are uncomfortable with accessing their own and other people's feelings, the social worker might need to tread a fine line between those communications that appeal to cognition and those that appeal to emotion. Some recognition and acknowledgement of feelings and how they affect body language, facial expressions, and what is being said might be explored, but the worker has to proceed with care. The idea is to help clients do what defensively they have learned not to do in order to feel safe. The worker is helping them to think about feelings, to recognise and reflect on emotions, both in the self and others. This is just one example of a very small step in helping avoidant personalities feel safe when feelings are aroused. The more affect and cognition can be coupled, the more able avoidant clients are to self-regulate.

In contrast, many clients show behaviours and relationship patterns that suggest an ambivalent-preoccupied type of attachment organisation.

For example, Deanna has been a long-standing client of a social work agency. She was the third of four children, each with a different father. Deanna's mother often said that she was on this planet to enjoy herself. It seemed to Deanna that men were more important to her mother than her children and that when her mother was in-between relationships she would swing unpredictably between being angry, depressed and vengeful. Although her mother would often tell her children that they were the most precious things in her life, it was hard to square this with her behaviour and life style. Deanna said she never really felt loved.

The mother of three school-age children herself, Deanna is currently without a partner. She now says she has given up on men: 'You give them everything, they take everything, and they give you nothing back.' Home life is chaotic. There are weekly crises that typically end up with Deanna visiting the social work office demanding that the children be taken into care and fostered, or complaining that no one gives a 'shit' about her and that she might as well be dead 'and who would look after the children then, eh?' She regularly runs up debt, gets into arguments with staff at the housing department and medical centre, and cannot stop eating and then gets depressed about what a 'fat cow' she is and that no man will 'fancy' her. She watches a lot of day-time TV and particularly enjoys the reality shows, believing that she learns a lot about 'human nature' and 'people's real psychology' from watching them.

But her most frequent gripe is the behaviour of the children. She says they take no notice of her. She tries her best to be a good mum, 'God knows I do', but 'they forever want this or that' and they are 'rude' . . . and it all begins to feel out of hand. She sees herself as a good person who would do anything for anybody, but no one appreciates her love and generosity, least of all her 'ungrateful kids'. The latest visit to the office saw Deanna in a highly distressed state. Before the social worker has a chance to say anything, Deanna tearfully launches into her current woes.

Deon [her son] has been sent home early from school for misbehaving in the classroom, again. 'He's getting a real pain and I can't cope with him any more. Those teachers should be able to control him. They've been trained, haven't they, they get paid lots of money for doing the job, don't they? Why should I be expected to cope? What help do I get? It's not fair. I don't get enough money to keep them decent. The dogs cost me a fortune to feed, but at least they're grateful and I wouldn't be without them. And do you know what's happened now? Roxy's started her periods! That's the last bloody thing I could be doing with right now. It'll be boys next, and one thing and another. I definitely do not want to be dealing with that. I can't cope, I really can't. What have I done to deserve all this? Nobody cares.'

The practice of a social worker guided by an attachment perspective takes note of Deanna's childhood history. The worker understands why so many other professionals, including some of her own managers, feel frustrated and exasperated with Deanna, that in spite of seemingly endless support, nothing changes, there is no apparent progress. Several times the social worker has been advised to close the case: 'Deanna is getting too dependent; she must learn to cooperate and stand on her own two feet.' When the case has been closed, it has usually been only a matter of a few weeks before Deanna crashes back into the office with a new crisis, a fresh drama.

The social worker knows that Deanna has deep anxieties about her own worth and lovability. She craves acceptance. But her anxious need to be loved and appreciated makes her go too far in relationships. She ends up placing huge emotional demands on others. It seems impossible ever to meet her needs. The outcome is always the same. People feel emotionally exhausted, cross and give up on her. Yet again she feels abandoned and frightened. The only way she can provoke recognition and response is to precipitate another crisis that cannot be ignored.

Patiently, the social worker knows that she must remain steady, available, predictable and reliable in all her dealings with Deanna. Calmness and structure have become her watchwords. Over time, in what sometimes has been dubbed 'managed dependency', the practitioner has become both a safe haven and a secure base for Deanna. The social worker's basic aim is to keep 'the show on the road' for as long as it takes. It might even be appropriate to consider the occasional use of brief, respite foster care for the children.

In cases like Deanna's it might be many years before the client begins to pick up and value some of the structure, logic and consequential thinking that the social worker always provides when she is working with her. Historically, Deanna has used anxious arousal and strong feelings as her guide to action. Thought and reflection have rarely entered the frame. However, feeling contained, acknowledged and understood by the social worker has allowed Deanna to find herself in a calm place, a safe haven. In the relationship with her social worker, she is slowly beginning to learn to stop and think before she feels and reacts. Knowing that the social worker is going to be there at times of need is actually helping Deanna to be less dependent and more confident. The social worker is becoming a secure base from which Deanna, with growing independence, can explore, learn, anticipate and plan. It is generally a case of two steps forward, one step back, but slowly, Deanna is relying less on feeling and more on thought. She is beginning to mentalise and reflect. As a result, the children feel less confused, less uncertain, less anxious, and better behaved as their mother learns to tune into their thoughts and feelings. She, too, begins to take on some of the attributes of a safe haven and secure base.

To recap

It is unlikely that social workers *en masse* will ever be trained to use the many formal instruments and measures that attachment researchers and specialist clinicians use to assess and classify children and adults.

Nevertheless, a good working knowledge of attachment theory helps social workers do a number of key things. It helps them make sense of, and keep their bearings in difficult cases. It encourages them to remain curious, fascinated and engaged with other people and their lives.

To be the subject of genuine interest and to be on the receiving end of a relationship in which the other is interested in you and wants to understand you and what the world looks and feels like for you, is a rare experience for most clients. It marks the beginning of a possible willingness to engage and for a working alliance to be forged. The worker–client relationship itself then becomes the major vehicle of support, change and progress. The worker acts as a safe haven, a secure base, a mentalising other, a transitional attachment figure. The relationship with the social worker becomes a place where clients feel a degree of safety. It becomes a place where they can begin to access, make sense of, and integrate their own thoughts and feelings, behaviours and reactions, hopes and fears (Baim & Morrison 2011). It marks the beginning of an improved ability to self-regulate. An attachment-informed social worker also knows when thoughts about feeling (say with ambivalent/preoccupied clients) or feelings about thoughts (say with avoidant/dismissing clients) might be introduced and explored. All of this is entirely compatible with interventions that might decrease stress, improve material resources, provide advice and guidance, promote insights, modify behaviour and set targets.

Attachment across the client groups

Child and family social workers traditionally have been the most regular and enthusiastic users of attachment-informed thinking. Attachment's presence has been most robust in child protection, adoption and foster care work. Although historically attachment's presence has been based on experience, practice wisdom and personal conviction, in more recent years, attachment-informed practices have been supported by a growing body of evidence-based research. For example, there is growing interest in employing attachment-based thinking in a number of preventive and early intervention services. Many of the positive parenting programmes and treatments designed to enhance the quality of early attachments are beginning to attract practitioners who work in support and early intervention teams and family centres (see Juffer and colleagues in Chapter 5, this volume). Social workers who work with disabled children and their parents are also beginning to see some value in taking an attachment-based perspective.

There is also a slow, but growing interest in attachment being shown by mental health social workers. As attachment theory and research advance in helping us understand some features associated with diagnoses such as Borderline Personality Disorder, Antisocial Personality Disorder, depression, anxiety disorders, eating disorders, and problems of substance abuse, so mental health social workers have begun to appreciate attachment's relevance and value in the assessment, treatment and support of patients with various mental illness (see Jeremy Holmes in Chapter 3).

Attachment is increasingly taking a lifecourse perspective on personality development and behaviour (Howe 2011). However, the growing literature in the field of adult attachments, whether generated by developmental psychologists or social psychologists, has yet to have a significant impact on social work thinking and practice. Nevertheless, there is potential to adopt and adapt many of the clinical practices being developed by attachment-based couple therapists (for example, see Johnson & Whiffen 2005) and family therapists (see Chimera in Chapter 4). Attachment theory and research can also be helpful in assessment work for courts that deal with issues of children's custody in divorce, separation and mediation cases.

And finally, attachment theory holds promise for social work with older people. This is an interesting client group from an attachment perspective (for example, see Magai 2008). As parents age and become more fragile, vulnerable and dependent, their roles and relationships with their children and others change from that of caregiver to careseeker. As Bowlby (1997: 207) observed, as peer relationships gradually disappear, older people's attachment behaviour is increasingly directed towards the younger generation – their own children, nurses, doctors and social care workers. Established attachment styles are still present and are likely to affect the way an old person responds to their own increasing dependency as well as their relationships with their adult children who may, or may not become willing carers.

Attachment is rather good at understanding the moral and behavioural consequences of the way we behave and have behaved in close relationships. As you
sow, so shall you reap, and what goes round comes round. This is particularly true
in the case of old age. Admittedly rather simplistic, there is some truth in the idea
that securely attached children are most likely and willing to take on the role of
caregiver for their parents. Elderly parents with avoidant, dismissing attachment
styles are not only more likely to want to remain independent for as long as possible, even beyond the time when it is no longer sensible, but are also more likely
to have adult children who are reluctant to assume the role of caregiver. Their
children might be the first to argue that perhaps residential care is the best option.

Old people whose attachment styles are ambivalent and preoccupied are
most likely to complain that their needs are not being recognised, that they feel
neglected, and that their children have a duty to look after them given all that they,
as parents, have done for their children over the years. Their children are likely to
feel that they are being emotionally blackmailed and although they might agree
that mum or dad can come to live with them, the role of caregiver for such a needy
parent is likely to be fraught with conflict, difficulty, exasperation and resentment.
Of course these mini-scenarios are caricatures, but they hint at some of the possible uses of an attachment-informed practice in the support and understanding of
old people and their families.

Conclusion

One of the more intriguing findings of attachment theory is the importance of
being sensitively kept-in-mind by others, particularly at times of need and stress.
This, in turn, helps people learn to keep others in mind. For social workers who
value the importance of the relationship in their work, these ideas help give shape,
substance and direction to their practice. The many different ways in which most
of social work's clients have not been kept safely in mind by the important people
in their lives explains their particular attachment style, behavioural traits and relationship conduct. Attachment, therefore, offers social workers a powerful model
with which to understand and work with people who have difficulties, are difficult,
or both.

References

Ainsworth, M. D. S., Blehar, M. C., Waters, E. & Wall, S. (1978). *Patterns of Attachment:
a psychological study of the Strange Situation*, Hillsdale, NJ: Erlbaum.
Baim, C. & Morrison, T. (2011). *Attachment-based Practice with Adults: understanding
strategies and promoting positive change*, Brighton: Pavilion.
Bateman, A. & Fonagy, P. (2006). *Mentalization-based Treatment for Borderline Person-
ality Disorder: a practical guide*, New York: Oxford University Press.
Bentall, R. (2009). *Doctoring the Mind: why psychiatric treatments fail*, London: Allen
Lane.

Bion, W. (1962). Psycho-analytic study of thinking. *International Journal of Psychoanalysis*, 43: 306–310.

Bower, M. (2005). Psychoanalytic theories for social work practice. In M. Bower (ed.) *Psychoanalytic Theory for Social Work Practice*, London: Routledge, pp. 3–14.

Bowlby, J. (1997). *Attachment and Loss: Volume I: Attachment*, London: Hogarth Press Pimlico Edition (Original edition 1969).

Crittenden, P. M. (2008). *Raising Parents: attachment, parenting and child safety*, Cullompton: Willan Publishing.

Crittenden, P. M. & Ainsworth, M. D. S. (1989). Child maltreatment and attachment theory. In D. Cicchetti & V. Carlson (eds) *Child Maltreatment: theory and research on the consequences of child abuse and neglect*, New York: Cambridge University Press, pp. 432–463.

Farnfield, S. & Holmes, P. (eds) (2014). *The Routledge Handbook of Attachment: assessment*, London and New York: Routledge.

Farnfield, S. & Stokowy, M. (2014). The Dynamic-Maturational Model (DMM) of attachment. In P. Holmes & S. Farnfield (eds) *The Routledge Handbook of Attachment: theory*, London and New York: Routledge.

Fonagy, P. (2006). The mentalization-approach to social development. In J. G. Allen & P. Fonagy (eds) *Handbook of Mentalization-based Treatment*, Chichester: John Wiley, pp. 53–100.

Fonagy, P., Gregely, G., Jurist, E. & Target, M. (2002). *Affect Regulation, Mentalization, and the Development of the Self*, New York: Other Press.

Gross, D. R. & Capuzzi, D. (2007). Helping relationships: from core dimensions to brief approaches. In D. Capuzzi and D. R. Gross (eds) *Counseling and Psychotherapy* (4th ed.) Upper Saddle River, NJ: Pearson, pp. 3–25.

Holmes, P. & Farnfield, S. (eds) (2014). *The Routledge Handbook of Attachment: theory*, London and New York: Routledge.

Howe, D. (2005). *Child Abuse and Neglect: attachment, development and intervention*, Houndmills: Palgrave Macmillan.

Howe, D. (2011). *Attachment Across the Lifecourse: a brief introduction*, Houndmills: Palgrave Macmillan.

Johnson, S. & Whiffen, V. (eds) (2005). *Attachment Processes in Couples and Family Therapy*, New York: Guilford Press.

Lyons-Ruth, K., Bronfman, E. & Parson, E. (1999). Maternal disrupted affective communication, maternal frightened or frightening behaviour, and infant disorganized strategies. In J. Vondra & D. Barnett (eds) *Atypical Patterns of Infant Attachment, Monographs of the Society for Research and Clinical Implications* 64(3): 67–96.

Magai, C. (2008). Attachment in middle and later life. In J. Cassidy & P. R. Shaver (eds) *Handbook of Attachment: theory, research and clinical applications*, New York: Guilford Press, pp. 532–551.

Main, M. & Cassidy, J. (1988). Categories of response to reunion with the parent at age 6: predictable from infant attachment classifications and stable over a 1-month period, *Developmental Psychology*, 24: 415–426.

Main, M. & Hesse, E. (1990). Parents' unresolved traumatic experiences are related to infants' disorganized attachment status: is frightened and/or frightening parental behaviour the linking mechanism? In M. Greenberg, D. Cicchetti & E. Cummings (eds) *Attachment in the Pre-School Years*, Chicago: University of Chicago Press, pp. 161–182.

Main, M. & Solomon, J. (1986). Discovery of a new, insecure disorganized/disoriented attachment pattern. In T. Brazleton & M. Yogman (eds) *Affective Development in Infancy*, Norwood, NJ: Ablex, pp. 95–124.

Meins, E. (1997). *Security of Attachment and the Social Development of Cognition*, Hove: Psychology Press.

Meins, E. (1999). Sensitivity, security and internal working models: bridging the transmission gap, *Attachment & Human Development*, 1(3): 325–342.

Robertson, J. (producer) (1953). *A two-year old goes to hospital: a scientific film record*. [Film]. Nacton, UK: Concord Film Council.

Shah, P. & Strathearn, L. (2014). Similarities and differences of the ABC + D Model and the DMM classification systems for attachment: A practitioner's guide. In P. Holmes & S. Farnfield (eds) *The Routledge Handbook of Attachment: Theory*, London and New York: Routledge.

Slade, A. (2008). Working with parents in child psychotherapy: engaging the reflective. In F. N. Busch (ed.) *Mentalization: theoretical considerations, research findings, and clinical implications*, London: The Analytic Press, pp. 207–234.

Stevenson, O. (1974). Editorial, *British Journal of Social Work*, 4(1): 1.

Van Rosmalen, L., Van IJzendoorn, M. H. & Bakermans-Kranenburg, M. J. (2014). ABC + D of attachment theory: The Strange Situation Procedure as the gold standard of attachment assessment. In P. Holmes & S. Farnfield (eds) *The Routledge Handbook of Attachment: Theory*, London and New York: Routledge.

Wilson, K., Ruch, G., Lymbery, M. & Cooper, A. (2011). *Social Work: an introduction to contemporary practice* (2nd ed.), Harlow: Pearson Education Ltd.

Winnicott, D. W. (1965). *The Maturational Processes and the Facilitating Environment*, London: Hogarth Press.

Index